evangelical awakenings
in SOUTHERN ASIA

Ex Libris

DARRELL A. HARRIS

evangelical awakenings
in SOUTHERN ASIA
J. EDWIN ORR

FROM THE LIBRARY OF
THE INSTITUTE FOR
WORSHIP STUDIES
FLORIDA CAMPUS

BETHANY FELLOWSHIP, INC.
Minneapolis, Minnesota

Copyright © 1975
J. Edwin Orr
All rights reserved

This edition is a revision and expansion of the book, *Evangelical Awakenings in India,* published in New Delhi by Masihi Sahitya Sanstha, copyright © 1970 by J. Edwin Orr.

Published by Bethany Fellowship, Inc.
6820 Auto Club Road, Minneapolis, Minnesota 55438

Printed in the United States of America

Library of Congress Cataloging in Publication Data:

Orr, James Edwin, 1912-
   Evangelical awakenings in southern Asia.

   Published in New Delhi, 1970, under title: Evangelical awakenings in India.
   Bibliography: p.
   Includes index.
   1. Revivals—India—History. 2. Revivals—South Asia—History. I. Title.
BV3777.I4077   1975   269'.2'0954   74-32019
ISBN 0-87123-127-1

TABLE OF CONTENTS

Introduction
EVANGELICAL AWAKENINGS   vii

1	THE SECOND GENERAL AWAKENING	1
2	ORGANIZING FOR ADVANCE	7
3	THE OPENING UP OF INDIA	17
4	THE THIRD GENERAL AWAKENING	22
5	WORK WIDENING AND DEEPENING	28
6	SOCIAL IMPACT OF REVIVAL	33
7	SOCIAL IMPACT ON INDIA	41
8	THE FOURTH GENERAL AWAKENING	50
9	AWAKENINGS IN INDIA, 1860—	56
10	MOVEMENTS AFTER REVIVAL	64
11	CHRISTIAN ACTION	73
12	MOODY AND THE STUDENTS	78
13	CONTINUED SOCIAL IMPACT	89
14	THE FIFTH GENERAL AWAKENING	99
15	THE EXPECTATION IN INDIA	107
16	THE AWAKENING IN ASSAM	112
17	THE AWAKENING IN ANDHRA	118
18	THE AWAKENING IN TAMILNAD	128
19	THE AWAKENING IN KERALA	135
20	THE AWAKENING IN KANARA	140
21	AWAKENINGS IN NORTH INDIA	144
22	PRE-INDEPENDENCE EVANGELISM	155
23	IN THE TRAVAIL OF NATIONHOOD	170
24	EVANGELICAL RESURGENCE IN INDIA	177
25	THE EVANGELIZATION OF SOUTHERN ASIA	191

Notes   201
Select Bibliography   227
General Bibliography   233
Index of Persons   237

Introduction

EVANGELICAL AWAKENINGS

An Evangelical Awakening is a movement of the Holy Spirit bringing about a revival of New Testament Christianity in the Church of Christ and in its related community. Such an awakening may change in a significant way an individual only; or it may affect a larger group of believers; or it may move a congregation, or the churches of a city or district, or the whole body of believers throughout a country or a continent; or indeed the larger body of believers throughout the world. The outpouring of the Spirit effects the reviving of the Church, the awakening of the masses, and the movement of uninstructed peoples towards the Christian faith; the revived Church, by many or by few, is moved to engage in evangelism, in teaching, and in social action.

Such an awakening may run its course briefly, or it may last a lifetime. It may come about in various ways, though there seems to be a pattern common to all such movements throughout history.

The major marks of an Evangelical Awakening are always some repetition of the phenomena of the Acts of the Apostles, followed by the revitalizing of nominal Christians and by bringing outsiders into vital touch with the Divine Dynamic causing all such Awakenings—the Spirit of God. The surest evidence of the Divine origin of any such quickening is its presentation of the evangelical message declared in the New Testament and its re-enactment of the phenomena therein in the empowering of saints and conversion of sinners.

It is more than interesting to compare the characteristics of the Awakenings of various decades with the prototype of evangelical revivals in the Acts of the Apostles, a perennial textbook for such movements.

Our Lord told His disciples: 'It is not for you to know the times or seasons which the Father has fixed by His own authority. But you shall receive power when the Holy Spirit has come upon you; and you shall be My witnesses ... to the end of the earth.' Thus was an outpouring of the Spirit predicted, and soon fulfilled.

Then began extraordinary praying among the disciples in the upper room. Who knows what self-judgment and confession and reconciliation went on? There were occasions for such. But, when they were all together in one place, there suddenly came from heaven a sound like the rush of a mighty wind and it filled all the house. The filling of the Holy Spirit was followed by xenolalic evangelism, not repeated in the times of the Apostles nor authenticated satisfactorily since.

The Apostle Peter averred that the outpouring fulfilled the prophecy of Joel, which predicted the prophesying of young men and maidens, the seeing of visions and dreams by young and old. He preached the death and resurrection of Jesus Christ. What was the response? The hearers were pierced, stabbed, stung, stunned, smitten—these are the synonyms of a rare verb which Homer used to signify being drummed to earth. It was no ordinary feeling; nor was the response a mild request for advice. It was more likely an uproar of entreaty, the agonizing cry of a multitude.

Those who responded to the Apostle's call for repentance confessed their faith publicly in the apostolic way. About three thousand were added to the church. Then followed apostolic teaching, fellowship, communion and prayers.

What kind of fellowship? Doubtless the words of Scripture were often used liturgically, but it is certain that the koinonia was open. What kind of prayers? There are instances of individual petitions of power and beauty, but there are also suggestions of simultaneous, audible prayer in which the main thrust of petition is recorded, as in the prophet's day.

The Apostles continued to urge their hearers to change and turn to God, which they did by the thousands. And no hostile power seemed for the moment able to hinder them. Persecution followed, but the work of God advanced.

The events recorded in the Acts have been repeated in full or lesser degree in the Awakenings of past centuries. From the study of Evangelical Revivals or Awakenings in cities and districts, countries and continents, generations and centuries, it is possible to trace a pattern of action and discover a progression of achievement that establish in the minds of those who accept the New Testament as recorded history an undoubted conclusion that the same Spirit of God Who moved the apostles has wrought His mighty works in the centuries preceding our own with the same results but with wider effects than those of which the apostles dreamed in their days of power.

Although the records are scarce, there were Evangelical Awakenings in the centuries before the rise of John Wycliffe, the Oxford reformer. But such movements in medieval times seemed very limited in their scope or abortive in their effect. What was achieved in the days of John Wycliffe—the dissemination of the Scriptures in the language of the people—has never been lost, nor has the doctrine of Scriptural authority. Thus the Lollard Revival led to the Reformation, which would have been unlikely without it; and the principle of appeal to the Word of God in the matter of reform has not been lost either. The Reformation thus led to the Puritan movement in which the essentials of evangelical theology were refined; and the Puritan movement prepared the way for the eighteenth, nineteenth and twentieth century Awakenings occurring in more rapid succession.

A student of church history in general and of the Great Awakenings in particular must surely be impressed by the remarkable continuity of doctrine as well as the continuity of action. Anyone could begin reading the story of the Gospels, continue on into the narrative of the Acts of the Apostles, then without any sense of interruption begin reading the story of the poor preachers of John Wycliffe, the itinerants of the Scottish Covenant, the circuit riders of John Wesley, the readers of Hans Nielsen Hauge in Norway, or the Disciples of the Lord in Madagascar.

Not only so, but the student of such movements would find in the preaching of the Awakenings and Revivals the same message preached and the same doctrines taught in the days of the Apostles. But non-evangelical Christianity, with its accretions of dogma and use of worldly power, would seem a system utterly alien to that of the Church of the Apostles, resembling much more the forces both ecclesiastical and secular that had opposed New Testament Christianity.

The reader of the Acts of the Apostles must surely notice that the Church began to spread by extraordinary praying and preaching. So too the 'upper room' type of praying and the pentecostal sort of preaching together with the irrepressible kind of personal witness find their place in Great Awakenings rather than in the less evangelical ecclesiastical patterns.

The first three centuries of progress were followed by a millenium of changed direction when the Church was united with the State and political force compelled the consciences of men. These centuries are rightly called the Dark Ages, though they were not entirely without light.

Before the fifteenth century, a change began, commencing a progression of awakenings that moved the Church by degrees back to the apostolic pattern and extended it all over the world. Not only were theological dogmas affected and missionary passion created, but society itself was changed.

From the times of the Lollards onward, the impact of the Evangelical Revivals or Awakenings was felt in the realm of personal liberty— knowing the truth made men free, and made them covet freedom for all. Thus the Social Rising of 1381 championed a charter of freedom based on evangelical conviction. Its daughter movement in Bohemia defended its freedom against the forces of tyranny for a century.

The consequent Reformation that soon began in Germany caused such a ferment in men's minds that a rising became inevitable— but it was crushed, only because some of those responsible for the hunger for freedom betrayed it. The hunger for righteousness of the early Puritans brought about another attempt to establish freedom under the law, but, like various ventures before it, the Commonwealth failed because it relied more upon secular force than persuasion.

In the eighteenth, nineteenth and twentieth centuries, the revived Evangelicals re-learned an earlier method. New Testament counsel began to prevail, helping persuade freethinkers and Christians, traditionalists and Evangelicals, that freedom was God's intent for every man, everywhere. Thus the nineteenth century became in itself the century of Christian action, taking Good News to every quarter of the earth, to every phase of life. Those whose hearts the Spirit had touched became the great initiators of reform and welfare and tuned even the conscience of unregenerate men to a sense of Divine harmony in society.

Yet Christians believed that the horizontal relationship of man to men was dependent upon the vertical relationship of man to God, that social reform was not meant to take the place of evangelism, 'so to present Christ in the power of the Spirit that men may come to put their trust in Him as Saviour and to serve Him as Lord in the fellowship of His Church and in the vocations of the common life.'

What may be called the General Awakenings began in the second quarter of the eighteenth century, among settlers in New Jersey and refugees from Moravia about the same time. The First Awakening ran its course in fifty years, and was followed by the Second Awakening in 1792, the Third in 1830, the Fourth in 1858-59, the Fifth in 1905.

1

THE SECOND GENERAL AWAKENING

The infidelity of the French Revolution represented the greatest challenge to Christianity since the time preceding the Emperor Constantine.[1] Christians had endured the threat of the northern barbarians, the assault of the armies of the crescent, the terror of the hordes from the steppes, and an eastern schism and a western reformation. But, until 1789, there had never been such a threat against the very foundations of the Faith, against believing in the God revealed in the Scriptures. Voltaire made no idle boast when he said that Christianity would be forgotten within thirty years.

In France, even the Huguenots apostasized.[2] Deism rode high in every country in Europe, and so-called Christian leaders either capitulated to infidelity or compromised with rationalism. The infant but sturdy nation on the American continent was swept by unbelief, so that the faithful trembled. Between the mailed fist of French military power and the insidious undermining of faith, there seemed no escape.

The spiritual preparation for a worldwide awakening began in Great Britain seven years before the outpouring of the Spirit there.[3] Believers of one denomination after the other, including the evangelical minorities in the Church of England and the Church of Scotland, devoted the first Monday evening of each month to pray for a revival of religion and an extension of Christ's kingdom overseas. This widespread union of prayer spread to the United States within ten years and to many other countries, and the concert of prayer remained the significant factor in the recurring revivals of religion and the extraordinary out-thrust of missions for a full fifty years, so commonplace it was taken for granted by the Churches.

The outbreak of the Revolution in France at first encouraged lovers of liberty in the English-speaking world to hope that liberty had truly dawned in France.[4] When the Terror began, and when military despotism rose, they were fearfully alarmed. The British people decided to fight. In the second year of the Revolution, John Wesley died.

The revival of religion, the second great awakening, began in Britain in late 1791, cresting in power among the Methodists who seemed unafraid of the phenomena of mass awakening.[5] It was also effective among the Baptists and the Congregationalists, though manifested in quieter forms. It accelerated the evangelical revival going on among clergy and laity of the Church of England, strengthening the hands of Simeon and his Eclectic Club and those of Wilberforce in his Clapham Sect—an Evangelical party in the Anglican Establishment which soon became dominant in influence.

At the same time, the principality of Wales was overrun by another movement of revival, packing the churches of the various denominations and gathering unusual crowds of many thousands in the open-air.[6] The revival accelerated the growth of the Baptists and Congregationalists, increased the number of Wesleyan Methodists, and caused the birth of a new denomination, the Calvinistic Methodist Church of Wales, now the Welsh Presbyterians, who separated from the Church of Wales because of its failure to provide either ministers or sacraments for its societies.

Phenomenal awakenings also swept many parts of the kingdom of Scotland, raising up such evangelists as the Haldanes,[7] and such pastoral evangelists as Chalmers in Glasgow and MacDonald in the North. The Scottish revivals began in the teeth of majority opposition in the Church of Scotland but within a generation had evangelized the auld Kirk. The coverage of the Scottish Revival was patchwork, its occurrence sporadic, because of the desperate state of the country. The light prevailed over the darkness.

Not for the first time, nor the last, the unhappy kingdom of Ireland, a majority of whose inhabitants were disfranchized, was rent asunder by turmoil that boiled over into the Rebellion of 1798. In the midst of strife, local awakenings occurred among the Methodists,[8] affecting the evangelical clergy of the Church of Ireland. The Presbyterians of the North were fully occupied contending for orthodoxy against a Unitarian insurgency. Revival brought forth societies for the evangelization of Ulster and the renewal of church life.

This period of revival in the United Kingdom brought forth the British and Foreign Bible Society, the Religious Tract Society, the Baptist Missionary Society, the London Missionary Society, the Church Missionary Society, and a host of auxiliary agencies for evangelism.[9] It produced also some significant social reform, even in wartime.

Before and after 1800, an awakening began in Scandinavia, resembling more the earlier British movements of the days of Wesley and Whitefield, though borrowing from the later British awakening in adopting its home and foreign mission projects, its Bible societies, and the like. In Norway, the revival was advanced by a layman, Hans Nielsen Hauge, who made a lasting impact upon Norway as a nation.[10] Another layman, Paavo Ruotsalainen, expedited the movement in Finland.[11] There were several national revivalists operating then in Sweden, but the influence of George Scott, a British Methodist, later exceeded them all.[12] In Denmark, the revival seemed less potent and was sooner overtaken by a Lutheran confessional reaction, which inhibited the renewal of revival in the 1830s—unlike Norway, Sweden, and Finland, which experienced extensive movements up until the mid-century, Gisle Johnson and Carl Olof Rosenius being the outstanding leaders in Norway and Sweden respectively.

In Switzerland, France, and the Netherlands, the general awakening was delayed until the defeat of Napoleon.[13] A visit to Geneva by Robert Haldane triggered a chain reaction of revival throughout the Reformed Churches of the countries named, raising up outstanding evangelists and missionary agencies. In Holland, the movement was somewhat delayed, and was sooner cramped by confessional reaction among the Dutch Reformed, some of whom objected to state control as well as evangelical ecumenism.

In the German States, the general awakening followed the defeat of Napoleon, and raised up scores of effective German evangelists, such as the Krummachers, Hofacker, Helferich, von Kottwitz, and the von Belows; German theologians, such as Neander and Tholuck; social reformers, such as Fliedner; and noteworthy home and foreign missionary agencies.[14] As in other European countries, the complication of state-church relationships provoked confessional reaction among Lutherans who repudiated the evangelical ecumenism of the revivalists in general. Next to British evangelical pioneers, the German revivalists achieved the most lasting social reforms. Close collaboration between British and German revivalists existed in home and foreign mission projects.

Confessionalism in Europe, whether Anglo-Catholic in England, Lutheran in Germany and Denmark, or Reformed in Holland and Switzerland, inhibited the renewal of revival in the 'thirties, unlike the United States, where the free church system accelerated it.

In the United States and in British North America, there were preparatory movements of revival in the 1780s that raised up leaders for the wider movement in the following decade. Conditions in the United States following the French Revolution were deplorable, emptying churches, increasing ungodliness and crime in society, infidelity among students. Sporadic revivals began in 1792. Then Isaac Backus and his friends in New England adopted the British plan for a general Concert of Prayer for the revival of religion and extension of Christ's kingdom abroad. Prayer meetings multiplied as church members devoted the first Monday of each month to fervent intercession.[15]

In 1798, the awakening became general. Congregations were crowded and conviction was deep, leading to numerous thoroughgoing conversions. Every state in New England was affected, and every evangelical denomination.[16] There were no records of emotional extravagance, and none among the churches of the Middle Atlantic States, where extraordinary revivals broke out in the cities of New York and Philadelphia as well as in smaller towns. In the western parts of New York and Pennsylvania, there were more startling displays of excitement.[17] The population of these eastern States was three million, and the extent of the revival therein was three times more considerable than in the frontier territories, with three hundred thousand people.

In 1800, extraordinary revival began in Kentucky, long after its manifestation east of the Alleghenies. Among the rough and lawless and illiterate frontiersmen, there were extremes of conviction and response, such as trembling and shaking—described as 'the jerks,'—weeping for sorrow and shouting for joy, fainting. Extravagances occurred among a comparative few, but were exaggerated by critics out of all proportion, so that twentieth century historians have stressed the odd performances and ignored the major thrust of the awakening in the United States, even pontificating that the awakening actually began, extravagantly, on the frontier— an obvious misreading of history. It cannot be denied that the revival transformed Kentucky and Tennessee from an utterly lawless community into a God-fearing one.[18]

On the frontier, there were minor schisms following the awakening, due largely to defects inherent in denominational organization than to the revival, which raised up voluntary evangelists among the laity. Reaction against evangelical ecumenism and lay evangelism forced some people out.

The awakening spread southwards into Virginia, North and South Carolina, and Georgia, again—as in Kentucky and Tennessee—attracting crowds so huge that no churches could possibly accommodate them, hence five, ten or fifteen thousand would gather in the forest clearings. The Negroes were moved equally with the whites.

In the Maritime Provinces of British North America, the revival of the 1780s was renewed among the Baptist and New Light Congregationalist churches. In Upper Canada—now Ontario—the Methodists promoted revival meetings and grew very rapidly, as did some Presbyterians and (later) the Baptists. American itinerants were most active in the movement, anti-American Churchmen and secular leaders most opposed to it. The war of 1812 interrupted the work, which resumed with the coming of peace, though still discouraged by conservative British leaders.[19]

As the influence of infidelity had been so strongly felt in the American colleges, so the blessing of revival overflowed in collegiate awakenings. Timothy Dwight, erudite president of Yale, proved to be the greatest champion of intelligent evangelical Christianity on campus, but the movement among students soon became a spontaneous, inter-collegiate union. The revived and converted students provided the majority of recruits for the home ministry, educational expansion, and foreign missionary effort.[20]

Revived Americans duplicated the formation of various evangelical societies in Britain, founding the American Bible Society, the American Tract Society, the American Board of Commissioners for Foreign Missions, the Foreign Mission of the American Baptists, and society after society. The order and extent of missionary organization reflected in some measure the degree of involvement of denominations in the Awakening.[21]

The Dutch colony of 30,000 at Cape Town experienced an awakening under the ministry of Dr. Helperus Ritzema van Lier, and thrust out local missionaries to evangelize the Khoisan (Hottentot and Bushmen) in the Cape hinterland.[22] A revival broke out in British army regiments in 1809, the Methodist soldier-evangelists gaining a hearing after an earthquake of great severity had shaken the Cape. There was little in the way of a free constituency to be revived in Australia, but the first chaplains to the settlements were Anglican Evangelicals, and revived congregations in Great Britain sent out evangelistically-minded laymen as settlers.

There is no doubt that the general awakening of the 1790s and 1800s, with its antecedents, was the prime factor in the extraordinary burst of missionary enthusiasm and social service, first in Britain, then in Europe and North America. Thomas Charles, whose zeal for God provoked the formation of the British and Foreign Bible Society, was a revivalist of first rank in Wales.[23] George Burder, who urged the founding of the Religious Tract Society, was a leader in the prayer union for revival. William Carey, a founder and pioneer of the Baptist Missionary Society, was one of a group who first set up in England the simultaneous prayer union that spread throughout evangelical Christendom and achieved its avowed purpose in the revival of religion and the extension of the kingdom of Christ overseas. The London Missionary Society and the Church Missionary Society grew out of the prayers of other Free Church and Church of England Evangelicals in the awakening. Methodist missions came from the same source, as did other Scottish societies and the Church of Scotland missions. The revival provided dynamic.[24]

The participation of Germans and Dutch in the Church Missionary Society and the London Missionary Society had its origin in the revival prayer groups in those countries, as did the proliferation of national missionary societies. A student prayer meeting in Williams College, the Haystack Compact, led to the foundation of the American Board and the American Baptist Missionary Union. The origins of the other denominational societies lay in the general revival.

It is all the more amazing to realise that these unique developments took place in Britain while that country was engaged in a titanic struggle with Napoleon, supported by ten times as many people. And the eager readiness of revived believers in Europe and North America transcended the political divisions and upheavals between them and Britain. The coming of peace in 1815 brought about a renewal of the revival in Britain, the rise of the Primitive Methodists to undertake an outreach to the masses somewhat neglected by Wesleyans.[25] In the Church of England, Charles Simeon was at the height of his influence, and the Church Building Society with government help was building hundreds of parish churches. The Baptists and Congregationalists were active in revival in England, and in Wales there were local revivals in many places. In Scotland, local awakenings and pastoral evangelism and social service built up the Church of Scotland Evangelicals. Revivals occurred in Ireland.

2

ORGANIZING FOR ADVANCE

It has been noted that there were sporadic movements of revival in Great Britain and the United States during the decade preceding the French Revolution, but that a general awakening began in the 1790s. The same pattern is seen in the formation of the evangelical societies founded to advance the work of evangelization, for most of them had their roots in the 1780s, but reached their organizational form between the dates of the Bastille and Waterloo in Great Britain, but after Waterloo in many other countries.

Latourette, in his consideration of the Great Century and the movements within Christianity through which the expansion of the faith had been chiefly accomplished, first noted the 'revivals' which were particularly effective in the United Kingdom and the United States; second, the organizations in large part growing out of them.[1] The European countries also shared fully in the movement.

It was in Great Britain that the first of these organizations had their beginning.[2] Reasons for prior British leadership included the effects of the Evangelical Revival on the thinking of Christians and the effects of the industrial revolution on the income of the people. With their desire to serve, the people were given the wherewithal to serve, an over-ruling of Providence later seen in other countries and in other centuries.

The rekindling of evangelical revival in Britain during the decade before the outbreak of revolution in France had caused a stirring in the hearts of dedicated Christians, and when the awakening became more general, their ideas were taken up and their burdens shared in a remarkable burst of organizing enthusiasm, all the more remarkable in wartime. In nearly every case, the initiative came from men who had been involved in local evangelical revivals, whether of the staider type within the Church of England, or the more dynamic kind occurring in companies of believers outside. Some of these founding fathers have been remembered for their works, the source of their dynamic forgotten.

To meet the demands of a population increasing in wealth and literacy, whose appetite for the printed Word was being whetted by the Awakening, spontaneous efforts were made. George Burder, a Congregationalist minister at Coventry, who had been influenced by George Whitefield and William Romaine, continued active as a pastoral evangelist. In 1799, he urged the formation of the Religious Tract Society to promote the diffusion of evangelical literature.[3] It was supported by both Church of England and Free Church folk, and its example was followed elsewhere, the foundation of the American Tract Society taking place a quarter of a century later, its avowed objective the providing of suitable Christian literature to the religiously destitute.[4]

The awakenings in Wales in the late 1780s had produced a hunger for the reading of Scripture among the common people. In 1787, an appeal was made from Wales for more Bibles in the Cymric tongue. The extraordinary revivals of 1791 onward catapulted Thomas Charles of Bala to the place of leadership in spiritual affairs in the principality. Thomas Charles continued active in these startling movements. When little Mary Jones tramped fifty miles over the Welsh hills with her six years' savings, only to find that the last copy of the Welsh Scriptures had been sold, she returned in tears to her home. Thomas Charles of Bala took up the matter with the Society for Promoting Christian Knowledge and, failing to persuade them, made a suggestion to the Religious Tract Society that a Bible Society be formed.[5] He returned to his work in the Awakening. The outcome was the foundation of the British and Foreign Bible Society in 1804. It was interdenominational in character, dedicated to the dissemination of the Scriptures without note or comment, at home or abroad. Its first officers largely were members of the 'Clapham Sect,' another expression of the awakening of Napoleonic times.[6] It is very clear that this history-making event resulted from the Awakening of 1791 onward in Britain. After the Battle of Waterloo, the American Bible Society[7] was formed to combine the efforts of several state-wide associations begun as a result of the American Awakening, and following the example in Britain. Bible Societies were formed in other European countries, generally after the coming of peace.

The Bible became the chief text-book of the Sunday School movement in Great Britain and the United States and elsewhere in the Protestant countries.

During the eighteenth century, many isolated attempts were made to evangelize children. Griffith Jones in Wales had concentrated upon teaching the young as well as adults to read. Hannah More, a godly Anglican woman committed to supporting the Establishment, circulated cheap tracts, and became concerned about the illiteracy of the rural folk in the Mendip Hills. While sharing a contemporary Anglican notion of full education for only the governing elite, Hannah More set out to provide elementary education for children in the rural countryside.[8] As her concern arose from her evangelical convictions, she too was interested in the Bible as a text-book. Just before the outbreak of the Revolution in France, she settled down in a country home near Bristol, and became wholly absorbed in the work of teaching the children. She was an intimate friend of Wilberforce and the Clapham Sect of Evangelical reformers encouraged her.

Joseph Lancaster, an evangelical Quaker, was likewise concerned about the hordes of illiterate and lawless children roaming the streets of London.[9] He devised a method of teaching a class of boys, then using them to teach a younger set while he taught them a second year, thus developing a school based upon the monitorial principle. In 1805, George III learned of the remarkable experiment whereby a single teacher kept order among hundreds of boys. The King asked how it could be done. 'By the same principle,' replied the Quaker, 'that thy Majesty's Army is kept in order!' So impressed was the King that he lent his support, and these monitorial schools fast multiplied. The Royal Lancasterian Society was formally constituted in 1810, becoming in 1815 the British and Foreign School Society. This monitorial school was a necessary development on the way to the public school system. It had its birth in the Revival.

In 1780, a social reformer named Robert Raikes stood among the unruly children of Gloucester's working class and asked himself: 'Can anything be done?' A Voice answered: 'Try.' And he tried.[10] He gathered the illiterate children on Sundays and taught them to read, using the Bible as the inevitable text-book. In 1803, the interdenominational Sunday School Union was formed, as much a product of evangelical revival as Raikes himself. One of the early promoters in London professed a desire to teach everyone in the world to read the Bible. Before the end of the second decade of the new century, the Sunday School movement in England and Wales had a half a million scholars enrolled.

It was in 1784 that John Sutcliffe called upon the Baptist Association of Northampton and Leicester Counties to set aside the first Monday of each month to pray for a general outpouring of the Holy Spirit and a spread of religion. John Sutcliffe had been challenged indirectly by Jonathan Edwards whose 'humble attempt to promote explicit agreement and visible union of God's people in extraordinary prayer for the revival of religion' included the advancement of Christ's Kingdom on earth pursuant to Scripture promises and the prophecies concerning the last time.[11]

Jonathan Edwards's writings helped Sutcliffe and others of Calvinistic conviction to reconcile their doctrine of Divine sovereignty with their notion of human responsibility. It is noteworthy that Sutcliffe served as pastor to William Carey and was an affectionate colleague of Andrew Fuller, the one becoming a pioneer of missions abroad and the other an advocate of missions at home.

Divine sovereignty and human responsibility were fused in the fire of the revival prayer meetings. It was natural that British intercessors were most concerned about the need of revival in Britain, but, when their prayers were happily answered, it was easy to direct the intercession into missionary enterprise, aimed at winning the whole wide world. Dr. R. Pierce Beaver, writing for an ecumenical readership, recognized the dynamic of prayer, affirming that 'the Concert of Prayer undoubtedly helped produce a climate favorable to the use of the missionary societies in the last decade of the eighteenth century.'[12] Another high authority, Dr. Ernest A. Payne, declared:[13]

> ... It was probably these prayer meetings, as much as any other single influence, which prepared the little group of ministers to venture on the formation of a missionary society.

The noted Anglican mission director, Dr. Eugene Stock, looking back after a century's success, picked the year 1786 as the 'wonderful year' in the development of missionary passion.[14] In that year, William Wilberforce resolved to live for God's glory and for the good of his fellow-men. It was in 1786 that William Carey first suggested to the group of Baptist ministers at Northampton that they must consider their responsibility to the heathen.[15] It was in 1786 that Dr. Thomas Coke initiated a Methodist mission to the people of the West Indies.[16] Many were the intercessors burdened for revival at home and missions abroad that year.

The answer to these prayers did not come until the last decade of the century. On 30th May 1792, William Carey at Nottingham preached a missionary sermon to assembled Baptist associates, urging them to 'expect great things from God: attempt great things for God.' Within six months, at a specially convened meeting of the association, what was soon to be called the Baptist Missionary Society was formed and Carey sailed for India in 1793.[17]

The founding of the Baptist Missionary Society is usually regarded as the inception of modern Protestant missionary enterprise. There had been several efforts to evangelize the non-Christian world before 1792, but they were limited in scope or in objective. The Northamptonshire shoemaker appears in retrospect to have been the first Anglo-Saxon of evangelical faith in either Britain or America to propose that Christians undertake to carry the Gospel to the world's unevangelized millions. A real enthusiast for geography and linguistics, he cobbled shoes, taught school, and preached the Good News.[18] Carey not only promoted but pioneered in missions; and he urged not only Baptists, but all Christians to share in the evangelization of every creature.[19]

Thomas Haweis, an Anglican Evangelical who had served the Countess of Huntington as a chaplain and who had been rebuked for so doing by an Anglican court, found himself superintending ministry in the revival years following 1791, when the Countess died. Still in Anglican orders, Haweis proposed the formation of the London Missionary Society, as an interdenominational organization, in 1795.[20] In 1796, the missionary ship 'Duff' sailed for the South Seas and so began the ministry of this remarkable society, which drew its support at first from Anglican and Free Church people revived in the Awakening, but later more and more from the churches of British Congregationalism.

In 1795, the Eclectic Society of Evangelical clergymen sponsored by Charles Simeon discussed a suggestion that a mission to the non-Christian world be initiated by members of the Church of England. From Simeon's prompting came the Church Missionary Society, founded in 1799 as a society for missions to Africa and the East. Strange to relate, the first missionaries of the Church Missionary Society were Germans trained at a missionary school in Berlin. The sponsoring Eclectic Society, of course, was comprised of ordained leaders of the Awakening among Anglicans in the revival times following 1791.[21]

In the year following the French Revolution, the British Methodist Conference set up a committee of management for the West Indian venture, and in successive steps finally committed its resources to the formation of the Wesleyan Methodist Missionary Society in 1817-18.[22]

In 1796, the Scottish Missionary Society and the Glasgow Missionary Society were formed by the leaders of the 1791 Awakening in the Lowlands of Scotland; but that year the General Assembly of the Church of Scotland rejected a proposal to begin a missionary enterprise. The opposition was spearheaded by the anti-Evangelicals, just as support was forthcoming from leading Evangelicals.[23] It was not until 1824 that General Assembly reversed its decision and sent missionaries out to India—including Alexander Duff, nurtured in the afterglow of the Scottish Revival.

Prior to the American Revolution, missionary-minded British Christians had sent support to missionaries on the American frontier engaged in evangelizing the Indians. It was natural that this interest should flag, and that loyal subjects of the King would be only too ready to turn over that responsibility to his former American subjects so very determined to be independent.

With the loss of the American Colonies, the fortunes of war and the blessings of naval supremacy made possible the building of a Second Empire, retaining Canada in North America but opening up India in Asia and Cape Colony in Africa. To these new fields, the main stream of pioneers made their way, but among the first enterprises was the mission to the South Seas, a no-man's-land of islands in the far Pacific. William Carey himself had thought of going to Tahiti, for he was an avid reader of Captain Cook's travels. There was no lack of opportunity for British folk.

At the end of the Revolution, American missionary work was in a sorry state. Christian Indians, whose missionaries had largely supported the Mother Country, found their tepee villages overrun by American forces, their congregations scattered, with some in flight to Canada.[24] The Scottish S.P.C.K. showed some interest in reviving their work, and the Congregational Establishment in New England decided to revive theirs.[25] In 1787, a Society for Propagating the Gospel among Indians and Others in North America was founded. Thanks to the revival in Virginia in 1787, the Presbyterians there recovered a missionary vision, and there was a measure of interest among the Reformed.[26]

ORGANIZING FOR ADVANCE

The early nineteenth century awakening had immediate effects upon the Negro inhabitants of the United States. In the North, Negro Baptist churches sprang up in Boston, New York, Philadelphia and other big cities. In 1800, the black members of a New York Methodist Episcopal Church withdrew quite amicably and formed Zion Church, which in 1821 took the lead in founding the African Methodist Episcopal Church, Zion.[27] Several years earlier, the Bethel Methodist Episcopal Church in Philadelphia, founded about 1792, had initiated the formation of the African Methodist Episcopal Church, with support from Bishop Asbury.[28] The two Negro denominations maintained their separate identity. In the South, Negro Baptists and Methodists continued to worship largely in white congregations, occupying humbler space.

Before long, the greatest work in evangelizing the Negro population was being done by black Christians themselves, but often with white encouragement. White Christians gave freely to Negro educational enterprises.[29] The standard of education among black ministers was inevitably low, and their churches were handicapped by the evil effects of slave relationships which often broke up families, leading to a laxity in marriage which persisted till modern times.[30]

* * * *

Heman Humphrey, president of historic Amherst College, reviewing the Second Great Awakening during the progress of the Fourth, delivered himself of an opinion which was formed close to the events themselves:[31]

> The organization of these institutions ... the Religious Tract Society ... the British and Foreign Bible Society the Baptist Missionary Society, the London Missionary Society, the Church Missionary Society, and kindred evangelical movements in the mother country, far spreading the gospel ... all are fruits of this blessed work of the Spirit graciously poured out about 1792, in a period of darkness when the hearts of Christians were failing them for fear.

Heman Humphrey lived through the Second Awakening, a young Christian; he became a leader in the Third, first in a Massachusetts pastorate, and then in successive revivals, generation after generation, in a collegiate community. His testimony confirmed what so few folk have realised that the great organizations of mission at home and abroad arose in the Second Great Awakening worldwide, not merely from a productive aftermath of the First Great Awakening.

The American Awakening of 1791 onwards had seemingly reached a climax in the New England and Middle Atlantic States within seven years, in the West and South within ten. Almost immediately, a missionary passion began to develop. In 1802, John M. Mason, Reformed divine, declared:[32]

> Let us not overlook as an unimportant matter the very existence of that missionary spirit... which has already awakened Christians... and bids fair to produce in due season a general movement of the Church upon earth.

The Concert of Prayer begun in 1795 had already moved believers to surrender to God for an outpouring of the Holy Spirit upon the whole country. As in Great Britain, it was not difficult to direct the prayers of intercessors towards missionary objectives. It was still a major problem to find new channels for the streams of intercession and sacrifical giving. American Baptists had begun to support the Carey project in India, but they and other Christians were looking for American-based agencies of enterprise.

In the autumn of 1796, a public meeting was held in New York to discuss the news of the foundation and progress of the interdenominational London Missionary Society, and, as a result, the New York Missionary Society was formed on similar interdenominational lines.[33] A missionary was sent to the Chickasaws of Georgia and another to the Tuscaroras in western New York State.[34] John Blair Smith, a revivalist, formerly president of Hampden-Sydney College, had become president of Union College in Schenectady, and in 1797 helped form a missionary society with Reformed backing, tackling the needs of the Oneidas.[35] In 1798, a missionary society was formed in Pennsylvania, and another in Connecticut.[36] In 1799, a society was formed in Massachusetts.[37] Each year brought forth new enterprises, dedicated in the main to a trans-cultural missionary evangelism in North America.

Meanwhile, associations of Baptist churches were taking on responsibilities for Indian missions as well as frontier evangelism, and other denominations were undertaking the same kind of work in their respective ways. Haweis of the London Missionary Society was quoted by his Connecticut Evangelical correspondents as declaring with his confreres that 'It revives our inmost souls to see the spreading of the sacred flame in America,' adding 'I trust that the sound will spread... till it shall reach... from the east to the west.' To Haweis,[38] Indian evangelism was foreign missionary work. It was still domestic to the Americans.

ORGANIZING FOR ADVANCE 15

The catalyst needed to convert such apostolic energy from home to foreign missions was supplied by the Awakening also, arising from the widespread revival of student Christianity, more particularly prayer meetings at Williams College.

One summer afternoon in 1806, five students at Williams College were driven from a maple grove where they were accustomed to meet for prayer.[39] They sheltered from the thunderstorm under a haystack, and there prayed about the need of reaching the unevangelized heathen for Christ.

The thunderstorm was of short duration, for the sun soon broke through the clouds as the light of a clear purpose broke upon their souls. Samuel J. Mills, impressed in the revival in Connecticut but fully committed at Williams College, gave the decisive word: 'We can do it, if we will!'

The students organized a society, youthful in spirit and habit, for they met in secret and in cipher recorded their minutes. They found no less than a score of students who sincerely shared their burden.

One among them, Adoniram Judson, was prepared to go out under the auspices of the London Missionary Society, but his friend Mills discouraged him, saying that it was not right that British friends should support their own mission and American volunteers also. In 1810, while completing final studies at Andover Theological Seminary, Mills and his friends went to the home of an interested professor to meet with a number of ministers of their denomination, the state establishment in Massachusetts.

The counsel of their senior brethren was divided. Some thought the proposition a premature one; others felt that it smacked of infatuation; others that it would be too expensive; but after one minister observed that they had better not try to hinder God, a majority supported their younger brethren. Soon the American Board of Commissioners for Foreign Missions was formed; hence out of the Haystack Compact there came the initiation of overseas missionary enterprise, and American foreign missions began their enlistment of the best-educated class in society in the United States.[40]

In 1812, a party of eight A. B. C. F. M. volunteers sailed for India. Before the ship reached Indian ports, war had been declared between the United Kingdom and the United States, and the officials of the East India Company, already prejudiced against British missionaries, were doubly hostile to the American project of evangelizing British subjects, of Hindu faith.

On the voyage to India, Judson and his bride, knowing that they would encounter William Carey, began to re-study the subject of believers' baptism. The Judsons and Luther Rice decided to embrace the Baptist viewpoint, and Rice returned to ask support of American Baptists, who in 1814 founded a general missionary convention of the denomination, later the American Baptist Foreign Mission Society. Forced out of India by an antagonistic British East India Company, the Judsons went on to Burma and wrought there a mighty work for God.[41]

In 1819, the Methodist Episcopal Church of the United States of America formed its missionary society.[42] The overseas missionary project of the Protestant Episcopal Church was begun two years later.[43] Presbyterians, divided by schism, took longer to establish an official missionary society, their Board of Foreign Missions being created in 1837.[44] In that same year, the missionary society of the Evangelical Lutheran Church in the United States took form and commenced operations.[45]

When, at the height of the 1798 Revival in the Eastern States, the New York Missionary Society was formed by the ministers of four denominations, the work was launched by redirecting the Concert of Prayer into missionary prayer sessions every second Wednesday of the month at candlelight, to entreat the outpouring of the Spirit with the proclamation of the Gospel to all nations.[46]

War was raging in January 1815 when the intercessors of the Concert of Prayer were asked to redouble their zeal and pray for a return of peace, a reformation of morals, and a general revival of religion. It was suggested that a return to the first Monday of every month would re-align the prayers of believers throughout Europe, America and the mission stations on other continents and islands. The response was gratifying, a large number of churches fully supporting the union of prayer.[47]

The Concert of Prayer for revival in the 1780s in Great Britain and in the 1790s in United States, and the renewed Concert of Prayer in both countries in 1815 and in several European realms besides, was clearly demonstrated to be the prime factor in motivating and equipping Christians for service in a worldwide movement which totally eclipsed the military might of the nations at the Battle of Waterloo. A century of comparative peace among nations made the great century of pioneer evangelization possible.

3

THE OPENING UP OF INDIA

After some tentative efforts, Indian Protestant missions began in 1706 with the commencement of an effort of Danish origin, of German staffing and of British support. The first of the volunteers for King Frederick IV's project were products of the Pietist Revival in Germany, Bartholomaus Ziegenbalg and Heinrich Plutschau.[1] The Danish Lutheran chaplains viewed the two evangelists with much disapproval, and other opposition made their life in India very trying.

After the untimely death of Ziegenbalg, other missionaries (chiefly German and Pietist) took up the challenge of the work. The Anglican Society for Promoting Christian Knowledge lent valuable aid to their efforts.[2]

A most outstanding missionary of the second half of the eighteenth century was Christian Friedrich Schwartz, who also was a product of Halle, the Pietist university.[3] He earned the respect of British East India Company officials and of many Indians, of high rank and low caste alike. Before the end of the eighteenth century, between eighteen and twenty thousand adherents had been gathered, chiefly Sudras, Pariahs and Eurasians of Portuguese extraction. Moravian enterprise flourished awhile and then failed.

The Evangelical Awakenings of the nineteenth century changed conditions enormously in the sending countries. This affected not only India but the whole non-Christian world.[4]

In the early years of the nineteenth century, the evangelical societies of the denominations awakened by the Revivals of the period sent out missionaries to South Sea Islanders and to Africans both in their home continent and in tropical America. These enjoyed a remarkable success among the former, winning whole peoples to the Gospel; and they made a fair beginning among the latter, laying the foundations of a work that made Christianity within the century the dominant faith in many tribes and nations.

In both cases, the evangelical missionaries were pitted against the dark forces of primitive paganism that was hardly able to stand its ground against an enlightened religion.

It was a very different story when the eager emissaries of the Evangelical Revivals tried to enter the homelands of rival religions—Islam in northern Africa and western Asia, Hinduism and propinquent systems in India, and Buddhism and propinquent faiths throughout the Orient. In these settings, New Testament Christianity was to encounter communities of interest or systems of philosophy that fiercely resisted the message of the Gospel. The command to go was followed by reconnaissance, then permanent residence.

The most hopeful opportunity was afforded in India, where extension of British commercial and imperial power opened a vast sub-continent to the influence of Europeans. In its early days in the middle of the eighteenth century, the East India Company in general practised a religious neutrality, which towards the end of the century became a handicap to the missionaries.

The renewal of the charter of the East India Company every twenty years—1793, 1813, 1833—proved to be of the utmost importance to the evangelization of India, for the friends of the missionaries used the debates in Parliament to insist upon far-reaching changes in Company policy.

The year 1793 marked a turning point in the evangelization of India. An Anglican Evangelical, William Wilberforce,[5] persuaded the House of Commons to make better provisions for chaplains for the Protestant employees of the Company. A number of these chaplains were strong Evangelicals, and seemed constrained to evangelize not only the Europeans but the Indian non-Christians.

There were many outstanding chaplains in the service of the East India Company during the first quarter of the nineteenth century, but the most remarkable was Henry Martyn. Martyn was born in Cornwall in 1781, and had a profound religious experience at Cambridge University at the turn of the century. He became a fellow of St. John's College and a curate to Charles Simeon in Holy Trinity Church.[6] He was called to overseas missionary service.

In 1806, Henry Martyn arrived in India, noting in his diary: 'Now let me burn out for God!' In six short years, his ambition was fulfilled, yet he became India's best remembered missionary. He was a manly disciple and a disciplined man, faithful in his duties as a chaplain, enthusiastic in his preaching to Hindus and Muslims, very brilliant in his work as a translator into Arabic, Persian and Urdu. He died on his way home to England.

THE OPENING UP OF INDIA

In 1793 also, William Carey arrived in India.[7] In spite of difficulties, the debts of a colleague and the insanity of his wife, the demands of his employment and the opposition of the authorities, Carey persisted, transferring his residence at the end of the century to Serampore, under the Danish flag. There he and Marshman and Ward set up a printing press, opened a school for the children of Europeans and preached to Indians. Their first convert was baptized in the year 1800.[8]

The energy of the Serampore missionaries was astounding. Not only did they translate the Scriptures into various Indian languages but they found time to experiment in the growing of sugar, coffee, cotton, cereals and fruit trees.

While in America and Europe the Evangelical Awakenings were making an impact upon the life of the United States and United Kingdom as well as Scandinavia, an early spiritual awakening had begun in the southernmost part of India.

Before the turn of the century, the numerous Nadar community who inhabited the hinterland of Cape Comorin were developing a lively interest in the Christian message. The able German missionary, Christian Friedrich Schwartz, based on Tanjore near Madras as a member of the English Mission, visited Palamcottah and found native Christians living there. He ministered in their villages.

Between 1795 and 1805, Schwartz and his European and Indian colleagues baptized upwards of five thousand professed converts,[9] laying the foundation of the Tinnevelly Christian community which maintained its own position as the most evangelized part of India for fully a century.

The Christians of the extreme south were left very much to themselves, the most able Tamil-speaking pastor being Satyanathan. To help them, the Church Missionary Society sent Karl Rhenius, a German graduate of the Bible School at Basel. Under the direction of Rhenius, catechists were placed in hundreds of villages, gathering groups of converts and building up little congregations.[10]

On the Travancore side of India's southern tip, another remarkable Tamil was converted, by name Vedamanikkam, soon becoming an ardent evangelist, winning a number of his own kindred to Christ.[11] Again, the Anglicans supplied a German overseer, W. T. Ringeltaube, who baptized a group of believers. The group began to grow. Although Ringeltaube was pessimistic to the point of eccentricity, considering only three or four genuine out of a total of six hundred, the passing of time showed their conversion to be a lasting experience. In 1810 came a movement in the local Nadar community. Ringeltaube doubted their sincerity, but baptized four hundred. Shortly after, Ringeltaube disappeared from ken. In December 1817, his successor (Reverend Charles Mead) received three thousand Nadars into fellowship. The transformation of the backward community into one of self-respecting Indians led to severest persecutions in South Travancore. The Hindus tried to forbid Christian women to wear jackets or blouses over their torsos, and the Nadars defied them. Christians were beaten and imprisoned after each protest, but persecution provoked more and more to apply for baptism.

To India, the London Missionary Society sent Nathaniel Forsyth in 1798,[12] but his work wore him out in Bengal within eighteen years. In 1813 a number of their missionaries were settled in Madras and the South.[13]

The year 1813 brought a time of missionary advance in India. The main factors that expedited the advance were the extension of the Company's rule in India, its change of attitude to missions, the conclusion of the Napoleonic Wars, and the increasing interest of the British, American and European Protestants in missions reinforced by 'the rising tide of religious revivals,' to quote Latourette.[14]

Restrictions on the residence of foreigners were lifted. In 1813, the American Board placed its missionaries in Bombay.[15] In 1813 also, Anglican Evangelicals in England persuaded the Company to provide a bishop and archdeacons for the supervision of missionaries in territory controlled by the East India Company forces.

During the decade following 1813, the Church Missionary Society sent twenty-six missionaries to India, eleven of them German Lutherans. In 1816, the Society began its Mission of Help to the ancient Syrian Church of Kerala far south.[16] It enjoyed good relations with its hosts for a while, then tensions developed, resulting in a number of Syrian Christians entering the Anglican fold and later in withdrawal of the more evangelical Syrians into a new denomination, the Mar Thoma Church, an evangelical-catholic-orthodox body of Christians under episcopal government.

In 1819, the British Methodists in Madras formed a missionary society, ministering to the British soldiers and civilians and to Tamil Indians. The work spread throughout the South of India.[17]

THE OPENING UP OF INDIA

The Serampore missionaries were of Particular Baptist affiliation. In 1821, the British General Baptists began a work in Orissa and a decade later the General Baptists from the United States joined them.[18] Other Baptists from the United States pioneered missions in Assam and Andhra, somewhat later.[19]

The Baptist Missionary Society also entered the island of Ceylon—Lanka—in 1812,[20] followed by the Methodists in 1814, alas without their leader, great-hearted Thomas Coke, who died during the voyage out.[21] In 1817, the Church Missionary Society sent four Evangelical clergymen to Ceylon,[22] and in 1815 the American Board commenced a mission to Indian Tamils in the Jaffna area of Ceylon.[23]

The Dutch Reformed Church in Ceylon was in decline in the early nineteenth century. With the change of government, nominal members relapsed into Buddhism, leaving Burgers (descendants of Dutch-Sinhalese unions) the sole support.

As in India, the sudden expansion of missionary enterprise was provoked by the missionary enthusiasm which arose from the widespread prayer unions that culminated in the revivals of 1792 onwards in Great Britain and the United States. This 'concert of prayer' was committed to intercession for 'the revival of religion' and 'the extension of Christ's Kingdom' overseas.[24]

As in the homelands, the movement was marked by the most cordial interdenominational cooperation, an evangelical ecumenism unprecedented in the history of Christianity. Carey was an ardent Baptist, but he urged Christians of all denominations to share in the evangelization of the world. Wilberforce was an ardent Anglican, yet he expedited the movement of Methodist missionaries overseas. Lutherans aided the Anglican enterprise and supplied many of the Church Missionary Society pioneers. Only the unrevived or reactionary traditionalists offered opposition. All this clearly reflected the interdenominational cooperation of the subjects of the great awakening in the sending countries.

4

THE THIRD GENERAL AWAKENING

As in Great Britain, revival was renewed in the United States and Canada after 1815, and for fifteen years there were revivals reported here and there.[1] This renewal saw the emergence of outstanding evangelists, such as Asahel Nettleton in New England, Daniel Baker in the South, and Charles Finney in the 'burnt-over' area of western New York State.[2] Local revivals continued in Great Britain, and a new surge of Methodism took denominational form.[3]

On the mission fields, the pioneers encountered three types of response to their evangelistic outreach and prayer: folk movements of unindoctrinated people, awakenings of instructed communities, and revivals of believers, in such places as South India, South Africa, Indonesia and Polynesia which were open to the Good news.

It seemed almost too good to be true that another general awakening of phenomenal power swept the United States in 1830-1831.[4] Whether in the eastern, western or southern States, it was without reported extravagance. The movement began in Boston and New York and other cities in summertime, 1830.[5] It began in Rochester, New York, during the autumn in Finney's ministry, and reached its peak in midwinter 1830-31, winning a thousand inquirers at the same time that a hundred thousand others were being enrolled in other parts from Maine to the borders of Texas.[6] Finney, as a national evangelist, was made by the revival of 1830-31, not vice versa. In these years, several smaller bodies of evangelistic folk unchurched by their denominations united in the virile Disciples of Christ movement.

Bishop Asbury told his Methodist preachers:[7] 'We must attend to camp-meetings; they make our harvest time.' The harvest was followed by as much work as that which preceded sowing. The Methodist Episcopal Church thrived in the 1830s, and doubled its numbers around 1840.[8] Likewise, the Baptists, carrying on their ministry by means of their 'farmer-preachers,' covered the country with a network of Baptist associations, founding a Home Mission in 1832.[9]

The revival of the 1830s was effective in Great Britain also, provoking local movements of great intensity among the various Methodist bodies in England, strengthening the Anglican Evangelicals and Free Churches.[10] It was inhibited somewhat by a confessional reaction, the Tractarian movement, which stressed a sacramental-sacerdotal churchmanship and opposed the evangelism of the awakenings.[11] James Caughey, an American evangelist, won many thousands in a series of campaigns in England—including William Booth, who commenced open air preaching.[12]

First South Wales and then North Wales were moved in awakenings in the 1830s.[13] Another general revival stirred Wales in the 'forties, influenced by Finney's philosophy of revival. In Scotland, revivals increased in number in the 1830s, culminating in an extraordinary outburst at Kilsyth under the ministry of William C. Burns, who witnessed a like revival in Dundee, then in various parts of Scotland, as spontaneous revivals broke out in the Highlands from 1839 onwards.[14] This Scottish Awakening prepared the way for the Disruption and the formation of the Free Church of Scotland, a protest against lay patronage and government interference. So great was the revival in Ireland that the bishops of the Church of Ireland were talking about 'a second reformation,' somewhat prematurely, for the converts of the time were lost to Ireland by emigration following the potato famine. In the North, Evangelicalism triumphed over Arianism among Presbyterians, who multiplied their congregations.[15]

The evangelical ecumenism of the times produced an interesting development. Dublin Evangelicals formed a group for 'the breaking of bread,' attracting many who were bewildered by denominationalism.[16] From this gathering came the Christian Brethren, miscalled Plymouth Brethren. John Darby became the leader of the Exclusive Brethren, George Muller of the Open Brethren, who promoted evangelism and missionary enterprise.

The ministry of George Scott in the 1830s precipitated a lasting revival in Sweden, Carl Olof Rosenius taking up his work after his expulsion, awakenings general in the 1840s, when revival was renewed in Norway, all Scandinavia being moved in the 1850s, despite a confessional reaction under Grundtvig.[17] There was confessional reaction in Germany also, although revivals continued. The continuing Reveil in France and Switzerland reached the Netherlands in 1830, provoking awakenings as well as a confessional reaction.

The 1830s were marked by some extraordinary revival-awakenings in Polynesia. In 1834, a phenomenal movement began in the kingdom of Tonga, described by the Wesleyan missionaries as a 'baptism from above.'[18] In 1837, a similar movement began in the kingdom of Hawaii, Titus Coan taking in 1705 tested converts in one day at Hilo, 7557 in one church during the movement.[19] Revivals were felt in other parts of Polynesia, and a movement in Tonga in the 1840s paralleled a great ingathering in the Fiji Islands, among a Melanesian fearfully addicted to cannibalism.[20] In 1822, missionaries of the Netherlands Missionary Society had entered Sulawesi in Indonesia.[21] While revival was moving the Netherlands, a folk movement of great proportions swept Minahassa, the northeastern peninsula, making that field Christian within a couple of generations.

In the 1830s, there were renewed revivals in Grahamstown in South Africa, and an overflow to the Bantu folk round about. Robert Moffat witnessed an ingathering in Botswanaland. At the same time, pioneers were pouring into southern Africa from missionary societies renewed or founded in the movements going on in the sending countries.[22] Pioneers were at the same time entering the Gold Coast and Nigeria, while freed slaves settled Sierra Leone and Liberia.

Missions of help to the Oriental Churches in the Near and Middle East resulted in revivals and awakenings, sometimes in disruption and reformation.[23] The pioneers coming from revived churches in Britain, Europe, and North America gained barely a foothold in China, where resistance to the foreign faith was strong. Japan and Korea remained closed to all missionary enterprise.

There were folk movements in various parts of India. Missionaries flocked to India after 1833 and accelerated the work of evangelism and social reform in the sub-continent. There were local revivals, among them a striking movement sparked by the ministry of Samuel Hebich.[24] A folk movement of the Karens of Burma to Christ followed the conversion of Ko Tha Byu through Baptist evangelism.[25] There was 'a time of revival' in Ceylon.

The work of James Thomson, who pioneered education and Bible distribution in the Latin American republics, was systematically destroyed in the political and religious reaction throughout the continent. In the West Indies, newly-liberated slaves flocked to the churches of the missionaries who had defended them against oppression.

After Finney became a national figure, he was invited to campaign in Boston, New York, Philadelphia and the larger cities.[26] His 'new measures' aroused opposition, and his theology moved away from the Presbyterian-Congregational brand of Calvinism to a middle course between Calvin and Arminius. He later espoused a perfectionism.

Finney's career proved most unusual in the history of evangelism. Reacting against a kind of fatalism in his own denomination, he deplored the notion that sinners should continue under conviction of sin until God should deign to grant them repentance; rather he felt that they should, by an act of the will, surrender to God. His preaching of this 'whosoever will' message achieved a powerful effect.

As a gospel tactician, Finney was second to none. As a strategist, his practice was better than his theory. Finney went to the extreme of stating that revivals of religion were nothing more or less than a result of the right use of the appropriate means.[27] His own expectancy of revival seemed justified by the results almost everywhere reported in his services. His theories, based on the assumption that times of refreshing were automatically assured, have not always applied during serious declines in community religion.

Unfortunately, besides encouraging many a local pastor or evangelist to expect revival, Finney's theory encouraged a brash school of evangelists who thought that they could promote genuine revival by means chosen by themselves in times chosen by themselves. The use of means was often blessed with Spirit-filled men, but with less-spiritual agents it gave rise to a brand of promotional evangelism, full of sensationalism and commercialism.

Neither the 1792 Awakening, at Finney's birth, nor the 1830 movement, nor the 1858-59 Awakening, nor the 1905 Revival after his death, was planned, programmed or promoted. It must be concluded that Finney's theory applied to evangelism, not outpourings of the Spirit.

One among many influenced by the writings of Finney, George Williams, converted in his 'teens, commenced in London in the 1840s the Young Men's Christian Association, at first as thoroughly evangelistic as it was social.[28] The formation of the Y.W.C.A. followed in the 'fifties. These movements experienced a remarkable expansion during the mid-century awakening in the United States and Great Britain and other countries. They were two of a host of voluntary organizations assisting the Churches.

There was nothing new in the theology of the 1830 Revival. All of its teachings were derived from the New Testament, its strong points the doctrines recovered in the Reformation and re-emphasized in the Evangelical Awakenings of the early and later eighteenth century.

Out of the evangelical ecumenism of the 1830s and 1840s came the Evangelical Alliance, founded in 1846 by leaders of the movement on both sides the Atlantic. Its doctrinal basis reflected the views of a majority of Protestants between 1810 and 1910 before broad church and high church partisans entered the cooperative movement.[29]

> I. The Divine inspiration, authority and sufficiency of the Holy Scriptures, and the right and duty of private judgment in the interpretation thereof.
> II. The Unity of the Godhead, and the Trinity of Persons therein.
> III. The utter depravity of human nature, in consequence of the Fall.
> IV. The incarnation of the Son of God, His work of atonement for sinners of mankind, and His mediatorial intercession and reign.
> V. The justification of the sinner by faith alone.
> VI. The work of the Holy Spirit in the conversion and sanctification of the sinner.
> VII. The resurrection of the body, the judgment of the world by the Lord Jesus Christ, the eternal blessedness of the righteous, and the eternal punishment of the wicked.

The Evangelical Alliance had adopted a final statement of faith—that of the Divine institution of the Christian ministry and obligation and perpetuity of the ordinances of baptism and the Lord's Supper. The records of the Awakenings reveal no departure from the points listed above, but they do indicate the participation of preachers and teachers, such as Brethren and Quakers, whose view of Christian ministry and ordinances differed from the other denominations.

In those times, the Roman Catholic and Greek Orthodox Churches offered no cooperation, but often persecuted the Evangelicals. Apart from the Anglican, Lutheran, Reformed and other neo-confessionalists, Protestants used the Alliance idea of Christian unity so widely that it led to a practice of fraternal fellowship having the force of a major doctrine. The revivalists, evangelists, pastors and missionaries at home and abroad worked together in evangelical comity.

3rd GENERAL AWAKENING

Meanwhile, the revivalists of the Third Awakening continued the drive for social betterment.[30] They achieved an emancipation of slaves, the protection of prisoners, the care of the sick, the improvement of working conditions, the safeguarding of women and children, and the extension of popular education, the founding of hospitals, asylums, orphanages, schools, high schools and colleges. The outstanding work of Wilberforce was followed by that of Fowell Buxton and Ashley Cooper, Earl of Shaftesbury. In Germany, Theodor Fliedner performed extraordinary social service. The more evangelistic Methodists in England provided leadership in the trade unions. In the United States, organized good works flourished as never before, promoted by societies that rose in the Awakening. On the mission fields, wherever permitted, missionaries became social activists in education, medicine, and other humanitarian projects.

The Third Great Awakening came to an end about 1842 in the United States. The unfulfilled predictions of William Miller regarding the Second Coming, the affluence of society in an expanding economy, and the divisive effect of chattel slavery tended to hinder further expansion of the Churches. In 1848, political turmoil affecting most countries brought it to an end in Great Britain and other parts of Europe. But after a decline which lasted about fifteen years, there came another great awakening, surpassing previous movements in its extent, wholesomeness, effects, and lasting impact, while sharing their theology and objectives.

5

WORK WIDENING AND DEEPENING

The renewal of revival in the sending countries, beginning 1830 in American cities and spreading around the world, was felt wherever there was an evangelical enterprise on the mission fields, in Polynesia, South Africa, and in due course in India from Bengal to Malabar.

In 1830, Scottish Presbyterian missionaries had arrived in India, their noted leader being Alexander Duff, a product of the nineteenth century awakening in Scotland, his family influenced by Simeon, himself a protege of Chalmers.[1]

Alexander Duff proved to be one of the most influential men to reach India. Not only did he leave his imprint upon the educational systems of India, including State schools, but he worked as an evangelist with a concern for souls: and he prayed for revival abroad and at home.[2]

Another famous Scottish missionary, John Wilson, had arrived in India the same year as Duff, under the auspices of the Scottish Missionary Society.[3] He too was a product of the Awakening of the early 1800s in the Scottish border country, and he too became a famous educator as well as an evangelist. He helped found the University of Bombay, but his monument was Wilson College.

Stephen Hislop, yet another Scots convert of the Revival in the border country, arrived in India during the 1840s and continued in educational work and evangelism in the Central Provinces.[4] Madras Christian College developed out of a collegiate institution founded by John Anderson, another of the Scottish volunteers.[5]

In Scotland, the revival in the days of Thomas Chalmers produced a passion for evangelism and education, and this was carried to India by younger men. Their loyalty to such evangelical revival was displayed at the time of the great disruption of the Church of Scotland, when the missionaries almost to a man gave up their security as established kirk ministers and allied themselves with Chalmers and the Free Church of Scotland, the revival party.[6] Scottish pioneering in India was very much the product of the Revival.

WORK WIDENING AND DEEPENING

After the triumph of Ulster Evangelicalism in 1840, the Irish Presbyterians began a work in Gujerat,[7] gathering their converts into villages. Welsh Presbyterians, hitherto working through the London Missionary Society, sent their own missionaries to the Khasi hill tribes of Assam in 1841, winning converts and founding little churches.[8] Both Irish and Welsh Presbyterian missions were revival produced.

Anthony Norris Groves of the Open Brethren brought out a dozen missionaries to India in 1836. Christian Brethren, be it noted, were thrust forth by the British Revival in its second phase in the nineteenth century.[9]

The renewal and revision of the East India Company's charter again in 1833 encouraged the entrance of non-British missionaries to India. Americans were quick to take advantage of the opportunities.

In 1835, American Baptists entered the northeastern province of Assam, pioneering in what was to become a very fruitful field, and the same society sent its pioneers to the southern province of Andhra, Telugu country, where one of the greatest ingatherings in history occurred later.[10]

After 1840,[11] American Presbyterians entered the Punjab, while John Scudder and other missionaries of the Reformed denomination in North America were gathering congregations at Arcot in the Madras area under the American Board— later transferred and supported by the Reformed Church.[12]

American Methodists did not pioneer in India until the 1850s,[13] when William Butler opened a mission in Bareilly, hitherto neglected in the staking out of mission stations. A significant work was begun in this territory.

In the second third of the century,[14] American Lutherans entered India and began operating a mission to the Telugus. German Evangelical Lutherans, later known as the Leipzig Mission,[15] entered the Indian field through Madras in 1840. Others, working through the Basel Mission, opened a work on the Malabar coast at Mangalore about that time.[16]

The Gossner Mission, founded by a converted Roman Catholic priest in the wake of the German Revival, sent its men to India and pioneered in various places, a significant work beginning at Chota Nagpur among a primitive people, the Kols, among whom a folk movement developed.[17]

The renewal of revival in the sending countries brought reinforcements to the missionary body in Ceylon also as they sought to reach the Sinhalese Buddhists and the Tamil Hindus and the Eurasian minority nominally Christian.

While most of the missionary effort in India was taken up with pioneering in unresponsive territories, there were occasional outbreaks of spiritual power—revival, awakening or folk movements of uninstructed people to Christ. These movements went largely unchronicled.

In 1832, the fervent preaching of Jenner and Deerr of the Church Missionary Society had won five converts in the Nadia district in Bengal, but between 1838 and 1840 a folk movement of Karta Bhojas to the Gospel gathered 1200 into the fold, and Bishop Wilson of Calcutta was described as 'full of thankful ecstasy.'[18] The folk movement continued for for some time, after which the Nadia Church institutionalized its Christian life.

On the opposite side of the sub-continent a revival began. One of the German missionaries who came out to India to serve under the Basel Mission in its work on the west coast was Samuel Hebich, whose remarkable zeal gained him an 'honourable mention' in Bishop Stephen Neill's history of Christian missions.[19] Hebich was converted in 1821, called to the mission field, arriving in Calicut in 1834.[20]

Hebich preached a simple Gospel, evangelical and direct. His outstanding success was with the officers of British regiments stationed nearby. His English vocabulary scarce exceeded 500 words, but his methods were witlessly naive and devastatingly effective. Scores of officers responded to his challenge, remaining true to God in the Queen's service. Some gained a certain fame as Christian laymen.

What was most significant about Hebich was that he was privileged to provoke both revival and awakening among the churches and community of his district, a remarkable work. This revival was wholly unexpected, observers declaring that it was the work of God's Holy Spirit, like 'the wind that bloweth where it listeth, and thou hearest the sound thereof but knowest not whence it cometh or whither it goeth.'

In August 1847, Samuel Hebich had gone with a European congregation to Chirakal to attend a meeting.[21] There the Indian catechists were so filled with the Spirit and spoke so searchingly that many of the Europeans were in tears.

On 16th September, the most obstinate of the padre's boys, David Jacobi, for whose conversion Hebich had often prayed in great anguish of spirit, came to him and of his own accord made a confession of his sins. When this was reported the following day to the united congregation, all hearts were stirred.

WORK WIDENING AND DEEPENING

A week later a school boy from Chirakal came running to the old pastor, crying 'Woe is me. I have mocked Jesus. I have said that He never lived. I have said that the padres teach only lies.' Hebich told him to be quiet, and taking the boy back to his home in Cannanore heard him in the study confess all his sins. The boy was admonished to look away from self and to look only to Jesus. Soon the boy found faith in Christ. His younger brother also came, making similar confession of sins. The two boys made public confession of their sins and of their newfound faith in Christ before the church in Chirakal and deeply moved the congregation.

'The fire' spread to Cannanore. Europeans made public confession of their sins in the prayer meeting, while the nationals came in groups to Hebich as to a priest, confessing to him their many sins of omission and of commission.[22]

Hebich during the revival season was almost beside himself. One day he rode to Tahy, a hamlet of fishermen, his soul all afire. When he entered the village, he called out to all: 'Repent! Repent! The day of the Lord is at hand.' The effect of this message was overpowering. None of the people could look up and all were silent before God. When he came to the mission house, he called out: 'Who will repent?' The people came crowding to the missionary, confessing their sins and praying God for forgiveness.[23]

On 6th October, Hebich rode to Tellicherry and confessed his faults and failings to his German brethren, who were not pleased at first. Later they followed his example. He told the national church of the revival in Cannanore. That evening, after he had returned to Cannanore, a revival began in Tellicherry that spread to Calicut and elsewhere. Everywhere the revival meetings continued far into the night. The heathen were filled with a spirit of great awe and nowhere was the voice of mockery heard; but most of them would not attend the revival meetings: a few who did were converted.

The one great defect deplored by his colleagues in this revival, wrote his biographer, was the emphasis that Hebich laid upon public confession of sins. Once convinced, he was hard to move. What Samuel Hebich failed to recognize was that while the intense conviction of sin bore the marks of its Divine origin—as the scripturally declared ministry of the Spirit of God—the varied responses to the conviction were attributable to human reaction, reaction as varied as human temperament, education and custom. And yet, after a lapse of many years, the revival was unanimously approved.

By the mid-century, the number of Protestant Christian Indians had reached approximately a hundred thousand. The various missionary bodies managed to maintain a surprising measure of comity and cooperation.[24] This they inherited in turn from the cooperation of revival evangelism.

In Ceylon, a greater response to the Christian message was evident among the Tamil immigrants than the Singhalese. This seemed to be the case in the work of the American Board, which reported local revivals in 1819, 1821 and 1824 —the last-named affecting all five stations.[25]

During the Third General Awakening in the 1830s, there were 'repeated seasons of the outpouring of the Holy Spirit' in Ceylon,[26] beginning in 1834 in the school at Batticotta, and continuing into 1835, as reported by Dr. John Scudder, the pioneer medical missionary, and renewing itself in 1838, when in a school of 170 boys (of whom about 45 were church members and 15 catechumens) there were about 50 professed conversions among the 110 'impenitent.'[27]

The British Wesleyan Methodists also relied on schools to open the doors, finding 'access to the heathen mind in its most teachable state' and sowing 'the seeds of eternal life in the rising generation.'[28] They too experienced times of refreshing in their schools in the 1830s.

The Baptists likewise were reinforced during the 1830s and expanded their work in several directions.[29] Anglicans, enjoying colonial patronage, also opened schools.[30] Church Missionary Society pioneers were supplemented by S.P.G. missioners, which tended to limit the evangelical operation in some ways. But the Anglicans registered converts, and built up a virile native clergy.

The land of Lanka, however, provided widespread and continued resistance to the Gospel. In spite of notable service rendered by the missionary societies, Ceylon— in the words of Bishop Stephen Neill—'remained a predominantly and obstinately Buddhist country.'[31]

Although indigenous revival movements occurred in the Indian dominions in the first half of the nineteenth century, the very rapid growth of the Church in India was not due to the vitality of existing Christian communities but to the indirect effects of the Awakenings in the Protestant nations of Europe and America, whose Churches took advantage of the extension of British rule to evangelize the sub-continent of people partly open to change.

6

SOCIAL IMPACT OF REVIVAL

To practise a selfish Christian faith seems impossible. 'Christianity,' said Wesley,[1] 'is essentially a social religion; to turn it into a solitary religion is indeed to destroy it.'

The sowing of the seed of social reform was carried out in the eighteenth century in Britain, just as was that of political liberty in America.[2] There were two main periods of harvest in the century that followed, coinciding in their beginnings with the early and the mid-century awakenings.[3]

Europe and America were convulsed by war in the days of Napoleon, hence it was to be expected that the flowering of social reform would follow the coming of peace after the battle of Waterloo. Peace made possible a way for social improvement not only in Great Britain and parts of Europe but also in the United States. The first period of impact came to an end about the time of the abortive revolutions of 1848 and the Crimean and American Civil Wars, and the second one commenced in the 1860s.

The first social impact was felt in the emancipation of slaves, in the protection of prisoners, in the care of the sick and wounded, in the betterment of the standards of workers, in the defence of women and children and of helpless animals, and in the establishment of systems of education.

By far, the greatest social evil was that of human slavery. Inter-tribal wars provided opportunities for slavery, which was the lot of the captured, not only in Africa but in many other parts of the world. The Arabs first introduced war for the capture of slaves for the Near Eastern market as a way of life in Africa, Europeans introducing the same objective (directly and indirectly) into West Africa for the overseas, rather than the overland trade. There is no escaping the responsibility for the active promotion of inter-tribal war, although (of course) such a state of affairs could not have occurred in the nominally Christian homelands, even then. The feudal system, with its institution of serfdom, a form of slavery, had passed away in most European countries, though persisting in the most backward.

The slave trade was a diabolical affair.[4] African chiefs often raided nearby villages at night and set fire to the huts, slaughtering the very old and very young and dragging the survivors in shackles to the coast. In the overseas trade, it was estimated that one in eight died during the voyage in which they were packed like logs in stinking holds, and that another one in twenty died in the port before reaching the auctioneer's block, twenty per cent dying within ten weeks of embarking, with no more than fifty per cent reaching the plantations. Likewise, in the overland trade, ten lives were lost for every slave who reached the coast and fifty per cent never reached a slave market,[5] according to Livingstone.

Thirteen years before the formation of the Committee for the Abolition of Slavery, John Wesley published his thoughts on slavery in a direct and penetrating argument against the inhuman traffic in human beings: 'Can human law turn darkness into light or evil into good? Notwithstanding ten thousand laws, right is right and wrong is wrong still.' [6]

Wesley declared all slave-holding absolutely inconsistent with any kind of natural justice, let alone Christian ethics. He declaimed that the whole business was hypocritically greedy, that slavery bred other vices. Men-buyers, he said, were no better than men-stealers. He denounced the wealthy slave-merchants as the mainspring that put into motion the slave-captains, slave-owners, kidnappers and murderers. They were all guilty.

These were strong words to use in 1774, when plantation slavery was protected by law, when philosophers of old and statesmen of the time were quoted eagerly to justify the outrageous institution. Wesley followed the example of the Quakers, who had spoken against slavery in the seventeenth century. George Whitefield declared less opposition. But the anti-slavery advocates were only a small, enlightened minority in both Britain and the American Colonies. Their voices were scarcely heard at first.

Slavery, though not practised in Europe, was prevalent in European colonies in the New World as well as in most Asian and African countries. In the nineteenth century, slavery was practised mainly in the plantation communities of the South in the United States and in the West Indies, as well as in the Ibero-American colonies. Yet the control of the machinery of slavery lay in the efficient shipping organizations of England, Old and New. And naval police power lay in the hands of the British Admiralty.

SOCIAL IMPACT OF REVIVAL 35

The pioneer advocates and engineers of the abolition of slavery within the British Empire were almost all products of the Evangelical Revivals. William Wilberforce and his colleagues were Evangelicals,[7] many of them the pillars of the then-derided, now-extolled Clapham Sect, a group of Church of England Evangelicals with Free Church adherents holding greater concern for the souls and bodies of men than for current ecclesiastical strife. As the abolition movement gained strength by spiritual persuasion, great men such as William Pitt, Edmund Burke and Charles James Fox, and others of like rank, joined the Evangelicals in their grand objective,[8] as did liberals with ethics inherited from their own Christian forebears.

From the time that Lord Mansfield declared in a famous case in 1772 that any slave brought to England was automatically free, anti-slavery agitation made progress; and the slave trade was abolished in 1807.[9]

That abolition of the slave trade had been achieved in Britain was of utmost importance. Had another country so decided, only a good example at the least would have been forthcoming. After Trafalgar, however, Great Britain's naval might was unchallenged for a century, and it was used to dissuade other nations from slave-trading. The nations at the Congress of Vienna agreed that the slave trade should be abolished, and country after country took legislative action until it was internationally outlawed by the civilized nations, and by some less-civilized countries as well.[10]

At first, the patrol action of the British navy against the slave-ships in the Atlantic and Indian Oceans had the effect of worsening conditions on the voyage to slave-markets, for up to two-thirds of the human cargoes were lost, some being thrown overboard to avoid detection and capture. And thus the dwindling supply of slaves caused much overwork in the West Indian plantations.[11]

Sir William Fowell Buxton led the agitation, until in 1834 Emancipation of the Slaves came into law throughout the British Empire.[12] No less than 750,000 in the West Indies alone were proclaimed free men, their chapels being crowded at midnight July 31, while the day of liberation, far from being one of bloodshed as predicted, became a day of order, reverence and rejoicing, the Negro having been prepared for his liberty through the influence of evangelical missions. Parliament cheerfully paid twenty million pounds sterling to recompense the slave-owners.

It took another thirty years to bring about the emancipation of the slaves in the United States. The successes in the early nineteenth century of the British Emancipation had dealt a staggering blow to the American institution of slavery, but it took more agitation by tender-conscienced Christians and yet another Evangelical Awakening, before a majority of the people were ready to abolish slavery. The Finneyan Revivals had a powerful effect on anti-slavery agitation in the North, not always appreciated.[13]

* * *

In prisons was held another reservoir of human misery. Already in the eighteenth century significant prison reform was under way.[14] The conditions of life in prisons were at that time indescribably foul. Old, decrepit buildings were commonly used as prisons; strait-jackets, irons and chains were added for security on the slightest excuse. The prisons were dens of despair with disease, drunkenness, indecency and debauchery forced on their inmates. Not only were the vicious criminals so incarcerated, but also first offenders and even persons already declared not guilty of any crime.

An Evangelical, John Howard, took up the challenge and gave his life as well as his private fortune.[15] John Howard received the official thanks of Britain's House of Commons. He[16] was recognized as the father of modern prison reform, inspiring others to take up the task only barely begun in his lifetime.[17] Evangelicals took the lead, followed by the free-thinkers, who tackled the reform of the penal code.[18]

A young Quaker mother who raised eleven children became burdened for the women, desperate and depraved, whom she found in the notorious Newgate prison that Wesley had called the earthly equivalent of hell. Elizabeth Fry not only read the Scriptures and prayed with these unfortunates, but also opened successful prison schools for them.[19] In 1817, Mrs. Fry founded a society for prison reform, dedicated to those principles now taken as elementary; separation of the sexes, classification of criminals, useful employment, secular education, and religious instruction with a view to restoring the prisoners to society.

One of those directly influenced was Theodor Fliedner, born in the first month of the year 1800, son of a Lutheran pastor.[20] Unconverted, he had attended the Universities of Giessen and Göttingen, but his faith was deepened elsewhere. A greater influence upon his life was the evangelical impact of Halle,[21] the university where August Francke had served.

In due course, Fliedner was called to the cure of Kaiserswerth, a Protestant parish in the midst of a Roman Catholic population.[22] A threat of foreclosure of a mortgage sent him off to Holland and England to collect funds. It was in London that the effect of the Revival dispelled finally any trace of rationalism in Fliedner's mind.[23] In 1823, Theodor Fliedner met Elizabeth Fry in the British capital.[24]

> I learned to know a whole host of institutions that minister to the bodies and souls of men. I inspected their schools and prisons. I observed their homes for the poor and the sick and the orphaned. I studied their missionary societies and Bible societies and their societies for the improvement of prisons and so forth. And I particularly noted that practically all of these institutions and organizations were called into being by a living faith in Jesus Christ and that nothing but this vital faith sustains them.

On his return to Germany, Fliedner requested voluntary imprisonment, but was refused. In 1826, he organized a prison society, the first of a series of philanthropic ventures. He built a home for discharged women prisoners, another for men, another for orphans, a hospital for the sick, an asylum for the insane. He urgently needed nurses to help, but in those days an educated woman would not stoop to empty a bucket. Fliedner decided that, if a farmer's daughter could be trained to look after helpless animals, she could be trained to look after sick people. He put girls in uniform and called them deaconesses.

Florence Nightingale, an English gentlewoman, was much intrigued by a report of the ministry of Theodor Fliedner at Kaiserswerth where the sick were lovingly cared for by the German deaconesses, all of them of peasant stock as were Elizabeth Fry's, nursing being regarded as too low for ladies. Soon she took her training in nursing at the obscure village on the Rhine.[25] Looking back years later, she deplored the backwardness of the hospital but commended its tone as 'excellent.' She recalled that she never had met with a higher tone, or a purer devotion. She returned to London to apply the lessons she had learned in the same evangelical way.

Before she died at the age of ninety, the lady with the lamp had revolutionized the life of the private soldier. She became generally regarded as the founder of modern nursing. And historians have conceded not only her training at a school born of evangelical revival but her debt to Evangelicals for her lifelong simplicity of purpose.

Secularists have contended that Florence Nightingale betrayed an anti-evangelical spirit by deriding prayer for the sick. This was a strange misrepresentation of fact. The attitude of the famous nurse was that of the modern Christian doctor. What was the good, she asked, to pray for deliverance from pestilent plague while sewers ran into the Thames?[26]

The greatest Evangelical reformer of all was Shaftesbury. At the base of the Shaftesbury Memorial in the heart of Piccadilly Circus in London is carved a striking inscription composed by W. E. Gladstone: 'During a public life of half a century, Lord Shaftesbury devoted the influence of his station, the strong sympathy of his heart and the great power of his mind to honouring God by serving his fellow-men— an example to his order, a blessing to his people, and a name to be by them ever gratefully remembered.'[27]

Great Britain was the first of the countries of the world to become industrialized. The Industrial Revolution brought about a sorry exploitation of the toiling masses, for whom Deism had done little.[28]

Shaftesbury described himself as 'an Evangelical of the Evangelicals,'[29] and this called him into a crusade for the betterment of humanity and gave an unparalleled demonstration of Christian love rather than of class hatred, love harnessed to the improvement of the lot of the working poor.

Before Lord Shaftesbury's reforms, workers were caught in a treadmill of competitive labour which served to keep them straining for sixteen hours a day. Shaftesbury and his friends put an end to that by legislation limiting operation of factories to ten hours a day, introducing a Saturday half-holiday, and abolishing all unnecessary Sunday labour.[30]

Shaftesbury's Mines and Collieries Act made impossible any further exploitation of women or children in coal mines where they had been used to drag coal in heavy wagons along darksome tunnels. His Chimney Sweep Acts prohibited the use of little boys to clean narrow factory chimneys of soot— many a child had suffocated in the task and others had been maimed therein. He also delivered children in the country from an agricultural exploitation as terrible as that of the factories. Shaftesbury, by his Lunacy Acts, transformed the lot of the insane from abused prisoners to patients.[31]

Shaftesbury promoted public parks, playing fields, gymnasia, garden allotments, working-men's institutes, public libraries, night schools, choral and debating societies, and other opportunities of self-help.[32]

Even Kenneth Scott Latourette in his weighty volumes has confessed that there is not enough space to list more than a few of the reformers and reforms impelled by evangelical motivation.[33] Nine out of ten of Lord Shaftesbury's colleagues in social and industrial reform were as much the products of Evangelicalism as the Earl himself.[34] A cotton-mill owner, John Wood, provided most of the money needed for the Ten Hours' Crusade. Richard Oastler, who did so much for the factory children, was a Methodist lay preacher. Others in the crusade were active in the lay preaching of the gospel. The Ten Hours' Act proved to be the Magna Carta of the liberty of industrial workers, closing factories at 6 p.m., keeping them closed for twelve hours, preventing labour from being robbed of evening and Sunday leisure.[35] After so many years of exploitation, it was a deliverance.

It is significant that trade unionism grew during this period of the social impact of the gospel. British trade unionism owed much to the six Dorchester labourers who were transported to the Australian penal colonies for seven years of servitude.[36] Their crime was that of forming an agricultural union to resist further depression of their wages as farm hands, wages already cut to a below-subsistence level of a shilling a day.[37] These labourers were guilty of no violence and no intimidation, not even a strike. In 1834, all six were dragged from their homes and condemned, then shipped off to Tasmania.

These Dorchester labourers, often called the 'Tolpuddle martyrs,' included three Methodist local preachers and two others active in the Tolpuddle Methodist Chapel.[38] A sixth man professed no religious convictions, but was so impressed with the religious life of one of his companions, who slaved with him in a convict gang, that he became a Christian and a Sunday School superintendent in later life. An aroused public opinion forced the early pardon of these working-men and their transportation home. The trade union cause had won a round in its battle for working men's elementary rights. Christian leadership continued for a hundred years in British trade unions. The Liberal Prime Minister, David Lloyd George, paid an unusual tribute to evangelical influence in the trade unions in these careful paragraphs:[39]

> The movement which improved the condition of the working classes, in wages, hours of labour, and otherwise, found most of its best officers and non-commissioned officers in men trained in institutions which were the result of Methodism ... John Wesley

inaugurated a movement which gripped the soul of England, that deepened its spiritual instincts, trained them and uplifted them; the result is that when a great appeal is made to either England or America, there is always the response . . . and it is due to the great religious revival of the eighteenth century.

Thus it was in the nineteenth century largely that the great Wesley-Whitefield Revival bore the fruit cultivated by converts of later awakenings in Britain and in the United States and elsewhere.

It cannot be denied that the influence of Great Britain on the United States of America was a powerful force, especially in the realm of social progress. As Great Britain was first industrialized, the hitherto unknown problems of industrial life were therein first encountered and overcome.

The decades following 1830 in American life have been called by historians[40] 'The Sentimental Years,' for it was a time when organized good works flourished as never before. There was scarcely an object of benevolence that lacked a dedicated society or institution,[41] and all of the organizations (whether church-related or not) were directly indebted to the Evangelical Awakening of the late eighteenth century, or the early nineteenth.[42]

In the United States, there were societies to promote education, to reform prisons, to stop prostitution, to colonize Africa with freed slaves, to advance the cause of peace, to provide social and spiritual amenities for sailors in port—not to mention the multitude of home and foreign missionary societies, Bible and tract societies, Sunday School associations and temperance clubs.[43]

Out of the Revival in Britain came the monitorial school system of Lancaster and Bell, a prelude to mass education. Schools and high schools and colleges were founded in the United States as a result of the Awakenings of 1800 onward in many churches and colleges, awakenings which provided not only founders but teaching staffs. Most of the denominational schools and high schools gave way to free public school systems in turn.

Of these developments, Latourette declared:[44]

> Even more important, the initiative and the early leadership in the creation of the system of free public schools supported by the state came largely from those who seem to have caught their inspiration from the Protestant wing of Christianity.

7

SOCIAL IMPACT ON INDIA

The rightful pride of Indian nationalism can claim with justice the many benefits brought by the dedication of great patriots to the land of their passionate loyalty. What other people have done for the country is often gratuitously attributed to imperialism, commercialism or self-interest.

The missionaries who invaded India with the Good News of Jesus Christ were agents neither of imperialism nor commercial enterprise. The East India Company provided the major opposition to their entry and penetration of the country. Nor were they there for self-interest. A quick glance around the graveyard in Serampore indicates the terrible toll of disease and death paid by the families of pioneer missionaries in India.

Of course, there was a connection between the work of the missionaries and the rule of British imperialism in India in the nineteenth century. There were missionaries in other parts of the mainland of Asia, but nowhere was there such a social impact as upon the Indian sub-continent. This can be explained primarily by the fact that ultimate power was in the hands of the British Parliament, not of indigenous emperors, kings or petty princes. There was no organized Indian public opinion capable of agitation for reform.

Dr. Kenneth Ingham's scholarly pen has noted that 'in the field of social progress emphasis has been placed upon the activities of the Brahma Samaj, the Arya Samaj, and more recently the Congress Party, rather than upon the work of Europeans.'[1] But the debt of indigenous reform movements such as Brahma Samaj to evangelical ideas and action must be considered, and even the debt of the Congress Party to the democratic ideals of the Anglo-American peoples who owed them both directly and indirectly to Christianity of the evangelical type. Quoting Ingham again:

> the history of Christian missionary achievement is older than any of these indigenous movements, and prepared the way for them to a degree far greater than the number of Christians in India might now suggest.

That there were reforms at all cannot be attributed to imperialist or nationalist initiative in Britian or in India prior to the advent of, or during the first thirty years of missionary work. The majority of the British people were apathetic to the problem of reform in India, just as the bulk of the Indian classes and masses were indifferent.

It was the minority of Evangelicals at work in the governing echelons of British imperialism and the tiny minority of Evangelicals agitating on the field in India who aroused public opinion in Britain and forced Parliament to legislate.

It has been shown that the movement for the abolition of slavery and the emancipation of the slaves in the English-speaking world owed its inception and conclusion both to evangelical impulse.

The abolition of slavery in all of the British possessions overseas was enacted as early as 1833 but the implementation of the legislation in India came gradually following the abolition of the legal status of slavery in 1843, twenty years before emancipation in the United States.

The Indian social order was based upon the maintenance of caste,[2] by which the lowest level of the population lived in a serfdom akin to outright slavery, and the lower castes were held in limited bondage. Even the high castes suffered a regimentation of privilege far removed from the blessings of personal liberty in a free society.

It could be said that while Islam tolerated the system of slavery, Hinduism maintained the system of caste which supported the authority of its priesthood and sustained the survival of archaic customs deemed socially inhibitive or viciously evil. Christianity came into an uneasy tension with the caste system and its supporters.

The Roman Catholic missionaries prior to the nineteenth century had reached no consensus of opinion regarding the caste system. Officially, the authorities in Rome distrusted caste, but on the field in India it was more often regarded as a civil or social affair, of no religious import.[3]

The Protestant missionaries, settled chiefly in the South of India, were somewhat uneasy about the Roman Catholic example, yet they themselves by no means uniformly condemned caste distinction in the Church. Some missionaries recognized caste, some tolerated it, some tried to ignore it and others, in growing numbers, began to oppose it. As early as 1822, missionaries of the Church Missionary Society and of the London Missionary Society decided to preach and teach the equality of castes.[4] This was most difficult to apply in the schools, where high caste parents might object to permitting their boys to associate with the lower caste lads, yet more and more schools began to open their classes to all comers.[5]

Among converts, the Indian Christians themselves concluded that conversion and caste were incompatible, and their former caste associates confirmed this by rejecting them from fellowship. In effect the Christians had become a new caste in the sight of the general public, a caste difficult to place in order of rank.

In 1833, the Anglican Bishop Daniel Wilson was scandalized by the prevalence of caste distinctions in parts of South India among church members. Lower and higher caste Christians were seated in different parts of the churches, and were buried in different parts of the graveyards. The Bishop issued a pastoral letter [6] in which was ordered that 'the distinction of caste must be abandoned, decidedly, immediately and finally.' This caused a measure of indignation among the higher caste Sudras, who switched to the Leipzig Lutheran Mission which discreetly tolerated caste distinctions.

But distaste and intolerance of caste in the churches grew more and more, and in later decades the influx of lower caste and outcaste folk into the churches demonstrated the real impact of Christianity upon the caste system, uplifting the despised classes and educating them, until their children were better equipped for life than some of those who affected to despise them.

The missionaries soon felt compelled to act against the degrading cruelty that marked some of the great idolatrous festivals. The East India Company levied a pilgrim tax upon those coming to some of the great shrines, using the money for the upkeep of the temples and their idols, of their priests and acolytes.[7]

The missionaries appealed over the heads of the Company officials to public opinion in Great Britain. Some missionaries tended to exaggerate the evils associated with the adulation of idols, as at Jagannath, and Company officials tended to minimise them. From 1814 to 1831,[8] a profit of about a hundred thousand pounds was made by the Company through this Jagannath pilgrim tax alone. In 1833, the agitation of the missionaries ended in the abolition of pilgrim tax as uncalled-for support of religion.

William Carey at Serampore became concerned with the practice of some parents of sacrificing infants to the gods in the sacred waters of the mouths of the Ganges.[9] This practice was outlawed. It took much longer for the Government to outlaw satisahagamana or the 'voluntary' burning of widows on the funeral pyre of their dead husbands.[10] Suttee, as it was called, aroused the anger of civil servants as well as of the missionaries.[11]

It was the missionaries who crusaded against the practice. The Anglican chaplain, Buchanan, calculated on the basis of population figures and the detailed reports of the Serampore missionaries that there were ten thousand widows burned alive in India annually.[12] But Buchanan's application of the Baptists' careful observation of one area to the whole of India was subject to dispute, but William Wilberforce used the Bengal figures in his speech on the renewal of the Company charter in the House of Commons in 1813.[13] Fowell Buxton, also Evangelical, added his influence to that of others in 1821. A Society for Promoting the Abolition of Human Sacrifices in India was formed. Meanwhile, the authorities vacillated. Enlightened Hindus, such as Ram Mohan Roy, also opposed the practice. Finally, Lord Bentinck in 1829 forbade widow-burning in the Presidency of Bengal, and Madras and Bombay followed suit.[14] The upheavals predicted by critics of the action failed to materialize, and suttee died away.

Missionaries in their crusade against suttee became aware of the suffering of Indian women in lesser ways, the ill-treatment of widows, the marriage of children, the seclusion of women. They determined to end the more glaring of these evils.

Few Indian leaders approved of their plans. Charles Grant, of the Clapham Sect and also of the Court of Directors of the East India Company, published his opinion that the lot of Indian women was one calling for pity.[15] Ram Mohan Roy pointed out that a widow was entitled to a fair share of her husband's property and a daughter a quarter inheritance,[16] but practice denied the Hindu theory.

Before the end of the first quarter of the new century, missionaries had begun educating girls. Prejudice and poverty were the main obstacles, for not only were women kept in subjection but their daily grind of labour prevented any escape.

The success in the face of difficulties encouraged the missionaries and inspired their Indian allies, including enlightened Hindus and Muslims. But it was only after the 1858-59 Awakenings that the programme gained momentum.

Missionaries from the start provided shelter for orphans and destitute children. Their limited resources hindered them from introducing a widespread programme of relief, but they dealt with local problems and offered an example for public and private bodies to follow. It was as a drop in the ocean of poverty.

The long battle of the missionaries against suttee convinced their leaders that education was needed to impel the Indian people themselves to welcome reform. But what kind of education?

Before 1793, the Europeans in India had little part in educational projects in India. Whatever education there was for Indian children was in the hands of missionaries, with rare exception. As early as 1781, Warren Hastings had founded a college for Muslims to study Muslim law, but less than a hundred students were involved.[17] Lord Wellesley established a college in 1800, without missionary initiative, but Evangelicals such as David Brown, Buchanan, and William Carey soon took part in the teaching.

By 1813, evangelical associations in Britain had persuaded Parliament to provide a hundred thousand rupees from Company revenue to promote education. Important as were the school projects which received financial support from the Government, they were far surpassed by the projects of the missionaries themselves. In 1819,[18] the Baptists reported 7000 children in their own schools, the Anglicans and London Missionary Society 4000 each, perhaps 50,000 in all schools of the various Societies in 1824. No government projects could remotely match this achievement. The Baptists at Serampore reported printing 71,000 school-books in various languages by 1828, and other Societies produced similar outputs.

A controversy developed between the Orientalists and the Anglicists regarding the medium of school instruction. Both agreed that the vernaculars should be used for elementary instruction, and both agreed that the vernaculars were inadequate for advanced studies. The Anglicists advocated teaching advanced subjects in English, the Orientalists in an Oriental classical language.

By 1824, the Directors of the Company were being persuaded that English was needed for the kind of education designed to help Indian people.[19] Most of the missionaries favoured a compromise at first, but Anglicists among them increased in influence. The Serampore missionaries taught Sanskrit also, but only for a better understanding of its daughter languages, not for its religious literature.

The Evangelical Awakening in Scotland[20] had begun to shape the educational system of that forward-looking nation. It was the Church of Scotland which sent out several men who were to influence educational policy in India.[21] Alexander Duff introduced far-reaching new methods in the missionary approach, developing Christian institutes of higher learning using English with an expectation of attracting young men of the higher castes desirous of a European education. And the occasional converts of these colleges provided an educated leadership for the emerging Indian churches. Duff advocated schools for women too.

Duff, in his educational programme was often opposed strongly by the missionaries, with one illustrious exception, William Carey.[22] But his programme won its way. It is significant that Duff was supported by the enlightened Hindu Ram Mohan Roy when he opened his first school in Calcutta, attracting a couple of hundred boys to study in English and the provincial Bengali.

Duff's success had a powerful effect upon the educational policies of the Government. Such Anglicists as Trevelyan and Macauley were beginning to win support, and in 1835 Lord Bentinck threw his support to the use of English as the medium of instruction. Within twenty years, the main lines of education for India were laid down.[23]

John Wilson, like Alexander Duff, a product of the local Revival in Scotland, arrived in Bombay in 1830, and in 1832 started a school which soon became a high school out of which Wilson College grew.[24] John Anderson similarly founded a work in Madras which became Madras Christian College. Yet another convert of the same Scottish Revival, Stephen Hislop,[25] founded a college in the central city of Nagpur. Schools and colleges began to spring up all over the country as missionaries adopted educational programmes for secular and spiritual betterment.[26] Converts from the higher castes became Anglican clergymen and Presbyterian ministers, national pastors and teachers, to provide needed leadership for the growing churches.

One of the greatest of all educationalists in India, Sir Philip Hartog, paid his tribute as a Jew to the work of the Christian missionaries:[27]

...imbued from the first with a zeal not only for religion but for spreading secular knowledge in the vernacular as well as in English... a great and inspiring influence in Indian education in all its stages... As one who belongs to another faith, I desire to bear my testimony to the noble and unselfish work of Christian educators in India, men and women.

Philip Hartog cited the missionaries among 'non-governmental agencies destined to exert an immense influence on Indian popular education.'[28] Through the influence of Grant, Wilberforce, and Zachary Macaulay and others of the Evangelical party, the East India Company was induced to set aside a sum of a hundred thousand rupees annually for the revival of literature and introduction of science in India. This was the beginning of an official system of education in India.

Yet, in forty years' time,[29] the total number of educational institutions managed, inspected or aided by the Company was no more than 1474, in which 67,569 pupils were instructed.[29] In the same period, the Protestant missionary societies alone raised their total of schools to 1628 (exclusive of 1867 Sunday Schools) with 64,043 pupils (exclusive of Sunday School pupils).[30]

Realizing the paucity of such missionary financing, one well-informed surveyor, M. A. Sherring, declared: 'One is amazed and almost overwhelmed at the stupendousness of this undertaking.'[31]

Foremost among the centres of education in all of India was Serampore, which Sir Philip Hartog declared 'the most famous missionary centre in India and one of the great influences in Indian education and culture.'[32] (Serampore was honoured by the Republic of India a century and a half later)

The Baptist Missionary Society entered the Orissa field. The London Missionary Society started elementary schools all over the South and several other places. The Church Missionary Society established centres in Calcutta, Madras and Bombay and moved into the provinces; in Tirunelveli district alone, at the tip of India, the C.M.S. operated 107 schools with 2882 scholars in 1835. The British Methodists (Wesleyan) soon established schools in Madras and Mysore. The Scottish Presbyterians entered the Indian field, and made their greatest strides when men like Alexander Duff, John Wilson, and John Anderson arrived after the second decade of the century.

The missionaries generally worked among the lower classes, hence they developed a strong emphasis upon vernacular education. They also opened schools for orphan children, and began a programme of education for women (in the teeth of strenuous opposition) not only in day schools for girls but zenana work among women in homes.[34]

As Dr. Ingham observed: 'The promotion of Christianity called for the extension of education to assist in the attack upon the superstition and mental slavery fostered by ignorance.'[35] This was reason enough.

The missionaries soon found themselves in a programme of translation into the vernacular languages of India. Centuries before, Francis Xavier had published his translations of the Ten Commandments and the Apostles' Creed, but no translation of the New Testament into Tamil, for instance, appeared for two hundred years until the evangelical missionary Ziegenbalg published his translation in the year 1714.[36]

The enterprise of William Carey and his colleagues at Serampore was astounding. Within two decades of arrival in India, they were preparing or printing portions of Holy Scripture in Sanskrit, Assamese, Bengali, Oriya, Hindi, Marathi, Gujerati, Kashmiri, Telugu and other tongues, with Chinese included. Within thirty years, they had the whole Bible ready in five languages and the New Testament in fifteen more.[37]

The other Societies were equally busy and the newly-formed British and Foreign Bible Society lent valuable aid. The knowledge of the Word of God spread throughout the land. But secular and classical literature was not neglected, for the Serampore Press published histories and geographies, grammars and books of instruction.

Indians tend to take for granted a lively and provocative popular press of newspapers in the vernaculars and in English. The first newspaper to gain a steady circulation in India was named Dig Darshan (The Signpost), published in 1818 by the Serampore Baptists.[38] Their second venture stimulated Ram Mohan Roy, the Hindu reformer, to publish his own newspaper in defence of his liberalized Hinduism, which provoked the orthodox Hindus to publish another to attack both Ram Mohan Roy and William Carey and to offer support for the practice of widow-burning.[39]

Serampore's Samachar Darpan continued to lead in influence and circulation,[40] and missionary enterprise in the vernacular press developed all over India, helping systematize the languages in their publication infancy. Who can estimate the influence of the Church Missionary Society press at Kottayam in Kerala upon Malayali progress? Linguistic talent was combined with a technical skill in many mission centres. If Carey was a genius in linguistics, William Ward was first-rate in printing techniques.

Indian literature and journalism scarcely had scope in the eighteenth century. It blossomed in the nineteenth century, and missionaries sent out by the Evangelical Awakenings contributed most in its development. This also paralleled the work of missionaries in other parts of the world where it was necessary to reduce languages to writing.

Indian friends, from acquaintances high in the echelons of Government to students low on the academic ladder, have expressed to the author with diffidence or vehemence the suggestion that if missionaries had concentrated upon social uplift and disowned any attempt at evangelization, their work would have met with uniform praise.

This suggestion ignores entirely the historical fact that in nearly every case these social reforms proposed by the missionaries met with strongest opposition. It also ignores the religious fact that the social programme of the missionaries stemmed from their evangelistic burden. It has been truly said:[41]

> Every missionary will claim that the mission school in India has a definite purpose. He may be specific and say that the function of mission schools in India is to lead boys and girls to Jesus Christ.

The dynamic for social action, according to the obvious motivation of missionaries past and present, is not sociological enthusiasm but theological evangelism. Missionaries have known, of course, that copyists and competitors would repeat their good works without the evangelism, and this has occasioned them no distress; but the fact remains that the original motive for all Christian social activity is evangelistic—not that the missions would have refused to do good works apart from evangelistic success!

8

THE FOURTH GENERAL AWAKENING

The Evangelical Awakening which began in the United States before the end of 1857 and in the United Kingdom in early 1859 spread all over the world and remained effective for at least forty years.[1]

The preliminary prayer meetings were commenced in New York City before the sudden bank panic of October in 1857, and the extraordinary conviction of sin in evangelism was first manifested in Canada, which was not immediately affected by the bank panic.[2] (That bank panics do not cause religious revivals may be seen in the results of the crash of the stock market in 1929 and on earlier occasions.)

How did this great Awakening manifest itself? In the autumn of 1857 came the first signs of an awakening—great success in revival and evangelism in Canada, and an extraordinary movement of men to prayer in New York City which spread from city to city throughout the United States and over the world. Churches, halls, and theatres were filled at noon for prayer, and the overflow filled churches of all denominations at night in a truly remarkable turning of a whole nation toward God.[3]

The Awakening of 1858 was received with enthusiasm by the secular press, which testified gladly of the changes for good in every place.[4] With few exceptions, chiefly among doctrinaire anti-Evangelicals, the Awakening was supported by all the Protestant denominations, including the formalist Anglicans and Lutherans as well as informal Baptists and Methodists. The movement was singularly free of sectarian spirit. Its primary emphasis on prayer did not overshadow its augmented preaching of the Word. The meetings were commended for their quietness and restraint, and won the respect of citizens everywhere, enlisting some of the most mature minds of the community for Christ.[5]

In addition to uncounted multitudes of nominal church members transformed by the power of God, more than a million converts were added to the membership of major denominations during the height of the movement.[6] Beyond all else, it was a layman's movement, in which the laymen of all denominations gladly undertook both normal and extraordinary responsibilities in the service of God and humanity. Despite the outbreak of the most devastating and bloody war in all the world between the Napoleonic wars and World War I, the awakening continued effective in the armies of both North and South and in the civil population at home, and the coming of peace brought about a renewal of zeal.[7]

The social influence of the Awakening was felt in wartime services, but much impetus was held in suspense until the cessation of hostilities, after which the social conscience asserted itself, reinforced by the social achievements of the same Awakening across the Atlantic.[8]

The same movement also affected the United Kingdom, beginning in 1859 in Ulster, the most northerly province in Ireland. Approximately ten per cent of the population there professed conversion, the same in Wales and Scotland, and a great awakening continued in England for years, another million being added to the Churches.[9] Repercussions were felt in many other European countries, and in South Africa and Australia and elsewhere among European settlers.

The phenomena of Revival were reported in parts of India, South Africa, and the East and West Indies among non-European peoples. Any mission field that possessed an indoctrinated body of believers enjoyed the same reviving. In many countries, the reviving was followed by extraordinary evangelism and by folk movements of tribes and castes.

Out of the 1859 Awakening in Britain arose a phalanx of famous evangelists—aristocrats and working men. Spurgeon built his Tabernacle on the crest of this movement.[10] The intervention of the War between the States (in which there was extraordinary evangelism and revival in every theatre of operations) delayed the emergence of great American evangelists from the 1858 Awakening. Yet the greatest of world evangelists emerged in America in due course.[11]

There was not so much unanimity of approval in Great Britain as in the United States. While the established Church of Scotland and other Presbyterian bodies overwhelmingly endorsed the Revival, there was lukewarmness or opposition in the broad-church and high-church sections of the Church of England. The British Free Churches fully supported the Awakening.[12] Many of its supporters questioned the value of the physical prostrations which marked the outset of the movement, but these died away under sober direction.

The 1858-59 Awakenings extended the working forces of evangelical Christendom. Not only were a million converted in both the United States and the United Kingdom, but existing evangelistic and philanthropic organizations were revived and new vehicles of enterprise created—Bible Societies flourished as never before, Home Missions and the Salvation Army were founded to extend thus the evangelistic-social ministry of the Awakening in worldwide projects. The impact on the youthful Y.M.C.A. organization was noteworthy.[13]

The mid-century Awakenings revived all the existing missionary societies and enabled them to enter other fields. The practical evangelical ecumenism of the Revival was embodied in the China Inland Mission founded by Hudson Taylor in the aftermath of the British Awakening, the first of the interdenominational 'faith missions.' As in the first half of the century, practically every missionary invasion was launched by men revived or converted in the Awakenings of the Churches in the sending countries.[14]

For example, the first permanent missions in Brazil followed the 1858-59 Awakenings. In Indonesia and India, folk movements to Christianity followed. China was penetrated by the converts of the Revival from many countries. The missionary occupation of Africa was rapid, and the liberated Negro in the Anglo-American territories was hopefully evangelized.

In the 1870s, D. L. Moody rose to fame as a world evangelist. Beginning modestly in York in 1873, Moody progressed through Sunderland, Newcastle, Edinburgh, Dundee, Glasgow, Belfast, Dublin, Manchester, Sheffield, Birmingham and Liverpool, using the methods of the 1858 Revival in prayer and preaching. About 2,500,000 people aggregate heard him in twenty weeks in London.[15]

In 1875, Moody returned to his native land a national figure, campaigning equally successfully in Brooklyn, Philadelphia, New York, Chicago, Boston and other cities. From then onwards, he ministered in cities on both sides of the Atlantic. A flock of successful evangelists was associated with him. Perhaps his greatest campaign was conducted at the World's Exposition in Chicago in 1893. Moody died in action in 1899.

In the Moody period, another awakening began in Sweden, extending the work of the National Evangelical Foundation (EFS)[16] and an offshoot, the Evangelical Mission Covenant (SMF). Revivals continued in Norway, Denmark and Finland.

4th GENERAL AWAKENING 53

As a result of the impact of Anglo-American Revivalists —including D. L. Moody—a Thirty Years' Revival began in Germany, from 1880 until 1910. Outstanding leaders were Theodor Christlieb (who founded the German Committee for Evangelism and Gemeinschaftsbewegung), Elijah Schrenk and Samuel Keller.[17]

In the same period, there was revival among the Ukrainian peasantry and evangelism among the Russian upper classes, the latter done by British gentlemen, Radstock and Baedeker. I. S. Prokhanov, converted in 1886, founded the All-Russian Evangelical Union which in the next century united in denominational organization with the Baptists.[18]

It is curious to notice that Charles Darwin's most significant publication (1859) occurred at the time of the Awakening in Great Britain and the United States, heralding a clash between sceptics who interpreted many new scientific conclusions as anti-theistic and traditional theologians who too readily agreed with such a faulty interpretation.

Yet far from antagonizing the academic world, the Awakening resulted in the most extraordinary invasion of the universities and colleges by the Christian message and the most successful recruitment of university-trained personnel in the history of higher education and evangelism.

In the 1858 Awakening in the United States, revivals among students resulted in the formation of the College Y.M.C.A.s, and in the following year, prayer meetings at Oxford and Cambridge gave rise to Christian Unions which later united to form the Inter-Varsity Fellowship. In the local student fellowship at Princeton in 1875 were several outstanding young men—Robert Mateer, who became leader of the Inter-Seminary Missionary Alliance; T. W. Wilson, who became president of Princeton University and later (as T. Woodrow Wilson) President of the United States, and Luther Wishard, who as organizer and evangelist of the Inter-Collegiate Y.M.C.A., pleaded with a reluctant Moody to minister to a sincerely interested student constituency.[19]

In 1882, Moody was persuaded to campaign in Cambridge University, where at first he stirred up scornful opposition. Out of the awakening, the Cambridge Seven (C.T. Studd and other first-rank varsity men) stirred the student world and proceeded to China as missionaries.

Thus encouraged, Moody acceded to Wishard's promptings to arrange a conference for students at Mount Hermon, in his home state. A youthful delegate, Robert Wilder, presented the claims of the mission fields and a hundred of the 250 present responded—within an academic year, two thousand from American universities and colleges. Thus was born the Student Volunteer Movement, with their watchword—to 'evangelize the world in this generation.' Under the direction of men like John R. Mott, Volunteers multiplied on every continent, as recruits or as emissaries.

Out of the 1859 Awakening arose the Keswick Movement for the Deepening of the Spiritual Life (1875). In the eastern hemisphere, it became a unifying force in Evangelicalism, a missionary recruitment rally of the highest quality. Out of the same agitation in America, the organization of the Holiness Movement resulted in splintering, giving birth to vigorous denominations in the Wesleyan tradition.[20]

Christian Endeavor, a movement for training young people in church-related activity, began in a local revival in Maine in 1881, under Francis E. Clark. Within fifteen years, there were more than two million members in forty thousand local societies: they were ecumenical and evangelical. A number of the denominations promoted comparable young people's organizations on the same plan.[21]

Toward the end of the century, an Anglican, George Grubb, excelled as evangelist in the British Empire countries, as did Gipsy Smith, Hay Aitken, John McNeill and Andrew Murray.

Singular advances were made in Africa. Charles Pamla continued preaching as the leading Bantu evangelist; Spencer Walton began a new missionary enterprise; an extraordinary awakening began in Uganda, Christianizing the country.[22]

The 1880s witnessed advances in the evangelization of China, as well as a remarkable seven years' revival in Japan, but the years of rapid growth in the island empire were followed by a decline caused by an onslaught of rationalist theology among national pastors.[23]

The awakenings in sending countries caused an extension of missionary enterprise on every continent. Albert B. Simpson, a convert of the 1858 Revival in Canada, founded the Christian and Missionary Alliance in 1886, at first as an interdenominational organization but later itself becoming a denomination as missionary minded as the Moravians.

In the social impact of mid-century Revivals, greater effects were realized in the industrialized United Kingdom. Lord Shaftesbury continued his extraordinary parliamentary projects for the betterment of humanity. Great orphanages were begun. A Society was formed for the Prevention of

Cruelty to Children (1889), while Josephine Butler rallied evangelical opinion to abolish the licensing of prostitution in Great Britain (1886).[24] Aroused evangelical interests motivated much of the agitation for the betterment of conditions for working people, many leaders in the Labour Party itself being avowed evangelical Christians. In the United States, there also was a growing concern with purely social issues such as rights of the working man, poverty, the liquor trade, slum housing and racial bitterness.[25] Overseas, social action excelled in missionary education and medical services.[26]

To achieve this reform, the crusaders of the Evangelical Awakenings did not stoop to engage in class warfare. Rather, under the guidance of the Spirit, they enlisted the privileged to serve the poor. The Seventh Earl of Shaftesbury singlehanded accomplished as much in his lifetime as had been achieved by any parliamentarian, yet remained an aristocrat.

Out of this evangelical concern grew a liberal social gospel whose advocates became indifferent by degrees to the dynamic of the Christian gospel, the transforming of individual lives by the power of Jesus Christ.

Some effects of the 1858-59 Awakening were not immediately apparent—the relationship of the conversion of hundreds of thousands who soon developed an insatiable desire for education to the transformation of the public school systems; or the evangelical conversion of Keir Hardie under Moody's ministry and the introduction of that evangelical spirit into the Labour Movement in contrast to the atheism of Continental socialism. This evangelical leadership among British workers continued for three generations.[27]

Unlike the Reformation, Puritanism and the Evangelical Revival, the Awakening of 1858-1859 onwards produced no cleavage among the Christian denominations, rather sewing together the rent patches of Evangelical Christianity with the thread of spiritual, if not organic, unity. The Anglo-Scottish Reformation rent the major part of British Christianity from the body of Roman Christianity.[28] Puritanism led to the expulsion of the Baptists and Congregationalists from the Anglican Established Church, and the Evangelical Revival resulted in the separation of a considerable part of the religious population from the Church of England. But the Evangelical Awakening of the mid-nineteenth century produced no further divisions and rather indicated that the tide in inter-church relationship had begun to flow in the opposite direction.[29]

9

AWAKENINGS IN INDIA, 1860—

Apart from India, there were not many Evangelicals in Asia at the mid-century. Did the 1858-59 Revival affect them in any way? The reports were as scattered as the churches in Asia themselves.

Before 1860, there were neither Evangelical missionaries nor Evangelical churches in either Japan or Korea. There were both—but in very limited numbers— in the Empire of China which constituted at that time the greatest missionary challenge and opportunity in the world. There were only 115 Protestant missionaries in the whole country, chiefly concentrated in the coastal cities and river ports.

In 1860, a revival began among the missionaries in the port of Shanghai. At the same time, there were stirrings in the tiny Christian assemblies of Chinese, as (for example) the remarkable work of grace at Lauling, near Tientsin, in the 1860's, described as 'wholly a work of God,' in which seventy men, fifty women and twenty young people requested baptism, an unheard-of thing in those days of antagonism and opposition.[1]

At the opposite end of Asia, American missionaries were reporting a religious awakening in Beirut, in Lebanon, in the 1860s.[2] There was also an awakening in 1861 among Armenians in Central Turkey, beginning at Marash, where in private homes prayer meetings multiplied, attended by Roman Catholics and Gregorians until crowds of a thousand to fifteen hundred gathered. An evangelical church that had six members in 1855 increased from 182 to 275 in 1862. It was a movement that brought results for years.

In the 1840s, there had been a remarkable awakening of Nestorian Christians in Iran, marked by its suddenness. A dozen years later, in 1859, revivals began among them again. It was said: 'The effects of these revivals are by no means limited to the souls converted. An enlightening, softening, and elevating influence of unwonted power has gone forth from them, affecting large masses of people.' Again, this movement proved effective.[3]

AWAKENINGS IN INDIA 1860—

At the middle of the nineteenth century, the population of India was approximately one hundred and fifty million people. Of these, there were 91,092 Evangelical Christians, of whom fifty-one thousand were living at the tip of India, in the Anglican mission-field around Tirunelveli and the Congregational mission-field in South Travancore,[4] where awakenings had occurred on either side of the Ghats at the beginning of the century. Less than forty thousand Christians were scattered over the rest of the huge sub-continent in tiny groups.

Throughout India, there were perhaps about six hundred missionaries, mostly ordained men and their wives. But these missionaries were overwhelmingly evangelical and evangelistic. It is certain that they had a burden for the rapid evangelization of India.

In 1857 the First War of Independence began.[5] It was limited to the Ganges Valley, from Delhi to Calcutta, and few other parts were affected. In the South, where Christianity had made its greatest gains, there was no uprising at all.

The ostensible reason given for 'the Mutiny' was the use of grease, presumably of cow or pork fat, on the cartridges of army rifles. One was offensive to Hindus, the other to Muslims. Despite a quick decision to use ghee, clarified butter, the damage was done. The anti-British rebels had found a cause for revolt.

There were other reasons, doubtless, among which was the disastrous defeat of the East India Company's British and Indian forces in Afghanistan in 1842. The prohibition of suttee and of female infanticide, the protection of the lower castes and outcastes against discrimination, and the many social reforms introduced through both evangelical and liberal political pressure helped to alarm the conservative upper classes.

The Uprising was not specifically directed against Christianity, but against British rule and military severity. But the 'mutineers' and their helpers fell upon civilian Europeans and native Christians, dispatching them in Delhi and elsewhere. The number of the Christians murdered was not large, a total of three score chaplains, missionaries, national Christians and families.

In the field of the Lutheran Mission, at Chota Nagpur, there was fierce persecution during the period of the Mutiny, but, in tribute to the depth of the work of grace among these people, it was said that 'During the persecution, not a single Christian denied the Lord Jesus, nor did anyone renounce Christianity.'[6] Although the Mutiny and its sad antagonisms poisoned Indian-British relationships, it was no more than a slap to Christianity.

While the phenomena of evangelical revival were being reported from over the United States in 1858, a company of American missionaries in Ludhiana (Northwest India) asked all Christians to set aside the second week of January 1860, for united prayer for Divine blessing.[7] The response all over the world was phenomenal. In India, for years to come there was unusual blessing.

News of the 1858-59 Awakenings in America and Ireland caused excitement in all the Evangelical communities in India. An outstanding leader in the resultant movement of prayer was Alexander Duff, who declared his support of the worldwide Awakening in unmistakable language:[8]

> In the face of the myriads instantaneously saved under the mighty outpourings of the Spirit of grace, I feel no disposition to enter into argument, discussion or controversy with anyone.

In Calcutta, Dr. Alexander Duff sponsored united prayer meetings, supported by Anglicans, Baptists, Congregationalists and Presbyterians.[9] Similar prayer meetings were begun in Madras, Bombay and other cities. A great and increasing spirit of prayer prevailed among the Christians, but no one was sure how these prayers would be answered. 'Something like a Revival movement seems to be springing-up in Bombay and Poona,' it was reported, and a call to prayer was issued urgently by the Bishop of Bombay for all Christians.

One of the greatest missionaries in the middle of the nineteenth century to serve India was George Bowen of Bombay. After describing Bowen's calm, phlegmatic temperament, his biographer, Robert E. Speer, stated illuminatingly:[10]

> Once however in 1859, on the day the news came of the great Revival in the North of Ireland, he was greatly moved and seemed almost beside himself. The possibility of such a work in India seemed for the first time to fill all his thoughts.

George Bowen spent upon occasion most of the night in prayer for revival in India.[11] There were many others like him, not only among the missionaries, but in the European military and civilian population of the British cantonments.

AWAKENINGS IN INDIA 1860— 59

India had just emerged from the trying days of the great Indian Mutiny. Among the British garrisons were many outstanding Christians, and, thanks to the humanitarian but imperialist zeal of the Clapham Sect in London, there were also many ardent Christian men in the Indian Civil Service. So the general movement to prayer in 1860 helped to bring about local revivals among Europeans, as at Sialkot, where officers, men, and civilians were converted.[12]

But the significant thing about the impact of the 1858-59 Awakening upon India was not the stirring among European missionaries and civilians, rather the outbreak of revivals among indigenous Christians, and the folk movements of Indian communities to Christianity that resulted therefrom.

In far-off Assam, the period following 1861 saw a revival among the churches of the Brahmaputra towns,[13] Gauhati, Nowgong and Sibsagor, besides tremendous growth in both the Garo Hills and Upper Assam. From this movement came the pioneer evangelists who initiated work among the other head-hunting tribes in the hills.

The mid-nineteenth century awakening in the Tirunelveli district of Tamilnad commenced in the ministry of a national evangelist, one who had been influenced by the best among the Christian Brethren as well as among the Anglicans.

John Christian Arulappan was born near Tirunelveli in 1810.[14] He entered mission work in 1825 and was influenced both by Anthony Norris Groves and the German Rhenius. In 1859, Arulappan read how God had visited both America and Great Britain in reviving power. He began to pray soon for a movement of the Spirit in India, a movement which anyone in his right mind would have judged as likely as snow in summer. The burden became an obsession with him.[15]

In the same locality, a poor woman suffered a very vivid dream about an awe-inspiring man who severely questioned her:[16] 'What has Christ done for you? What love has He shown you?' She shared her concern with another woman, and both were so distressed that they came to Arulappan for his counsel. They could not eat, and they trembled and cried. Arulappan requested the women to read the First Epistle of John, which concerns confession of sin.[17]

A 'wonderful work of the Spirit' began on the 4th March 1860, and in May the Spirit was poured out openly upon the congregations.[18] Some there were who prophesied and rebuked the people and others beat their breasts in contrition, and some fell down, wept bitterly and confessed their sins.[19]

What was startling about this outburst of the phenomena of revival was that it was occurring among people who never expected it, nor did the missionaries who had brought them the Gospel.[20] There were tongues, visions, and prophecies, none of which were familiar to the godly clergy of the Church of England. Some reacted against the movement immediately: 'I wrote disparagingly in my last letter,' said one, but added: 'The effect of their proceeding has been extraordinary.[21] The heathen listen to them attentively. Their doctrine is sound and pertinent, exhibiting a right understanding of Law and Gospel.' The Anglicans reporting were astounded,[22] for the movement among the nominal Christians and unevangelized villagers produced the same sort of prostrations and outcries noticed within the year in the 1859 Revival in Ireland. There were thousands of lasting conversions.

Another Anglican missionary commented that the Church of England clergy were backward in accepting such movements as these; but soon the testimony became decided and unanimous.[23] They were willing to proclaim it indeed a new era in Indian missions, that of lay converts going forth without scrip or purse to preach to their fellow-countrymen. This, the dream of the pioneers, almost too good to be true, was being realized. The testimony of the Church Missionary Society veteran, David Fenn, was simple and direct:[24]

> What a mighty change has come over this people for the better. Those who were at enmity with each other have become reconciled of their own accord. They show great eagerness to learn the Word of God.

The revival appeared in 1860 and lasted with vigour until the end of 1865. At the end of that decade, the Anglican missionaries reported that this remarkable work had proved permanent in general effects up to the time of writing,[25] 1869. In the next decade, it was to appear in Kerala among the Malayalis.

There was severe persecution of the Nadars in Travancore in 1858. The enemy over reached himself, for in 1859 Sir Charles Trevelyan, the Governor of Madras, delivered a proclamation permitting clothing above the waist. By 1870, Christian adherents numbered 30,969; of these, 2,331 were communicants.[26]

In 1861, the Church Missionary Society gave thanks for the conversion of a Brahmin family,[27] and from this event came both blessing and distress to the Christian community in Kerala. In 1865, one of the family, Justus Joseph, received ordination in the Anglican Church; and later, his brothers Matthew and Jacob formed an evangelistic team, one preaching and the other singing.[28]

Syrian Christians in the area were divided in loyalty, some affiliated with the Roman Catholics, some maintaining connections with the Jacobites in Syria, and others reformed within the Church of England in India.

The influence of the Church Missionary Society's Mission of Help had produced tension between the more evangelical and the more traditional parties in the Syrian Church. In the 1830s, a Malayali professor of Syriac,[29] Abraham Malpan of Maramon, had tried to effect a reformation in the Church, and, failing, had sent his nephew—a keen scholar in the C.M.S. college at Kottayam—to Syria to seek consecration as a bishop by an Orthodox Jacobite patriarch. He returned as a Metropolitan, Mar Athanasius, but found himself in the midst of determined opposition to reform.[30]

Of the four parties mentioned, the Anglicans and the Reform Party of the Syrians (later the Mar Thoma Church) under their Metran only proved susceptible to evangelical influences radiated by the Awakening.

Prayer meetings were continuing throughout South India from the 1860s into the '70s.[31] The Archbishop of Canterbury had appointed 3rd December as a worldwide Day of Prayer. Church of England missionary editors in Madras announced late in 1873 'Signs of a Religious Awakening in Travancore' —the report apparently from the pen of David Fenn, veteran Anglican missionary.[32] Revival began in the Mavelikara and Tiruvalla sections,[33] in districts where missionary efforts had been most concentrated and the work of the reformation most marked and active in the Syrian Church. A visit of followers of the Tamil teacher, Arulappan, stirred folk:[34]

> ... In July last, in Mankuzhi, a woman of our congregation had a remarkable dream. A dark cloud seemed to come down ... and at the same time she heard a voice saying to her 'Except you repent, you will perish.' About the same time, the wife of an evangelist, a truly Christian woman, had a similar vision. The two women began to speak and pray with others earnestly. Soon after this, a C.M.S. schoolmaster in Kattanam was struck down, his body trembling and his mind overpowered with a sense of his sins. Others in Kattanam were similarly affected ... The movement spread till it reached into all nine congregations of the C.M.S., and into thirteen of the Syrian Church.[35]

The Metran, Mar Athanasius, acted towards the movement judiciously and sympathetically,[36] and gave leave for special services and prayer meetings in Syrian churches and parish rooms.

At Chengannur, in a Syrian Reform Church, Fenn found a congregation of two hundred, all on their knees and in a state of excitement.[37] There were violent outbursts of grief over the sufferings of the Saviour and over their sins which had caused them. This was followed by 'united' prayer, no doubt, simultaneous and audible prayer.[38]

At Puwattur, in an Anglican parish, the local Anglican missionary, J. M. Speechly, declared that the whole community had been quickened into renewed earnestness after Divine things. Prayer meetings were being held in churches and prayer houses for months on end. Suitable buildings for prayer had been erected, and in several of them there were daily meetings for prayer. 'The people could hardly bear to leave the churches and came to them day after day,' it was reported.[39]

Justus Joseph and his brothers became very active in the great awakening.[40] Other Anglicans took advantage of this revival. There were very successful meetings in Kottayam directed by the Rev. Henry Baker of the Church Missionary Society, wherein 589 converts were baptized in one day in January of 1875. Nevertheless, the Anglican missionaries were much concerned about 'the strange physical manifestations,' such as prostrations similar to those occurring in Tirunelveli in 1860.[41]

It is more than significant that the thirteen congregations of the Syrian Church moved by the Awakening formed the nucleus of the Mar Thoma denomination, the evangelical and reformed sector of the historic Syrian Church.

The Kerala Awakening was marked by intense sorrow for sin. It reformed the lives of drunkards, of deceivers and extortioners, and brought about a restitution of property wrongly acquired. It increased the sale of Scriptures, a 70% increase in 1874, and promoted the earnest evangelization of the heathen, as well as diligence in attending the services of Divine worship and prayer meetings.[42] The most stirring lyrics of Malayali Christians had their origin in the 1873 Kerala Awakenings.[43] It was this Awakening which enabled the Syrian Mar Thoma Church, about to lose its property, to build and to fill its parish churches. It also expanded the work of the Anglicans.

AWAKENINGS IN INDIA 1860—

The major proportion of the fruits of revival were conserved in the fellowship of the Syrian Mar Thoma Church and that of the Anglicans in Kerala. But a minor part became schismatic—3000 Syrians and 200 Anglicans led astray.[44]

As one of the leaders in the Kerala Revival, Justus Joseph aimed to conserve and perpetuate the blessings of the work, but he made the usual mistake of confusing the human response to the Spirit's working with the working of the Holy Spirit Himself.[45] There had been emotional outbursts in some of the meetings, so he tried ardently to conserve all the emotional patterns. This led to sheerest emotionalism, which meant the manipulation of emotional response. And there had been cathartic confession of sins also. Justus Joseph sought to perpetuate the confession of sins in detail. This led to shocking exhibitionism which disgusted saner worshippers and brought ridicule.[46]

Another leader, Kudarapallil Thommen of the Chengalam parish, professed to receive a divine revelation of the Second Coming of Christ within six years. The prophet of the Six Years' Advent predicted days of darkness between 10th and 12th August 1876; and there was a merciful falling away from the fanaticism through the non-fulfilment of prophecy.[47]

It was unfortunate that the minor movement called itself 'the Revival Church,' which served to discredit the major movement in the memory of some churchmen. Proper perspective is seen in the fact that the strength of the Revival Church dwindled down to 1051 by the year 1901, while the Mar Thoma Church and the Anglicans continued to build the converts and their succeeding young people into their parishes. Walker of Tinnevelly not only redeemed the good name of evangelism but influenced hundreds of the Six Years' Advent people to re-enter the major Evangelical Churches.

That the Anglicans gained from the 1873 Awakening is seen in the fact that adult baptism was given 4632 people in the 1870s, 2497 in the next decade.[48] In the confused state of Mar Thoma affairs, statistical records are lacking, but it is well-known that their numbers increased by the thousands annually, in spite of the vicissitudes of reformation.

10

MOVEMENTS AFTER REVIVAL

Dr. Donald A. McGavran has pointed out that Revival, in the classic sense, does not occur in unevangelized or Bible-ignorant communities. In the so-called Christian countries, a renewal of Bible study and an interest in Bible doctrine has preceded the Great Awakenings; while on the mission fields, phenomenal revival has occurred only after a Christian community, however small, had been gathered.

In a certain sense, evangelism must precede revival. There must be a gathered community to be revived, and that is why so often mightily-used evangelists, such as W.C. Burns, proceeded from a great awakening in the homeland (such as then occurred in Scotland) to a field of pioneering (such as was China) and worked patiently without seeing any outpouring of the Spirit—rather the discouraging, one-by-one growth of the Church.

But, in India, because of the peculiar stratification of the population by the caste system, the way for both evangelism and revival was often prepared by what have been described as mass movements, people movements or folk movements.

As has been stated, some observers have considered an ingathering of great numbers into church membership a Revival! In the United States, any successful evangelistic campaign is described thus—but, even so, it is assumed that a majority of inquirers receiving counsel would testify to an individual experience of conversion.

This was not the case in folk movements. They seemed simply the movement of unindoctrinated people seeking a better way of life in Christianity. Group or multi-individual decisions resulted. The evangelization of such people, by pastors, teachers, and evangelists, became the first order of the day for their spiritual mentors, and when the body of believers became indoctrinated, they in turn became subject to spiritual outpourings.

Even so, there seemed to be some connection between ingatherings in folk movements[1] and antecedent phenomenal revivals—demonstrable both generally and particularly.

Many of the folk movements cited by Bishop J. Wascom Pickett in his study of Christian mass movements in India occurred shortly after the 1859 Revival.

During this period, the Lutheran Mission at Chota Nagpur working among a primitive people enjoyed a folk movement, and by 1868 they had baptized ten thousand converts. In sixty years, their Christian community increased to nearly four hundred thousand people.[2]

There was a similar movement among the Chuhras in the Punjab that resulted in an awakening among the lower caste people and added multitudes to the churches in the 1870s. During the 1880s, this vigorous folk movement quadrupled the number of Protestant adherents in the Punjab, three out of every five joining the churches being Chuhras won by the American United Presbyterian Mission.

Before 1860, there was an attempt to evangelize Mazhabi Sikhs, a 'tribe' of professional thieves. By 1881, these folk were Christianized and transformed into useful citizenry, a census of India showing that the numbers of Christians had increased as the number of 'thieves' declined.[3]

In 1871, there arose a folk movement to the Christian faith among the caste of Sweepers and this added a quarter of a million adherents to the churches. The first convert was made in 1860, the year of the prayer revival in India.[5]

Around Moradabad, a folk movement of the Chamars had begun in 1864.[5] The movements among the Nadars south in Travancore have been cited already. These folk movements among unconverted, and even utterly unevangelized people seemed to follow a pattern in following believers' revival.

The connection is best seen in Andhradesa's experience of revival and folk movements. In 1862, a total abandonment of the Telugu mission was urged at the annual meeting of the American Baptist Missionary Union.[6] It was a hopeless fruitless, discouraging field. But the Baptists refused to give up their 'Lone Star Mission.' The Anglicans, working through their Church Missionary Society, found the Telugus equally a hard people to move. So did the Brethren of the Godavery Delta Mission, and so also the Lutherans. In the 1860 meetings, missionaries of all kinds were praying.

News of the 1858-1859 Revivals in America and Ireland caused reactions in all the evangelical communities in India, and this was true in parts of Andhradesa also. Narsapur and Palakol Christians were deeply moved, and from September onward in 1860 special united weekly prayer meetings were held there alternately with attendances which exceeded fifty adults, converts coming from at least twenty-two villages.[7]

At least fifty adults! What was that among the millions of Telugu-speaking people? It was not the size of the meetings but the depth of the prayers which counted. Within a generation, the number of Telugu-speaking Christians had increased from a few hundreds to a few hundred thousand!

Later that year, the word of the revival farther south in Tirunelveli under Arulappan reached the Godaveri delta and stirred hearts afresh.[8] In December, a scholar was reading a portion of Scripture when taken with great trembling and so was thought to be dying. He revived and testified to all his students that they were sinners and needed to repent and to believe in Christ. A little later, a young man was struck down in the open field and bore testimony without fear to all around. A notable feature of this revival in 1861 was its effect on Brahmins. A Brahmin convert preached in Palakol market place to large audiences.[9]

Thirty miles from Vijayawada, in the village of Raghavapuram, a Mala outcast highway robber by name Pagolu Venkayya, heard rumors of a missionary who had said, 'Idols are no gods. A carpenter makes them and a painter paints them.'[10]

Venkayya began to pray, 'O great God, what art Thou? Where art Thou?' He had a dream of a man of singular beauty who looked kindly on him and told him that he was his friend. Shortly afterwards, he was sorely troubled by the death of his little girl, but he found no comfort.[11]

Venkayya watched one day a Hindu festival at Vijayawada. As the pilgrims bathed in the sacred waters, Venkayya protested: 'This water can never wash away sin.' A Brahmin priest, overhearing him, told him 'Go to him in the house on the hill and he will tell you how to get peace with God.' Venkayya sought out the teacher.[12]

Meanwhile the Anglican missionary Darling had preached for months without response. He was resting in the heat of the day when six men came to see him. His Hindu butler angrily drove them off, forbidding them to disturb the master. The missionary was wakened by the noise, and inquired what was the matter. Venkayya came forward with outstretched hands and said: 'Sir, we are men without knowledge. Please tell us about the true God, the Saviour whom you know.'

That very day, the missionary had poured out his heart in desperate prayer, ready to give up if no one showed any interest. He welcomed the six men with thankfulness. They went on their way rejoicing, asking the missionary to visit them and tell them more.

When Darling visited their village, the whole male population attended upon his preaching. He baptized sixteen on the 9th March 1859, forty-eight being confirmed in 1864. Venkayya himself won 700 converts in twelve years. In 1859, the Church Missionary Society had 200 converts in Andhradesa; in 1891, there were 10,000.[13]

It was the influence of these 1860 prayer meetings that produced the destined leaders of a far greater movement, according to John Clough, an American Baptist missionary whose own conversion took place during the 1858 Awakening in Iowa, and who later baptized 9606 believers in a matter of a few days in Andhra. Clough himself observed:[14]

> If Vongole Abraham had not settled in the north of Andhradesa and become a man of Christian character, his kinsman, (Yerraguntla Periah) might never have become converted and the mass movement in Andhradesa might never have happened.

Thus the key missionary and the key community leaders were moved by God at the same time of revival. The circumstances were these.[15] Cattle disease in the Rajahmundry and Machilipatnam districts in the north of Andhradesa brought an influx of shrewd Madiga merchants, leather workers and therefore outcastes, mostly from the Nellore district. A stranger had been seen in the tiny Brethren congregation in Palakol,[16] with far-reaching consequences, for he spent a week with William Bowden, a dedicated Brethren missionary, then visited F. W. N. Alexander, a missionary in Eluru, and was baptized as Vongolu Abraham, a new and happy Christian who settled in Eluru.

Abraham had a distant relative, Yerragunta Periah, who also encountered Alexander in 1862.[17] Periah then visited William Bowden in Palakol but was told there to wait until missionaries came to his own district. He walked forty miles to Ongole to seek out missionaries, but met instead a local civilian lady, Mrs. Shilling, in the street at dusk and respectfully asked her to tell him about the Lord Jesus. She read the third chapter of the Gospel of John, as a result of which he was 'born again.' He returned to his home town where his wife Nagamma and his friends also believed.[18]

Itinerant preachers sent to Tullakondapad were amazed to find the new convert, Periah, far outstripping them in zeal for souls.[19] (He continued thus until his death in 1897.) Periah was not content to be an isolated layman. He was determined to enlist a missionary from Nellore to build a work in Ongole. So he set out on foot and arrived at the Nellore compound.[20]

'Where is the white teacher?' asked Periah. 'I believe in Jesus Christ. I want Christian fellowship.' Thus it was Periah who called Clough to Ongole, where a church was organized on the 1st of January 1867.

The worldwide movement of prayer continued from 1860. 'We began 1869,' reported John Clough to the American Baptist Telugu Mission, 'with a week of prayer.'[21] There followed a spontaneous revival that year, the beginning of a folk movement. And the year 1869 became a great year in their history. The converts had been coming in by tens; they now began to come in by hundreds.[22]

There came the great famine of 1877-78 in which five million people perished. Clough was a trained engineer, so he offered to help British engineers construct a section of the Buckingham Canal paralleling the coast. He organized working gangs and paid them.

To avoid the charge of using famine relief to make proselytes, Clough and his friends for fully fifteen months—from 11th March 1877 till 16th June 1878—had not baptized a single person.[23] An earnest Roman Catholic missionary announced, in fraternal concern, that if the Baptists soon did not baptize their converts, he would baptize them. At last, when believers' baptism was administered, converts baptized in one day numbered 2222, in three days 3536, in thirty-nine days 8691, in all 9606 before the end of 1878.[24]

In 1890, there was another great ingathering at Ongole district, 1671 being baptized in four hours and thirty minutes. In three months, the total baptized at Ongole was 3765, at Kumbum 1466, in all 5231 converts without famine relief.[25]

From 1860, the mission field of the Leipzig Evangelical Lutheran Mission grew into a vast area in South India, and evangelistic work was done wherever it proved possible. There was a steady increase in the number of converts won, 4846 in 1860, but 13,720 in 1885.[26]

In the highlands of Bihar, primitive tribes proved more receptive to the Gospel than people of the plains. Lutherans of the Gossner Mission (the fruit of revival in Germany) settled in Ranchi and by 1857 had baptized nearly a thousand converts, who remained true through trying times.[27]

MOVEMENTS AFTER REVIVAL

In 1860, a new generation of missionaries arrived, and friction developed with their elders. What opposition from without could not do, the schism in the church succeeded in doing.[28] The Church Missionary Society refused to receive the dissident missionaries, but the S.P.G. did. The Anglicans thus built up a diocese, and the Lutherans started building again. Their 20,000 Christians baptized by 1873 (600 or so communicants) became in 1895 a full 40,000, with 12,732 communicants.[29]

In the days of revival in Europe, Boerresen, a Dane, and Skrefsrud, a Norwegian, were converted. The latter joined the Gossner Mission in the Hills in 1863, followed by the Boerresens. They founded their own mission among Santals farther east, and won a Christian community of multiplied thousands. Their dynamic was that of the Scandinavian mid-century Evangelical Revival.[30]

Evangelism in the North of India sprang from revival. One of Methodism's greatest missionaries, J. M. Thoburn,[31] was called of God in the year of Revival in the United States in 1858,[32] during which he received an infilling of the Spirit. He proceeded to India and spent the rest of his life therein. Although many cities of India had shared in the prayer movement of 1860, Thoburn found the work discouraging:[33]

> Revivals and all forms of revival work were unknown in India. The great cities were well supplied with Christian churches but nothing like revival had ever been witnessed in any city of the Empire. A growing feeling of despondency had taken possession of many missionaries, and not a few of those who had witnessed revivals at home were inclined to think it would be too much to expect a time of refreshing in India.

Elsewhere, Thoburn asserted that up to the close of the fifth decade of the nineteenth century no instance of a religious revival in the popular sense of the term had been reported in any part of India—which opinion ignored Hebich, for one.

The 1858 Awakening was extended to all six continents by the remarkable ministry of a very unusual Methodist, William Taylor, who proved to be one of the most versatile evangelists of all time, a follower of Wesley who made the world his parish in a way that few in history ever did.[34]

Taylor was born in Virginia in 1821, converted in 1841, and a year later began to work with the Baltimore Conference of the Methodist Episcopal Church. In 1849, Taylor followed the Gold Rush to California.[35] Lacking a church or hall, he used a wooden box as a platform on the wharf at San Francisco, and soon gathered his congregation. Taylor became known up and down California as 'the street preacher.' He returned to Eastern States and Canada to share in the aftermath of the 1858 Revival and a few years later heard a call to a world-wide ministry.[36]

In 1870, word came that 'a great evangelist named William Taylor,' who had won great fame in Australia and South Africa, was on his way to India, and would probably begin his work in the city of Lucknow.[37]

Taylor commenced preaching in Lucknow on November 25th, and within three weeks had won a hundred or more converts in a thorough awakening[38] which marked the introduction of a newer and higher standard[39] of piety and Christian fidelity among those bearing the Christian name. The spirit of revival which had been kindled in Lucknow burned brightly throughout the year, and both European and native Christians were powerfully influenced by it. The work of grace was deep and powerful, while some of its manifestations surpassed anything of a similar kind which had ever been seen by Thoburn in his lifetime.

Taylor preached[40] in Kanpur, Shahjahanpur and Bareilly, then Meerut and Delhi and other northern cities. There was a searching energy in the preaching of the Word which seemed to find out hidden sin, and a power in the Gospel so proclaimed that saved to the uttermost. Repentance, confession, forgiveness of sin, and renewal of character—all were illustrated before the eyes of the hitherto discouraged missionaries in the lives of people well-known to them.[41]

In December 1871,[42] William Taylor arrived in Bombay. He followed up the successful work of revival and evangelism by forming fellowship bands, which carried the work much further. A large number of men and women of all communities had been converted, and the lasting success of his mission was recognized in the testimony, given decades later, that the work did not cease with his departure but went on growing.[43]

Taylor remained in the Bombay Presidency, including the Poona cantonment, for a full year. He commenced in January 1873 his campaign in Calcutta, with much the same sort of success,[44] his legacy to the Methodists being still appreciated a century later, though only thirteen converts had applied for membership in April 1873.[45]

A missionary observer said of Taylor: 'What a flame of revival he had become. The living God was with him and pentecostal fire fell upon the people wherever he went.'[46]

In 1874, the evangelist sailed for Madras, in which on 10th February he packed out a hall which seated 300— with 'a great awakening' ensuing.[47] He moved to Memorial Hall with 600 seats, referring converts connected with Baptist and Wesleyan causes to their own churches, and organizing all other inquirers into classes meeting locally in houses. That work became permanent.[48]

In August 1874, Taylor hired the Clarendon Hall in the cantonment city of Bangalore, and filled its 300 seats fully, winning 140 converts of whom a hundred formed a local church. That work also became permanent.[49]

Taylor's autobiographical writings are anecdotal, without the perspective needed by the historian. Others' opinions have given a far better picture of the impact upon Indian Christians and non-Christians.

George Bowen commented that the awakenings in India under Taylor's ministry exposed certain preachers of great reputation as utterly useless in leading souls to Christ.[50] And Bishop Thoburn averred in long retrospect that the revival influence, widely felt, really marked the beginning of a new day in the mission fields of India.[51]

The quickening of interest in some circles in Ceylon was followed by a definite Buddhist revival in 1862-1864.[52] The obvious good accruing to Christians in this resurgence of the ancient faith was a recognition by many concerned that they could not be nominal Christians and nominal Buddhists at the same time, a fallacy lingering on since Dutch days.

Evangelical Anglicanism suffered a setback in the 1870s when a brilliant young Oxford don, R. G. Copleston, was appointed bishop.[53] High Church in upbringing, Copleston sought to effect changes in the Anglican operation of such a dialectical nature that he was opposed by the missionary body, whereupon he withdrew from all of them the license to minister, 1876-80. Deadlock ensued till the Archbishop of Canterbury with consummate tact effected a compromise. Copleston later became Bishop of Calcutta and Metropolitan of the (Anglican) Church of India, a dedicated churchman.

It was not until the arrival of the Rev. George Grubb in the late 1880s that anything resembling a general awakening of evangelical Christianity occurred in the beautiful island of Ceylon. But still there was steady, if slow, growth.

Beginnings had been made in the northwest Muslim areas of India, but scarcely among the Muslims. Afghanistan remained a closed land, fanatically bigoted. Footholds had been won in the ancient Christian communities of Persia, and revival and evangelism enlarged the churches. In the 1870s, American Presbyterians and the Church Missionary Society opened up work in Iran.

American Board teachers established a college in Beirut —later named the American University—and in Istanbul— Robert College. These were aimed at undermining Muslim resistance, which was strong.

American Board missionaries reported an evangelical revival in the year 1889 among the Armenians. The chief evangelist of the movement was the Rev. Haratune Jenanian of Tarsus.[54] There were three large Evangelical churches in Aintab, a town of 35,000. Response began in the smallest and spread to the other two. Half the hearers were of the Gregorian faith. So great was the movement that missionaries and helpers from all around joined in the work, the attendances ranging from a thousand to two thousand, taxing all available space. In several weeks, more than a thousand announced their conversion to God, among them drunkards and gamblers, and five hundred joined the church in two Sundays' services.

In the lands of the Crescent, except where there were ancient Christian communities as in Persia and Turkey, or where there were pagan minorities as in Northwest India and Indonesia, the phenomena of evangelical awakenings appeared to be unknown. Likewise, the growth of Christian churches—apart from the minorities—was discouragingly feeble. Yet missionaries persisted, seeking the glory of the impossible.

11

CHRISTIAN ACTION

The population of the United States was approximately thirty million in 1860,[1] of the United Kingdom slightly less. It has been shown that about a million new converts were added to the Churches of each country during the scope of the 1858-59 Awakening, a vast addition to the reservoir of Christian strength, and one that provided resources for a great forward movement in the next half-century.[2]

Not only did the membership of the churches, as well as church attendance, increase by twenty per cent, but there were entirely new developments in the life of the churches, activities taking an entirely new direction in some cases. There were not only new societies, but new kinds of societies in operation. There were reinforcements of older objectives and there were objectives clearly seen for the first time. Most significant in the 1858-59 Awakenings was the rise of the laity to play a fuller part in the affairs of the churches of Protestant Christianity. Bishop Warren Candler said:[3]

> The working forces of the churches were immeasurably increased. The Revival of 1858 inaugurated in some sense the era of lay work in American Christianity. Wesley's system of class leaders, exhorters and local preachers had done much at an early date in the same direction but now the layman's day fully dawned on all churches. No new doctrine was brought forward but a new agency was brought to bear in spreading the old truth through the efforts of men who, if they could not interpret the scriptures with precision or train souls to perfection, could at least help inquiring sinners to find the Lord by relating how they themselves had found Him.

In both America and Britain, the organizers of the union prayer meetings were businessmen warmly supported by clergy who were delighted to find the laymen willing, and gospel meetings were arranged by Christian laymen for their associates in industry, the services, the colleges and the professions.[4] In Indian cities, lay people often initiated both prayer and gospel meetings.[5]

G. E. Morgan commented on developments in Britain:[6]

In surveying the vast growth of Home Missions, the conviction gains force that the period following the Revival of 1859 was one of the most fruitful in the annals of Christianity in this country; and also that in these later days, when so many criticize and scepticize about Revival, it cannot be too strongly emphasized that the entire Home Mission Movement was not only inaugurated and manned, but financed by the revival converts and sympathizers.

As a natural corollary of the movement of the laity, the trend toward a practical interdenominational unity developed rapidly. Generally, lay movements are interdenominational, and usually revivals of religion also are interdenominational. Furthermore, in the Awakening of 1858-59, the various denominations were so busy trying to cater for an influx of new members that there was scarcely room for sectarian jealousy. With hardly an exception, the Churches were all working together as one man. Arminians and Calvinists so ignored their differences; Baptists and Pædobaptists were blessed together, and everything was almost too good to be true. By common consent, the doctrinal controversies were left alone, and the idea worked well.[7]

These factors held true in both America and Britain—countries of undivided loyalty—and had considerable force in multilingual India, in which the Evangelicals of Aryan, Dravidian or other stock, or of Arminian or Calvinistic theology were equally benefitted in the Awakening.

With the Revival of 1858 came the successful introduction of the Y.M.C.A. to American cities, and the flowering of the movement in the United States.[8] The influx of converted young men into Christian churches found an excellent outlet in the evangelistic activites of the early Christian associations of young men. The Y.M.C.A. took the initiative in the evangelizing of the masses.

From the beginning of the Revival in Britain, the Y.M.C.A. not only shared in the ingathering, but often sponsored the meetings which brought Christians together for united prayer and united evangelism. A conference of provincial and city Y.M.C.A. delegates met in London at the start of the Revival, and reiterated an early principle of the Y.M.C.A., binding it on all branches—a decided and authenticated conversion to God as the requirement for membership. From that time forward, the Y.M.C.A. increased with the Awakening.[9]

The lasting effect of the 1858-59 Revivals on the Y.M.C.A. is scarcely mentioned in standard histories on the subject.

CHRISTIAN ACTION 75

The year 1864, indeed, is officially recognized as 'the turning point of the Y.M.C.A.,[10] the beginning of certain success.' The 1864 Edinburgh Conference of the Y.M.C.A. laid the foundations of the movement with its liberal provision for all-round requirements of young men, spiritual and social, physical and individual, initiated in evangelism.

In 1890, David McConaughy organized the Madras Indian Y.M.C.A., and thirty-five associations met in the first 1891 national convention. Sherwood Eddy and Robert P. Wilder— Student Volunteer leaders—promoted work among students.

The most significant and fascinating home missionary development of the 1858-59 Awakening was the birth of the Salvation Army, which extended the evangelistic and social ministry of the more general movement.

The achievements of the husband-and-wife evangelistic team, William and Catherine Booth, during the years of the Revival were notable. Booth's experience in Cornwall taught him a connection between holiness of Christian living and power in successful evangelism, for he preached one to achieve the other.[11] His experience in the Black Country Awakening taught him that the masses could be most successfully reached by their own kind bearing witness. His frustration at the hands of unsympathetic denominational directors must have determined him to shape an organization of his own. He was an interdenominationalist, yet his Wesleyan convictions were strong; so his creation, the Salvation Army, became interdenominational in the support commanded from all manner of Christians, yet denominational enough to be reckoned a convinced Arminian fellowship, more Wesleyan than contemporary Methodists in doctrine and practice.

Prophetically, in the New Year of 1861, a conference was called in Sussex Hall, Leadenhall Street, in the City of London to consider the appalling need of the slums of the East End.[12] The Reverend Baptist Noël there predicted that some far-reaching work was about to begin, and so the East London Special Services Committee began operations.

Six months later, William Booth visited London friends to seek employment in a home mission capacity, and was put into contact with leaders of the East London committee. They invited him to become their evangelist, but four years of success in revival ministry elsewhere elapsed before Booth accepted their invitation. Into this opportunity for service, William Booth poured his passion for soul winning and his experience of ministry in the Awakening. The committee became the Christian Revival Association; then the East London Christian Mission; then, as its efforts were extended, the Christian Mission, which Booth finally named the Salvation Army.[13]

The Salvation Army thus arose as a lasting extension of the 1858-59 Revival in its double ministry of evangelism and social uplift. Many activities developed by Booth had already been initiated by other workers in the Awakening—its indoor and outdoor evangelism, its mission to fallen women, to criminals, its welfare work, and its missionary enterprise.

While the Army bore the indelible stamp of the personalities of William and Catherine Booth, it was cast by them in the mold of the 1858-59 Revival; and its pioneers entered country after country, becoming a world-wide movement still committed to evangelism and social welfare. In 1882 the Salvation Army under Frederick Tucker entered India— and soon adapted itself to local conditions of urban life.

The mid-nineteenth century Revival brought expression to a concern for the evangelization of children, as distinct from their general welfare. This had its effects in church related teaching as well as in specialized evangelism.

Edward Payson Hammond was born in the Connecticut Valley in 1831.[14] He was converted seventeen years later, and participated in the American Revival of 1858. Visiting Scotland for purposes of self-improvement, Hammond was asked to preach in Musselburgh in 1860, during the Scottish Awakening. Having left his greatcoat in the vestry, he went there but found the door bolted. A tiny little girl opened it and explained that 'a wheen o'us lassies' were praying there. Hammond overheard a tiny tot offer so touching a prayer that tears sprang to his eyes. His ideas were revolutionized. He became the children's evangelist, and foster-father of the Children's Special Service Mission. Hammond accomplished his greatest work in revival services in the Vale of Dumfries and in the city of Glasgow. His success prepared the way for a fruitful campaign in Boston, followed by great awakenings in the state of Maine, which made him a sought-after missioner from Philadelphia to San Francisco. E. P. Hammond revisited Britain, and maintained a transatlantic usefulness at a time when the exchange of talent was lively both ways. He campaigned also in Canada.

But Hammond's lasting work was as a winner of children to Christ. In the late 1860s, Spurgeon filled the Metropolitan Tabernacle with 8000 children to hear Hammond preach.

CHRISTIAN ACTION 77

Seventeen years later, Payson Hammond returned to find that many of the child converts had become Spurgeon's most valued congregational officers and workers.

Likewise, the Awakening of 1858-59 infused new vitality into the Sunday School movement.[15] A Chicago businessman, Benjamin Franklin Jacobs, began his Sunday School career during the 1858 Revival, at a time when the Sunday Schools of the country were crowded with children. Jacobs engineered the International Sunday School Convention within seventeen years. Henry Clay Trumbull, likewise active in the Revival, became the leading Sunday School editor in 1875. In Ulster, the Awakening crowded the Sunday Schools, and the upsurge was felt in all three Kingdoms.[16] The statistics of British Churches showed some denominational gains in numbers of pupils in Sunday School as high as 33% to 50% in seven years. Sunday Schools multiplied throughout India after the 1858-59 Awakenings. Child evangelism was likewise introduced. The use of simple methods practised by Children's Special Service Missioners won many youngsters to vital faith.

The British and Foreign Bible Society had celebrated its jubilee in 1854. Five years later, the Awakening brought a host of helpers to the band of workers in the noble enterprise. Little credit is given by historians to the cause of the sudden expansion of the 1860s, although it is noted.

The circulation of Scriptures among revived and converted multitudes in Ireland soared, and the Hibernian Bible Society became a supporter instead of a subsidiary[17] of the parent society. In 1861, the National Bible Society of Scotland was founded. The 1860s were years of expansion for the Bible Society's Welsh auxiliaries.[18] Advances were made in every direction in England, and by 1863 'there was scarcely a city or town in England which had not its Biblewoman supported by local contributions.'[19] At the same time, the circulation of the Scriptures at home and abroad exceeded two million, a 50% gain over the Jubilee figures.[20] During the War between the States, the presses of the American Bible Society were working at full pressure to keep up with the demand for Bibles, and these were supplied to both armies, while the financial response of civilians increased in proportion. The sale of Dutch Bibles increased in South Africa after 1860, a similar increase in English after 1865. And the sale of New Testaments and Bibles and scripture portions increased by the year in all parts of India. Scripture contributed to literacy, and literacy to the sale of Scripture.

12

MOODY AND THE STUDENTS

The impact of the 1858-59 Awakening was felt in the field of evangelism for more than forty years—the span of D. L. Moody's ministry—and continued on until the outbreak of World War I, before which disaster another worldwide awakening had become interdenominationally effective.

As the figure of Charles Grandison Finney dominated American evangelism in the middle third of the nineteenth century, so the figure of Dwight Lyman Moody dominated the final third, not only in the United States but Britain. Finney was a well-educated scholar; Moody an uneducated countryman who never learned to spell or punctuate his pungent speech. This they had in common, that they were full of zeal to win men and women to Jesus Christ.

In Northfield, a pretty village in rural Massachusetts, family circumstances scarcely suggested a career as a world evangelist for Moody.[1] His father had died when Dwight was four years old, leaving his mother and eight other children (including twins born posthumously) without provision. Nor did family religion suggest it. All the Moody children were christened in the local Unitarian Church. As an eighteen-year old lad in Boston, Moody was professedly converted. It proved to be a simple rather than a profound experience, for when he was examined for admission to church membership, he had so little to say that his candidacy was deferred until he had learned a little more.[2] A little over a year later, Moody moved to the frontier town of Chicago. It was here that his great career began.

The Awakening of 1857-58 in Chicago made a profound impression on the life of the zealous young man from New England.[3] The churches of every denomination were packed to overflowing, yet the rapid growth of the town provided all the raw material for evangelism needed.

In Chicago, Moody became interested in winning young folk to Christ through the Sunday School and through the Young Men's Christian Association. So successful was he that he became an expert in 'drumming up' scholars for

MOODY AND THE STUDENTS

Sunday School.[4] In 1858, he started a Sunday School of his own in a vacant saloon, and before long it was the largest Sunday School in Chicago. All the while, he continued active in his business as a salesman.

Moody's Sunday School developed into a church. In 1860, Moody decided to give up his business income (then bringing him $5000 a year) and to 'live by faith' (which brought him $150 the first year).[5] In 1864, the congregation occupied its own building on Illinois Street, and next year Moody was elected president of the Y.M.C.A. in Chicago. He remained a layman.

His first trip to Britain Moody made in the year 1867, seeking out leaders of the evangelical movement there, such as C. H. Spurgeon, George Müller, George Williams, Lord Shaftesbury, R. C. Morgan, Henry Varley, Harry Moorhouse, and those who seemed to Moody to have something to share with him in the work of the Lord.[6]

Events in Chicago encouraged Moody to revisit Britain. In 1868, the great Farwell Hall of the Y.M.C.A. was burned. Harry Moorhouse, a product of the Revival in Manchester, several years earlier, came to visit Moody, and was asked by him to preach—a mistake, everyone thought at first. Moorhouse preached for a week on the love of God, using the text, John chapter iii, verse 16.[7] He profoundly moved D. L. Moody, whose preaching was never the same again, and who became a preacher of a new message in a new spirit.

Moody had been married in 1862 to a young English-born girl, Emma Revell. In 1870, he met a helpmeet of a different kind, Ira D. Sankey, who became his soloist in his world ministry. In 1871, a great fire destroyed the city of Chicago, reducing to ashes fifty churches and missions. In 1871, while visiting New York, Moody experienced a mighty enduement of the Holy Spirit, an answer to two old ladies' prayers.[8]

In 1872, Moody paid a second visit to Britain. After a night of prayer in Dublin, Henry Varley said to him: 'Moody, the world has yet to see what God will do with a man fully consecrated to Him.' That comment startled Moody.[9] His visit brought a local awakening in a North London church and a number of invitations to return to Britain for a wider ministry followed. An Anglican clergyman, William Pennefather, sent him an invitation by letter to America.[10] Moody tried to settle again in Chicago, but he felt restless until he decided to return to Britain and win 10,000 souls to Christ there.

Moody persuaded Sankey to go along. Their plans made, in June 1873, the Moody and Sankey families arrived in Liverpool to learn that Pennefather had died.[11] Moody crossed to York and commenced meetings on short notice. The response was slow but definite. There was still no movement in the next campaign, in Sunderland. But in Newcastle-on-Tyne, Moody and Sankey's evangelism enjoyed success.

From there, the evangelists proceeded north to Scotland. A turning point in Moody's ministry came in their Edinburgh Campaign. Despite the local Calvinistic conservatism, the evangelist won the enthusiastic approval of the people, both inside and outside the churches. The ministers studied the movement carefully, then began to back it without reserve. Moody introduced the noonday prayer meeting of the 1858-59 Revival again. His evening meetings were crowded, taxing the largest auditoriums.[12]

After three weeks in Dundee, Moody began a mission in Glasgow that made a lasting impact on the city. Not only were thousands converted, but the United Evangelistic Committee transformed itself into the Glasgow Evangelistic Association and maintained a dozen subsidiary organizations of evangelism and relief work.[13]

Thus encouraged, the evangelists crossed over to Ireland. The Belfast Mission of the Moody and Sankey team commenced in the autumn of 1874. A daily noonday prayer meeting was begun in a Donegall Square church. The evening meetings attracted an enormous attendance of young men. The Anglican, Presbyterian and other ministers reinforced them. Dublin's Roman Catholic majority noted Moody's own avoidance of affront to their faith, and proved friendly, if not enthusiastic.[14] Again, there were several thousands of professed conversions. The Irish had seen the greatest expression of evangelism since the '59 Revival.

The Manchester, Sheffield, Birmingham and Liverpool Missions followed, each with success. They were moving towards a climax in London. Twenty thousand people nightly heard them in the Agricultural Hall in Islington. While William Taylor of California continued there, D. L. Moody preached in a tabernacle in Bow to the poor and in the Opera House in the Haymarket to the rich each evening. The London meetings lasted twenty weeks and attracted 2,500,000.[15]

As in Scotland, Moody's work in England gave birth to many Christian enterprises besides giving a breath of revival to existent organizations. It made such an impact that

Friedrich Engels, the collaborator with Karl Marx in his Communist propaganda, explained the whole business as a plot of the British bourgeoisie to import Yankee revivalism to keep the proletariat contented.[16]

In August 1875, Moody returned to the United States and commenced a campaign in Brooklyn in October, followed by a greater in Philadelphia in late November. Vast crowds attended, for news of success in Britain had enthused the American church people. In February 1876, Moody held a campaign in New York, where the New Yorkers attended in tens of thousands, many responding.[17]

Moody returned to Chicago to campaign in the winter of 1876, and received a hero's welcome from a city which claimed him as a son. Early in 1877, he commenced ministry in Boston, another city of his youth, but there he encountered opposition from both Roman and Unitarian sides. A year later, he was still campaigning in New England. Sankey parted from him to conduct a singing ministry in England, but failing there returned to work with Moody as before. In 1880-81, together they ministered in cities across the country as far as the Pacific Coast.[18]

In Newcastle-on-Tyne, Moody began his second British campaign in October 1881, again moving north to Edinburgh for six weeks, then to Glasgow, in which metropolis he held forth for five months. He then conducted short series of meetings in Welsh cities and towns and in provincial cities in England.[19] In 1883, Moody conducted an eight months' mission in London. Two large temporary structures were built, one in North London and the other in South London. As soon as a three weeks' mission had been completed in one, it was soon transferred to another location on the same side while the other building was being used across the river.[20]

After 1884, Moody conducted his evangelistic campaigns in smaller American cities,[21] besides giving much of his time to educational promotion at Chicago and Northfield, and to Bible conferences. It was rare for him to visit non-English-speaking countries, though in 1894 Moody preached in Mexico City, contributing to a most significant year.[22]

Moody conducted a great campaign in 1893 at the World's Columbian Exposition in Chicago. Approximately two million visitors attended this evangelistic series at the World's Fair, sponsored by Moody with the help of his Bible Institute. Points of preaching were chosen on the north-side, west-side and south-side of Chicago, and, on Sunday mornings, Moody rented a huge circus tent near the lake front. To reach those speaking French, German, Polish and other languages of Europe, Moody invited Monod of Paris, Stoecker of Berlin, Pinder of Poland, and other European notables to conduct special meetings, and he also shared ministry with Thomas Spurgeon of New Zealand, Henry Varley of Australia, John McNeill of Scotland—famous English-speaking evangelists, and warm admirers of Moody.[23]

In Kansas City, Missouri was held Moody's last series, commencing November 1899. His committee was composed of Anglican, Baptist, Congregational, Disciples, Methodist and Presbyterian ministers.[24] There were the usual great crowds, but Moody showed signs of exhaustion. He told his friends: 'This is the first time in forty years of preaching that I have had to give up my meetings.' He rushed home and lingered little, leaving his loved ones 22nd December 1899, mourned by multitudes who rejoiced in his works.

Moody's ministry was a puzzle to unbelieving scholars. The distinguished historian, William Warren Sweet, insisted that 'the attempts of sociologists and psychologists to explain him seem trite and foolish.'[25]

It seems appropriate to point out that Dwight Lyman Moody was an evangelist, and that his organized campaigns of evangelism were not necessarily 'revivals' in the historic sense of the word, and that his calling cannot therefore be described as a revivalist, if such a word is also used to describe the ministry of men such as Evan Roberts.

Among classes that despised his homely ways, Moody stirred up supercilious enemies, yet he also inspired both loyalty and esteem in the best products of the universities. A man is known by his associates and his friends. Moody's co-workers were extremely able men. He made use of the musical talents of Philip P. Bliss and George C. Stebbins, besides those of Ira D. Sankey. Associated with him in preaching were men like D. W. Whittle, Reuben A. Torrey, A. C. Dixon, and J. Wilbur Chapman, Americans; and from Britain, Henry Varley, John McNeill, Henry Drummond, G. Campbell Morgan, and F. B. Meyer.

The story of what God had accomplished through Moody in Great Britain and the United States created quite a great interest in evangelism and revival in Australia, New Zealand and South Africa,[26] even though the American evangelist was never to visit these southern commonwealths. His influence was likewise great among English-speaking Indian churches.

Also of deep significance to all-India Christianity was the Keswick Convention for the Deepening of the Spiritual Life, an evangelical movement with a truly worldwide influence, budded at gatherings in London, Oxford and Brighton in 1873, '74 and '75, and blossomed into early maturity at a Lake District resort in 1875; but the seed was sown in the great Revival of 1858-59 in the English-speaking world. Its origins may be traced to the American Middle West.

William Edwin Boardman had published at the height of the Awakening of 1858 a treatise upon the 'Higher Christian Life.' He was a zealous young Presbyterian businessman when he started his search in the 1840s for a holier life. His book was a huge success on both sides of the Atlantic (circulation, 200,000), being published in Britain in 1860.[27] It produced its greatest effect in the Old Country.

The year 1860 dated the conversion of a young English clergyman, Evan Hopkins, and it was not long before a copy of Boardman's treatise found its way into the eager hands of Hopkins, then engaged in an engrossing revival ministry. It was on 1st May 1873 that Hopkins with fifteen other people met in Mayfair to discuss the subject of the deepening of the Christian life. He entered a fuller experience so real that his wife was the first to follow him into it.[28]

In July 1874, a conference was conducted at Broadlands estate in Hampshire, the seat of Lord Mount Temple, the leaders being Mr. and Mrs. R. Pearsall Smith. Before he could participate in a conference announced for 1875, Smith suffered a nervous breakdown, brought about by charges more serious than the indiscretion which provoked them.[29] It is of interest that Pearsall Smith's daughter married Lord Bertrand Russell, which added to his anti-Christian bias.

Meetings for promoting Scriptural holiness were begun at Oxford in August 1874, with the help of Canon Cristopher. The Convention at Oxford was followed by a larger one at Brighton, begun on 29th May 1875.[30] Henry Varley, of 1859 Revival fame, spoke several times. D. L. Moody in London sent the good will and prayers of eight thousand people then attending his mass meetings.

The Vicar of St. John's, Keswick, Harford Battersby, had been active in the 1860 Awakening in Carlisle[31] He attended the Oxford Convention, committing himself. He invited his friends to the Lakeside town, and thus began the conventions for deepening of the Christian life that gained for 'Keswick' a unique place of leadership in the evangelical world. A majority of its leaders were either evangelists or converts of the 1859 Revival, as were a number of new speakers.

Canon Harford Battersby continued to preside until his death; Evan Hopkins emerged as the leader; William Haslam ministered; Theodore Monod participated. After an address by Evan Hopkins, Handley C. G. Moule was moved to stand publicly as a seeker after blessing, and as Principal of Ridley Hall, Cambridge or as Bishop of Durham, he warmly addressed the Keswick Convention thirteen times.[32]

Andrew Murray entered a deeper experience at Keswick in 1882, and became a mouthpiece of its message all over the world.[33] In 1887, a new speaker was F. B. Meyer, converted during the Revival in the 1860s in London.[34] Another was Charles Inwood, the Irish Methodist evangelist, whose ministry extended its message far and wide.[35]

The Keswick Convention became a missionary force after Reginald Radcliffe in 1886 borrowed its tent for a missionary meeting. Hudson Taylor and Eugene Stock used the Keswick platform to enlist young people for the mission fields. The Keswick line of teaching was supported within the United States by such evangelical leaders as D. L. Moody, Reuben Torrey, Adoniram J. Gordon, A. B. Simpson and J. Wilbur Chapman, but it never became the unifying force in United States that it had become in Great Britain.

Keswick borrowed its evangelical ecumenism, with its slogan 'All One in Christ Jesus,' from the Revival of 1858-59 and the movements which followed it. Unlike certain other products of the Revival, the Keswick Convention maintained its evangelical and evangelistic character.

Andrew Murray thus became a spokesman for Keswick in South Africa, and not only won the unchurched through his evangelism but nominal Christians to a greater commitment. Through his influence, an annual convention for the deepening of the spiritual life was organized at Wellington.

Keswick theology, mediated through a tract written by a Tamil evangelist, stirred up George Pilkington in Uganda and through him provoked an extraordinary awakening that added tens of thousands to the Anglican mission churches of East Africa.[36]

A Keswick speaker, Charles Inwood, brought the same message to Malawi, and witnessed another extraordinary revival of the Presbyterian churches and ingathering of the heathen, less than twenty years later, a comparable work of grace in Central Africa.[37]

The influence of D. L. Moody was profoundly felt among Christian students. Moody was not a theologian. His own theological convictions were strongly conservative, but he maintained cordial friendships with men of other points of view, including Professor Henry Drummond. But until the 1880s, Moody had avoided ministry to students, chiefly because he felt himself academically unequipped.

'There never was a place,' said Moody, 'that I approached with greater anxiety than Cambridge. Never having had the privilege of a university education, I was nervous about meeting university men.' He was not concerned without good reason, as events quickly proved.[38]

Well might Moody be anxious, for there were many high-spirited students lying in wait for him. There were hoots and cheers, fire-crackers and guffaws, but Moody kept his temper. His student sponsors had heavy hearts that 5th of November in 1882, but next day a ring-leader, Gerald Lander of Trinity College, called to apologize.[39]

Although seventeen hundred students had been counted in the first meeting in the Corn Exchange, only a hundred attended the second in a seated gymnasium, but they included Gerald Lander. On Wednesday, before a larger crowd, Moody gave an evangelistic appeal and after repeating it saw more than fifty men make their way to the inquiry room. One was Gerald Lander—afterwards Bishop of Hong Kong.

Next night, a hundred or more waited behind for counsel. All through the week, clear-cut conversions were professed by intellectuals and athletes, many of them proving to be both deep and lasting. The final meeting in the Corn Exchange brought eighteen hundred hearers, and concluded a mission which proved to be the beginning of a worldwide, interdenominational student movement.

The next day, without the benefit of a Sunday start, Moody opened his mission in the Corn Exchange in Oxford, which was filled to overflowing. Bolder, he quenched attempts at rowdyism several nights running and gained a hearing for his messages. Audiences moved from Clarendon Assembly Rooms to the Town Hall, where Moody gathered inquirers in an aftermeeting, and a number made personal decisions for Christ.[40]

Helping in Moody's evangelism, the two Studd brothers of cricketing fame, J. E. Kynaston Studd and Charles T. Studd, addressed one of Moody's Stepney mission meetings, and a young man named Wilfred Grenfell was converted.[41]

Sir Montague Beauchamp, William Cassels, D. E. Hoste, Arthur and Cecil Polhill-Turner, Stanley Smith and C. T. Studd, all Moody's helpers and some his converts, offered themselves to work in China under the China Inland Mission, They first became a remarkable witness team, named the Cambridge Seven, touring the British universities with their message, stirring up the students; then they sailed east.[42]

Meanwhile, in the United States and Canada, the Young Men's Christian Associations had become the main vehicles of religious life on the campuses of North American colleges and universities. The first Y.M.C.A.s for students were organized in the University of Michigan and the University of Virginia in 1858, during the Revival. Within ten years, there were forty such associations; and an Inter-Collegiate Young Men's Christian Association was founded in 1877.[43]

Two years earlier, a young man named Luther Wishard moved to Princeton University and found fellowship in the Philadelphian Society, a Christian union.[44] One of his friends therein was T. W. Wilson, known in class as Tommy, but better known later as Woodrow Wilson who carried his deep Christian idealism to the Presidency of the United States of America during critical times.

Luther Wishard became the mainspring of student Young Men's Christian Associations, and within another ten years there were two hundred and fifty associations on campuses with twelve thousand members.

A friend of Luther Wishard, Robert Mateer of Princeton, became director of an Inter-Seminary Missionary Alliance which held its first convention in 1880 with two hundred and fifty students from thirty or more seminaries present;[45] these missionary-minded students, like their Y.M.C.A. friends, were strongly evangelical and evangelistic.

Luther Wishard, as organizer and evangelist of the Inter-Collegiate Y.M.C.A., had tried hard to interest Moody in collegiate ministry, but had been rebuffed by the modest Moody, conscious of his academic deficiencies.[46] In 1884, after Moody's powerful impact on Cambridge became known, Wishard pleaded again with Moody, who consented to preach at a few colleges in 1885, including Dartmouth, Princeton and Yale. His college-slanted sermons, he knew, were few. He looked for help from his many faculty friends.

Meanwhile Stanley Smith, the Cambridge oarsman, and C. T. Studd, the Cambridge cricketer, had visited Edinburgh University in 1884 to make an impact on the four thousand students. Moody invited Kynaston Studd to spend an academic term in the autumn of 1885 in North American colleges, of which he visited twenty in thirteen weeks.[47] One of those he then challenged to a dedication of heart and life at Cornell University was John R. Mott, a law student who had been converted in a revival in Pottsville, Iowa at age 14.[48]

An outcome of Moody's growing interest in the student world was the convening of a college conference at Mount Hermon in Massachusetts in the summer of 1886, when some two hundred and fifty students from one hundred colleges attended, and Moody was as popular as any eminent lecturer. This first conference was entirely unprogrammed, and the students followed a course of lectures and activities which came about 'as the Spirit directed.'[49]

One of the college delegates was Robert P. Wilder, son of a retired missionary to India, who had already formed a student foreign missionary association at Princeton. The Wilder family, whose head had been one of the Williams College group of missionaries in the early 1800s, had been praying that a thousand students from American universities might be enlisted for foreign missionary enterprise. To every student who would listen, Robert Wilder presented the call of missions.[50]

Wilder succeeded in persuading Moody to set aside time for missionary talks, and this combination of prayer and presentation had its effect.[51] One hundred delegates signed a declaration signifying their willingness to serve overseas.

Robert Wilder and John Forman toured the universities and succeeded in enlisting about two thousand volunteers for missions. Moody was first cautious about the exuberant enthusiasm of the youngsters, but he continued to help them. The volunteers increased their own numbers to about three thousand in the academic year, 1887-88.[52]

Professor Henry Drummond of Edinburgh crossed over the Atlantic and addressed the students. He received a welter of invitations to address scientific societies, but refused almost all of them. He returned to minister in American universities, Williams College being stirred, Dartmouth suspending all classes, Princeton pre-empting his time from morning till night, Yale giving him one of the busiest weeks of his life. Even Harvard heard him graciously. Drummond was attacked by conservatives for his attempt to bring both religion and science into harmony, and, although Moody had lined up with the conservatives, he stood by Drummond as a zealous evangelist and a great scholar. Drummond so extended his student ministry around the world.[53]

Luther Wishard returned the British visitors' calls by touring the universities of Cambridge, Oxford, Edinburgh and Glasgow in the spring of 1888. The summer he spent in Germany, France, Switzerland and Sweden. Wishard extended his journey around the world, reporting conversions and calls to service everywhere.[54]

James B. Reynolds, another student volunteer, crossed the Atlantic to Oslo University. He also visited Stockholm, Lund and Copenhagen in 1889. In 1891, Robert Wilder visited universities in Britain, enlisting three hundred volunteers for missionary service.[55]

In 1893, a conference was called at Keswick, attended by a hundred delegates from twenty universities, and from it was created the Inter-University Christian Union.[56] Donald Fraser, later a missionary, became its first secretary.

The Student Volunteers sought to enlist every Christian in the objective of evangelizing the world. Their watchword was 'the evangelization of the world in this generation.' In their main objective, they were hugely successful, for in half a century, more than twenty thousand students reached the foreign mission fields of the Church, an astounding and heartening achievement. The greatest of church historians, Kenneth Scott Latourette declared his measured opinion that it was through the Student Volunteers in the various countries that a large proportion of the outstanding leaders in the spread of Protestant Christianity were recruited.[57]

In due course, the Student Volunteer Movement began to make its impact upon the Christian life of India, church and college and community. Another movement that made a contribution to church life interdenominationally was the Christian Endeavour Societies.

In the winter of 1880-81, there was a time of revival in Williston Congregational Church, in Portland, Maine. Its pastor, Francis E. Clark, wishing to conserve the blessing, organized a 'Young People's Society of Christian Endeavor' to call youth to greater dedication and service, training the young folk to participate in church activities.[58]

By 1895, there were thirty-eight thousand C. E. Societies in the world, with 2,225,000 members.[59] The movement was evangelical, evangelistic and church-related, suited to the climate of the day, which was evangelical and ecumenical. It was heartily welcomed in India.

13

CONTINUED SOCIAL IMPACT

Following the mid-century Awakening, Britain maintained the lead assumed fifty years earlier in undertaking social reform and relief. There were many reasons for this.

It is an American historical opinion that the 1858 Revival had little effect on the social welfare of the American people.[1] Rather its effects were suspended while the nation's energies were being consumed by the War between the States, a war with far-reaching social after-effects.

During that war, Christians engaged in social action; the United States Christian Commission brought spiritual good, intellectual improvement, and social and spiritual welfare to Federal troops; there were Christian organizations also that cared for the welfare of Confederate soldiers.[2]

Negroes were given as much protection as war permitted. Suddenly, in the course of hostilities, slavery was swept away.[3] What Christians were striving for by peaceful agitation became mandatory almost overnight by military decree. Emancipation, however, did not occur in a moral vacuum.

In post-war years, the American Evangelicals found British social enterprises ready to adopt. The 1858-59 Evangelical Awakening, while it was primarily evangelistic, had developed a humane spirit as liberal as its theology was conservative. Commenting on a single outcome of the great Revival, G. M. Trevelyan affirmed that it had 'brought the enthusiasm of "conversion" after Wesley's original fashion to the army of the homeless and unfed, to the drunkard, the criminal and the harlot,' treating 'social work and care for the material conditions of the poor and outcast as being an essential part of the Christian mission to the souls of men and women.'[4] This tribute belongs to the 1858-59 Awakening as a whole, not only to a very worthy part.

One of the first effects of the Awakening of 1858-59 was the creation of new and intense sympathy with the poor and suffering. 'God has not ordained,' protested Lord Shaftesbury, 'that in a Christian country there should be an overwhelming mass of foul, helpless poverty.'[5]

A revival school of Christian philanthropists soon arose, seeking to go straight to the heart of the slums with its practical Samaritanism, yet always ready to cooperate in all wise legislative improvements. So, as this Awakening intensified the fervency of faith, denominational schemes, organizations and committees were multiplied; numberless philanthropic institutions, asylums, homes, refuges, and schools were founded.[6]

As before, Shaftesbury was spokesman for evangelical social reform.[7] He originated more Royal Commissions of social investigation than any parliamentarian in all British history, extending benefits to all classes of working people.

During 1864 and 1867, Industrial Extension Acts were passed, practically universalizing provisions of workmen's protection. In 1865, Lord Shaftesbury tackled the problem of agricultural gangs and so relieved the children of the countryside from a bondage as brutal as that endured by their townsfellows in earlier decades. In 1872, Shaftesbury worked for the abolition of use of children in brickyards. His most striking victory was passing legislation forbidding the use of little boys to clean house and factory chimneys.

The Seventh Earl of Shaftesbury was not without faults, of course. As an aristocrat of class-conscious times, he upheld the superiority of his order, detested trade unions, and was occasionally a narrow-minded diehard. He bitterly opposed the Salvation Army and refused to reconsider an opinion hard to excuse.[8]

There is an immediate connection between an evangelical awakening and educational hunger.[9] In Great Britain in 1815, elementary schools were entirely private. Two decades later, Lord Ashley (later Shaftesbury) petitioned the Queen to provide education for the working classes. As insisted by Evangelicals, the State contributed a measure of support to elementary schools. In 1870, their recommendations were fulfilled in an Education Act, setting up public day schools. A million or more were in attendance in England in 1870; two million or more in 1885.[10] This had a profound effect upon the countries of the overseas Empire.

During the 1859 Awakening in Dublin, some members of a brilliant family named Barnardo professed to accept Christ as Saviour in the Metropolitan Hall series.[11] Two of these Barnardo brothers tried to persuade their younger brother, Tom, but he scoffed. Nevertheless he attended the meetings and witnessed the striking demonstrations of spiritual conviction. These he explained away as emotional hysteria and psychological phenomena, yet in spite of his subtle arguments he was set to thinking. An address by John Hambledon in the same place some weeks later caused him such conviction that long after midnight he sought, in great distress and with many tears, his brothers' help. Young Barnardo heard a call to missionary service and soon volunteered— but tragic discoveries in the dismal East End of London led him into his life-work, the founding of Dr. Barnardo's Homes, the world's largest private orphanage system. Other great orphanages were founded throughout the country.[12]

Young and Ashton, in their study of British social work in the nineteenth century, specified Evangelicalism as the 'greatest single urge' of humanitarianism, saying that the sentiment of human benevolence and its practical expression derived directly from religious influence. 'It came from the quickened knowledge, born of religious revivalism, that all men were the children of God and loved by Him.'[13]

The same forces were at work in American experience. A Christian man, John Augustus, a cobbler in Boston, offered in 1841 to bail out a drunkard. The Massachusetts Court agreed to it and, in the next two decades, this Christian man bailed out two thousand people who might have otherwise become criminals.[14] By the time of the Awakening, the vital experiment had succeeded. The example was followed.

The Probation of First Offenders became law first in the State of Massachusetts in 1878, and a similar law passed in Britain in 1887, though preceded there by the Youthful Offenders Act of 1854, and the Discharged Prisoners Act of 1862, likewise through Christian prompting.[15] Sarah Martin and Mary Carpenter, who achieved so much for the care of prisoners in Britain, were both dedicated Christian women who had before them Fliedner's example from Germany.

The Awakening of 1858-59 had an immediate effect upon the ancient practice of prostitution. It was a far cry from medieval days when the Bishops had licensed a row of houses of ill-fame near London Bridge; and a long time since the Puritans of Cromwell's day had made fornication a felony, punishable by death on the second occasion.

The industrial revolution aggravated the problem. Slum squalor and drunkenness made many women reckless. By the mid-nineteenth century, venereal disease was rampant in London, and in the 1860s became the target of regulative legislation, approved and disapproved on moral grounds.[16]

One of the first startling stories from the Ulster Revival of 1859 was that of a prayer meeting being held by the newly converted inmates of a brothel. A policeman reported seeing a group of fourteen prostitutes making their way to a home of rehabilitation, the result of a visit to a prayer meeting in Belfast. Dr. Hugh Hanna in the same city noted that prostitutes were prompted to seek salvation after seeing the falling off in business.[17]

In the earlier months of the 1860 Revival in the city of London, attempts were made to reclaim the prostitutes who frequented the West End. A series of evangelistic meetings was held for prostitutes only, arranged at midnight or later. At the outset, many fallen girls burst into tears when addressed by the saintly Baptist Noël who talked very tenderly to them. The sponsors took a score of penitents to houses of rehabilitation. A thousand women were rescued in a year of the operation of the mission.[18]

The work was carried on by a rare champion. In bereavement, Josephine Butler sought to share the greater pain of other unfortunates, and thus found her life work in social welfare in London. In visits to prisons, where she shared in the menial tasks of the women, Josephine Butler was confronted with the evil of state patronage and regulation of vice. She dedicated herself in righteous indignation to the abolition of the evil. Concentrating upon the inequality of suspected women before the law, Josephine Butler worked for repeal of the obnoxious legislation that made government the official supervisor of iniquity.[19]

By the year 1877, more than eight hundred committees (provincial and metropolitan) had gathered eight thousand petitions with more than two million signatures submitted to Parliament. A Select Committee of Parliament (1879 onward) reported adversely, so Mrs. Butler rallied Christian forces in prayer 'so that the prayers of the people of God would be as the incense of Aaron, when he ran between the living and the dead.' The Acts were suspended in 1883, and repealed in 1886.[20]

'No other woman in history,' said the social reformer, Dame Millicent Fawcett, 'had such a far-reaching influence or effected so widespread a change in public opinion.' Other victories, by Ellice Hopkins and by Bramwell Booth with his journalist-associate, W. T. Stead, were won.[21] In a major crusade against the white-slave traffic, Stead demonstrated (in a morally innocent but technically guilty way) that young girls could be inveigled into involuntary servitude of the most vicious kind. His crusade was followed by national and international action carried on by the League of Nations.

For ninety years, the charge was reiterated by enemies of the 1859 Revival that the excitement brought about a sad increase of sexual promiscuity. Even Charles Dickens was guilty of declaring that 'the most immoral scenes take place on Sunday nights.'[22] There was much evidence to the contrary, but the prejudice persisted.

Most of the instances quoted by observers of the Revival concerned the reform of professional prostitutes rather than promiscuity and its outcome, illegitimacy. There were no compulsory registrations of births in Ireland in those days, but the Scottish figures indicated a decrease in rural cases, and a considerable reduction of the annual increase in urban areas; the all-Scotland figures showed a tiny fractional rise in illegitimacy year by year, except in 1860, when the 1859 Awakening had its full effect.[23]

A charge of increased promiscuity is easy to make in the absence of statistics to contradict selected examples of sin. Since the first publication of the present author's studies on the subject, this charge has not been repeated. Without a doubt, the excitement of the times provided more temptation for young people, in sympathetic reaction, not more sin.

In the year 1859, the young Swiss businessman Henri Dunant followed the French Emperor Napoleon III to North Italy, hoping to arrange business contracts. Unwittingly he found himself a spectator at the bloody battle of Solferino, fought between the armies of the French and Austrians.

Henri Dunant was of a prominent evangelical family and already active in the Young Men's Christian Association of Geneva.[24] Among those who had made a profound impression upon his thinking were Elizabeth Fry, famed as a prison reformer, and Florence Nightingale, famed as a military nurse.[25] Dunant was expert in both business and evangelism and maintained his family interests.

Dunant was horrified by the suffering of the wounded and dying on the battlefield. He helped as best he could in the days that followed, noting the sincere if unskilled efforts of local people to alleviate their suffering. He wrote 'A Memory of Solferino' and published it in 1862, sending it to statemen and leaders throughout Europe. As a result, a Geneva Convention was held in 1864 and from its findings and decisions came the Red Cross Movement.[26]

Not everyone expected to help proved willing. Some of the military leaders resented the intrusion of civilians on the battlefield. To Henri Dunant's sorrow, even Florence Nightingale withheld her support,[27] saying that the succor of the wounded in war was the business of government. But there was enough help forthcoming to speed the Red Cross on its mission of mercy and it spread throughout the world, by no means an evangelical agency but an evangelical idea whose time had come.

Timothy L. Smith, in his able study of 'revivalism' and social reform, made a pertinent observation concerning conditions in the United States at that time:[28]

> The rapid growth of concern with purely social issues such as poverty, working men's rights, the liquor traffic, slum housing, and racial bitterness is the chief feature distinguishing American religion after 1865 from that of the first half of the nineteenth century.

The United States was being rapidly industrialized, and the Christian Gospel was beginning to influence the situation. Evangelical sentiment was expressed by Mrs. Barnardo thus: 'The State should deal with it, but does not: the Church of Christ must!'[29] Responsibility of the State was recognized.

The social influence of the 1858-59 Awakening carried over to the mission fields of the world. The influence of the missionaries was circumscribed by their relationship to the holders of power: in other words, in India and in southern Africa, the missionaries could appeal to the British as the colonizing or protecting power, either directly or by stirring up the evangelical conscience at home; whereas, in China or Japan, the missionaries had no lobbying lever.

Generally speaking, the colonial powers were indisposed to interfere with their subjects' way of life, providing the government and commerce were not disrupted thereby. They welcomed the aid of the missionaries, but supported them only up to a point, and, in certain countries, they opposed them and ardently defended the native religion and culture.

The missionaries were scarcely ever able to achieve results in such fields as the rights of working men, for the simple reason that the working force was nowhere as near full development as in the industrialized countries. There were other factors also, the gap between employers and employed in standards of living, which was considerable in countries of homogeneous race as well as in those where the race factor further complicated matters.

It was the same in other continents after 1860, as surely the social ferment caused by the leavening of Evangelical Awakenings spread far and wide. In India, it had resulted in the foundation of schools and colleges during the first half-century. After 1858-59, it produced yet another missionary initiative in the educational field.[30]

The curse of India in the nineteenth century was cholera. Epidemics swept huge areas, the fondness of Indian folk for pilgrimages and religious festivals multiplying the danger, wiping out tens of thousands.

Indian opposition to the practice of European medicine in India was varied. Long acquaintance with tropical disease had provided native doctors with proven remedies, but effectiveness was often nullified by mixed-in religious superstition. The problem of training Indian doctors in the practice of modern medicine arose. Dead bodies were defiling to the touch of a Hindu who therefore could not study dissection to learn anatomy. Alexander Duff's College students in Calcutta informed a government commission of inquiry that their studies in the English medium had removed their religious scruples in such matters. Hence, Indian practice of medicine moved into realms of the possible as a Medical College of Calcutta was founded to teach Western medicine to Indian students.[31]

Few of the missionaries sent out in the first quarter of the nineteenth century were medically trained, but all were 'well disposed' to medicine. The American Board of Missions first began to send out medical evangelists as such. Dr. John Scudder arrived in Madras in 1836,[32] and his son Henry Scudder began a medical work in Arcot in 1851 which in its second century is famed in all of Asia and the world as the Vellore hospital and medical college complex, developed by Dr. Ida S. Scudder and her colleagues.

It was after the 1858-59 Revivals in America and Europe that medical missionaries came alive in all India. The Scottish Presbyterians began a medical work in Rajasthan in 1860, employing medical evangelists who dispensed medicine and the Gospel.[33] Other Scots established hospitals at principal mission stations in the same period. Other missions adopted similar plans.

Before the 1858-59 Awakenings, there were no more than seven medical evangelists in the entire Indian sub-continent, but their numbers quadrupled by 1882 and increased to 140 in 1895, with 168 Indian doctors assisting them.[34]

In the decade of the Revival, Clara Swain as a fully qualified doctor began her work among Indian women at Bareilly, where she opened a women's hospital in 1874.[35] Other lady doctors followed, British sponsors founding Zenana Medical Missions to meet the needs of women, who were kept in purdah (seclusion) all the days of their married life, from puberty until death. This resulted in the education of women, first in purdah, afterwards outside the homes.

Christian Institutes for training doctors and nurses followed the foundation of hospitals. In 1881, a training hostel was begun at Agra, and in the years following, Dr. Edith Brown founded a School of Medicine for Christian women in Ludhiana, Dr. William Wanless one for men at Miraj, and Dr. Ida Scudder another for women at Vellore, serving north and central and south India, attracting capable students of whatever caste or class.[36]

Their standards were necessarily low, but, as a result of upgrading, the Medical Colleges at Vellore and Ludhiana and Miraj became fully-fledged Christian Medical Colleges for men and women from all parts of India. The writer was told by an Indian cabinet minister's lady that she chose outright to patronize a Christian hospital (at which he lectured in 1970) because of its 'tender loving care.'

The evangelical impact on nursing was felt in India too, and it is sufficient to say that 90% of all nurses throughout India (surveyed in World War II) were Anglo-Indian or Indian Christians, and that four-fifths of all Christian nurses were trained at mission hospitals.[37]

The missionaries tackled the 'white scourge.' The leading tuberculosis sanatorium in all India is that of the Union Mission in southern Andhra.[38] Sixty hospitals, homes and clinics for lepers are operated or subsidized by the Mission to Lepers which began in 1874 when three ladies in Dublin collected money for relief of leprosy. Cochrane and Brand, evangelical missionaries, are world famous specialists in Hansen's disease.

From the days of William Carey, evangelical missionaries sought to improve Indian agriculture. Carey had published valuable horticultural catalogues, and urged the missionary societies to send out men qualified to teach agriculture and to preach. The contribution of missionaries to agriculture in India is beyond computation. A case in point is Allahabad Agricultural Institute, founded by Sam Higginbotham,[39] the well-known agricultural missionary and evangelist.

CONTINUED SOCIAL IMPACT

Mission schools, although by no means 'the last word' in technology and education, introduced not only better animal husbandry and agricultural methods, but inculcated requisite ideas of personal and social hygiene, prophylaxis against disease and improvement of diet, resulting in a vast enlargement of living standards which discouraged superstition.

The 1858-59 Awakenings were felt in India in the 1860s. Not only did they bring out a contingent of dedicated missionaries, but they stirred the Indian Christian communities too. Kerala, at the southwest corner of India, shared in a like movement beginning in 1861 and climaxing in 1873. People in Travancore were 33% nominally Christian; their Rajahs were enlightened rulers; and among non-Christians, women were held in higher respect than in other parts of India.

Jawaharlal Nehru, in denigrating British imperial benefits in India, cited Kerala as an example of native superiority. The Church Missionary Society's entrance to Kerala had effected startling changes in the ancient Syrian Christian community there. English schools were begun in 1834, and thirty years later a vernacular education committee using Malayalam was established by the State.[40] Kerala early had the benefit of two Christian colleges, Kottayam begun by the C.M.S. and Alwaye, a wholly Indian Christian institution. A University was early established at Trivandrum.[41]

Within thirty years of 1860, there were 2418 institutions of all classes and grades with 104,616 pupils. Ten years or so later, there were a hundred and fifty thousand, 25% in state schools. In another generation, there were 2700 in the Kerala colleges, more than fifty thousand in English schools and half-a-million or more in primary schools, and Kerala led the rest of India in literacy, with 23.9%.[42] The initiative had come from the missionaries and Indian Christians.

Missionary education in China developed the same way as in India, with obvious differences, the absence of a conscientious colonial power, the lack of a caste system, the use of a hallowed system of classical education. Japan and Korea, likewise, experienced missionary stimulus to education.

What was true of Asian countries was even more true of the African continent, where (south of the Sahara) there was no indigenous religious system other than animism to hinder the work of the missionaries. The education of Africa was one of the greatest achievements of the missions. In a lesser way, so also was the education of the islands of the Pacific, and even Latin America owed much to Evangelical influence.

In the homelands of Evangelical Christianity, the step-by-step improvement of social conditions, the leavening of the lump by the Christian conscience, was accompanied by a development of a social impetus by Society itself, so that it was no longer necessary for Christians to initiate ideas for new social improvements—they simply joined efforts with other enlightened citizens.[43] Their ministry of pioneering was channeled more and more into needier fields abroad. There, where the social conscience was often feeble, they were free to combine their urgent evangelism with urgent social betterment, their hosts accepting the former so long as it was accompanied by the latter.

This Christian service was so very different from the practice of the Communists, who were often committed to the worsening of conditions so that bloody revolution would follow the frustration of social progress, an overthrow of the establishment providing opportunity for dictation.

Arnold Toynbee has described Communism as a Christian heresy, and certainly it sprang out of the Christian social conscience rather than out of Islam or Buddhism, even though it reacted bitterly against many basic Christian beliefs and practices.

Marx was in London during the great Revival of 1860 onward.[44] Marx founded his International in 1864 and stayed in its company or at the desks of the British Museum. He was a contemporary of Lord Shaftesbury and of his reforming friends, and he was still a resident of London when D. L. Moody came to preach.[45] He derided the Moody campaigns, if his friend Engels be accepted as a reliable authority. Marx became so obsessed with his dogma that he learned to hate Christians for doing good and so delaying the day of violence. He was impatient with the evolutionary methods of all Christian social reformers.

As Marx had rebelled against Christianity and its ethics and methods, he did not understand the Acts of the Apostles who turned their world 'upside down' by persuasion rather than by resort to violence. Christian meekness Marx considered cowardice; Christian humility he considered self-contempt; Christian steadfastness he put down as abasement; and Christian obedience he put down as subjection; while Christian kindness he called obsequiousness. For the rule of God in society he substituted a war of the classes; for love, he substituted hatred. He denied God's existence, and promoted atheism.

14

THE FIFTH GENERAL AWAKENING

The worldwide Awakening of the early twentieth century came at the end of fifty years of evangelical advance, following the outpouring of the Spirit far and wide in 1858-59 and the 'sixties. Thus it did not represent a recovery from a long night of despair caused by rampant infidelity, as was the case in the days of Wesley. It seemed, rather, a blaze of evening glory at the end of 'the Great Century.'[1]

It was the most extensive Evangelical Awakening of all time, reviving Anglican, Baptist, Congregational, Disciple, Lutheran, Methodist, Presbyterian and Reformed churches and other evangelical bodies throughout Europe and North America, Australasia and South Africa, and their daughter churches and missionary causes throughout Asia, Africa, and Latin America, winning more than five million folk to an evangelical faith in the two years of greatest impact in each country. Indirectly it produced Pentecostalism.

Why did it occur at the time it did? The ways of God are past finding out. One can only surmise. A subtler form of infidelity had arisen, a compromise between Christianity and humanism. A more sophisticated interpretation of human conduct, inspired by Freud, spoke of God as an Illusion.

The prescient widsom of its Author may also account for the sudden spread of the Revival of 1900-1910. Within ten years, the awful slaughter of World War I had begun, and a gentler way of life passed into the twilight of history.

Arnold Toynbee, reminiscing, recalled the trauma of the time, when half his classmates perished in battle. Oneself was a child when the news of the Battle of the Somme threw every family in his native city into mourning for the finest of their fathers and sons and brothers killed in action.[2]

The Awakening was a kind of harvest before the devastation of Christendom. It was Sir Edward Grey who lamented in 1914 that the lights of civilization were going out one by one, not to be lit again in his lifetime. The upheavals of war unloosed the times of revolution on mankind. A biographer of Wilbur Chapman observed:[3]

As we look back over these extraordinary religious awakenings which . . . so quickened the churches and so effectively pressed the claims of God upon the consciences of multitudes, we cannot escape the conviction that God in gracious providence was reaping a spiritual harvest before He permitted the outburst of revolutionary forces that have overwhelmed the world, impoverished almost every nation, produced economic and social chaos, and stained with dishonor the pride of Christian civilization.

In the history of revivals, it has often been noted that such restoral periods are a warning of, and synchronize with, impending judgment. The harvest is gathered before the field is doomed to death.

The early twentieth century Evangelical Awakening was a worldwide movement. It did not begin with the phenomenal Welsh Revival of 1904-05. Rather its sources were in the springs of little prayer meetings which seemed to arise spontaneously all over the world, combining into the streams of expectation which became a river of blessing in which the Welsh Revival became the greatest cataract.

Meetings for prayer for revival in evangelical gatherings such as Moody Bible Institute and the Keswick Convention greeted the new century—not surprisingly.[4] What was remarkable was that missionaries and national believers in obscure places in India, the Far East, Africa and Latin America seemed moved at the same time to pray for phenomenal revival in their fields and world wide. Most of them had never seen or heard of phenomenal revival occurring on missionfields, and few of them had witnessed it at home. Their experience was limited to reading of past revivals.

The first manifestation of phenomenal revival occurred simultaneously among Boer prisoners of war in places ten thousand miles apart, as far away as Bermuda and Ceylon. The work was marked by extraordinary praying, by faithful preaching, conviction of sin, confession and repentance with lasting conversions and hundreds of enlistments for missionary service. The spirit of Revival spread to South Africa in the throes of economic depression.[5]

Not without significance, an Awakening began in 1900 in the churches of Japan, which had long suffered from a period of retarded growth.[6] It started in an unusually effective movement to prayer, followed by an unusually intensive effort of evangelism, matched by an awakening of Japanese urban masses to the claims of Christ, and such an ingathering that the total membership of the churches almost doubled within the decade. Why did the Japanese Awakening occur in 1900? It would have been impossible four years later when Japan became involved in momentous war with Russia.

Significantly also for the evangelistic follow-up of the general Awakening, the Torrey and Alexander team found that unusual praying had prepared a way for the most fruitful evangelistic ministry ever known in New Zealand and Australia,[7] and the unprecedented success of the campaigns launched Torrey and Alexander (and later Chapman and Alexander) on their worldwide evangelistic crusades, conventionally run but accompanied by revival of the churches.

Gipsy Smith experienced much the same kind of response in his Mission of Peace in war-weary South Africa, successful evangelism provoking an awakening of the population to Christian faith. Gipsy Smith extended his ministry.[8]

Meanwhile worldwide prayer meetings were intensifying. Undoubtedly, the farthest-felt happening of the decade was the Welsh Revival, which began as a local revival in early 1904, moved the whole of Wales by the end of the year, produced the mystic figure of Evan Roberts as leader yet filled simultaneously almost every church in the principality.[9]

The Welsh Revival was the farthest-reaching of the movements of the general Awakening, for it affected the whole of the Evangelical cause in India, Korea and China, renewed revival in Japan and South Africa, and sent a wave of awakening over Africa, Latin America, and the South Seas.

The story of the Welsh Revival is astounding. Begun with prayer meetings of less than a score of intercessors, when it burst its bounds the churches of Wales were crowded for more than two years. A hundred thousand outsiders were converted and added to the churches, the vast majority remaining true to the end. Drunkenness was immediately cut in half, and many taverns went bankrupt. Crime was so diminished that judges were presented with white gloves signifying that there were no cases of murder, assault, rape or robbery or the like to consider. The police became 'unemployed' in many districts. Stoppages occurred in coalmines, not due to unpleasantness between management and workers, but because so many foul-mouthed miners became converted and stopped using foul language that the horses which hauled the coal trucks in the mines could no longer understand what was being said to them, and transportation ground to a halt.

Time and again, the writer has been asked why the Welsh Revival did not last. It did last. The most exciting phase lasted two years. There was an inevitable drifting away of some whose interest was superficial, perhaps one person in forty of the total membership of the Churches. Even critics of the movement conceded that eighty percent of the converts remained in the Churches after five years.[10]

But there was a falling away in Wales. Why? It did not occur among the converts of the 1904 Revival, other than the minority noted. Converts of the Revival continued to be the choicest segment of church life, even in the 1930s, when the writer studied the spiritual life of Wales closely. Two disasters overtook Wales.[11] The first World War slaughtered a high proportion of the generation revived, or converted, or only influenced by the Revival, leaving a dearth of men in the churches; the coal mines of Wales were hit in the 1920s by tragic unemployment, which continued into the thirties in the Depression; and the class under military age during the war, infants during the Revival, espoused the gospel of Marxism. The Aneurin Bevans replaced the Keir Hardies in the party.

There was yet another reason. The Welsh Revival took scripture knowledge for granted, and preaching thus deemed superfluous was at a minimum. The Welsh revival constituency was ill-prepared for a new onslaught of anti-evangelicalism which captured a generation of otherwise disillusioned Welshmen. The province of Ulster moved into the place held by the principality of Wales as a land of evangelistic activities.

The story of the Welsh Revival has often been told. Most Christian people, including scholars, have been unaware of the extent of the Awakening which followed in the English-speaking world—in the United Kingdom, the United States, Canada, South Africa, Australia and faraway New Zealand.

The Archbishop of Canterbury called for a nationwide day of prayer.[12] Thirty English bishops declared for the Revival after one of their number, deeply moved, told of confirming 950 new converts in a country parish church. The Revival swept Scotland and Ireland.[13] Under Albert Lunde, also a friend of the researcher in later years, a movement began in Norway described by Bishop Berggrav as the greatest revival of his experience. It affected Sweden, Finland, and Denmark, Lutherans there saying that it was the greatest movement of the Spirit since the Vikings were evangelized.[14] It broke out in Germany, France and other countries of Europe, marked by prayer and confession.[15]

It is difficult to count converts in the Church of England, but, in the years 1903-1906, the other Protestant denominations gained ten percent, or 300,000.[16]

When news of the Awakening reached the United States, huge conferences of ministers gathered in New York and Chicago and other cities to discuss what to do when the Awakening began. Soon the Methodists in Philadelphia had 6101 new converts in trial membership; the ministers of Atlantic City claimed that only fifty adults remained professedly unconverted in a population of 60,000. Churches in New York City took in hundreds on a single Sunday— in one instance, 364 were received into membership, 286 new converts, 217 adults, 134 men, 60 heads of families.[17]

The 1905 Awakening rolled through the South like a tidal wave, packing churches for prayer and confession, adding hundreds to membership rolls—First Baptist in Paducah added a thousand in a couple of months and the old pastor died of overwork. Believers' baptisms among the Southern Baptists rose twenty-five per cent in one year. Other denominations shared equally in the Awakening.[18]

In the Middle West, churches were suddenly inundated by great crowds of seekers. The 'greatest revivals in their history' were reported by Methodists in town after town; the Baptists and others gained likewise. Everyone was so busy in Chicago that the pastors decided to hold their own meetings and help one another deal with the influx. Every store and factory closed in Burlington, Iowa, to permit employees to attend services of intercession and dedication. The mayor of Denver declared a day of prayer: by 10 a.m., churches were filled; at 11.30, almost every store closed; 12,000 attended prayer meetings in downtown theatres and halls; every school closed; the Colorado Legislature closed. The impact was felt for a year.[19]

In the West, great demonstrations marched through the streets of Los Angeles. United meetings attracted attendance of 180,000. The Grand Opera House was filled at midnight as drunks and prostitutes were seeking salvation. For three hours a day, business was practically suspended in Portland, Oregon, bank presidents and bootblacks attending prayer meetings while two hundred department stores in agreement closed from 11 till 2.[20]

Churches of the various denominations, town or country, were moved from Newfoundland to British Columbia across Canada, in spontaneous prayer or ardent evangelism.[21]

Church membership in the United States in seven major Protestant denominations increased by more than two million in five years (870,389 new communicants in 1906) and continued rising.[22] This did not include the gains of the younger denominations of Pentecostal or Holiness dynamic whose rate of increase was considerably greater.

It is naturally difficult to estimate the gains in the Dutch Reformed Church in South Africa, for most converts therein already possessed family affiliation. The Methodist Church increased by thirty percent in the three years of revival.[23] No doubt, the same patterns applied in New Zealand, Australia and South Africa, all stirred by the Welsh Revival.

The writer has visited all the States of India, has addressed more than a million people there, and has lectured in twenty of their theological colleges, and to hundreds of missionaries and national pastors. And yet he encountered only one who knew of the extent of the Indian Revival of 1905-1906, a retired professor of theology. Yet the Awakening in India moved every province and the Christian population increased by seventy percent, sixteen times as fast as the Hindu, the Protestant rate of increase being almost double that of the Roman Catholic. In many places, meetings went on for five to ten hours.[24]

In Burma, 1905 'brought ingathering quite surpassing anything known in the history of the mission.' The A.B.M.U. baptized 2000 Karens that year, 200 being the average. In a single church, 1340 Shans were baptized in December, 3113 in all being added in the 'marvelous ingathering.'[25]

The story of the Korean Revival of 1907 has been told and retold. It is less well-known that the Revival came in three waves, 1903, 1905 and 1907—the membership of the Churches quadrupling within a decade, the national Church being created from almost nothing by the movement. Since then, the Korean Churches have maintained the impetus.[26]

The revival campaigns of Jonathan Goforth in Manchuria have been recorded and published, but the extent of the Awakening in China between the Boxer Uprising and the 1911 Revolution has not been apprehended. China's greatest living evangelist, survivor of the China-wide Awakening of 1927-1939, told the writer that he had not even heard of the Awakening (in every province in the 1900s) apart from the post-Boxer revulsion. Yet the number of Protestant communicants doubled in a decade to quarter of a million, twice that figure for the total Evangelical community.[27]

In Indonesia,[28] the numbers of Evangelicals, 100,000 in 1903, trebled in the decade of general Awakening to 300,000, and in subsequent movements of phenomenal power, the number of believers on one little island (Nias) surpassed the latter figure, winning two-thirds the population. Protestant membership in Malagasia increased sixty-six percent in the years of Revival, 1905-1915. And pioneering success was achieved in the newly-opened Philippines.

The Awakening had limited effect in the Latin American countries: unusual revival in Brazil, phenomenal awakening in Chile, with Evangelical membership in both countries starting to climb—until in our times it passed the number of practising Roman Catholics; pioneering continued in other republics with sparse results but promise of future harvest, since realised.[29]

The Edinburgh World Missionary Conference recognized that more progress had been made in all Africa in the first decade of the twentieth century than experienced hitherto. Protestant communicants in the African mission fields increased in 1903-1910 from 300,000 to 500,000, there having been many awakenings in various parts in those years.[30] But the full impact of the Welsh Revival was not felt until the war years, when phenomenal revival occurred among the Africans. In the next half century, the increase was double that of the general population.

It was most significant that the Awakening of the 1900s was ecumenical, in the best senses of the word. It was thoroughly interdenominational. The foregoing narratives have provided instances of Anglican, Baptist, Brethren, Congregational, Disciple, Lutheran, Methodist, Presbyterian and Reformed congregations sharing in the Revival. There is a total lack of evidence of any response on the part of Roman Catholic or Greek Orthodox communities, but this is not surprising, for it was so in the days of the Puritans, of Wesley, of Finney, and of Moody. Only in the mid-twentieth century, when their changing attitude to Scripture has accompanied a changing attitude to dissent, have heretofore non-evangelical church bodies been affected by evangelical movements.

During the Welsh Revival, there occurred charismatic phenomena—uncanny discernment, visions, trances—but no glossolalia. There was an outbreak of speaking in tongues in India in the aftermath of the Awakening. In 1907, there was speaking in tongues among converts of the Revival in Los Angeles, from which Pentecostalism spread widely.[31]

There is no telling what might have happened in society had not the First World War absorbed the energies of the nations in the aftermath of this Edwardian Awakening. The time, talent, and treasure of the people were preempted in any struggle for national existence, and what little is over is devoted to the welfare of the fighting men and the victims of war. This was the case in World War I.

Even so, no one could possibly say that the Awakenings of the 1900s in Great Britain or the United States were without social impact. In Britain, there was utter unanimity on the part of observers regarding 'the high ethical character' of the movement. The renewed obedience to the four great social commandments reduced crime, promoted honesty, inculcated truthfulness and produced chastity. Drunkenness and gambling were sharply curtailed. It was the same in the United States, for a wave of morality went over the country, producing a revival of righteousness. Corruption in state and civic government encountered a setback which was attributed by observers in church and state to the Great Awakening. For a dozen years, the country was committed in degree to civic and national integrity, until new forces of corruption triumphed again in the 1920s.[32]

In such awakenings, it seems that the individual response is much more immediate than the social response. British church leaders acclaimed 'the high ethical character of the movement.' The then largest denomination in the United States declared in review that the public conscience had been revived, overthrowing corrupt officials, crossing the party lines, electing Governors, Senators, Assemblymen, Mayors and District Attorneys of recognized honesty. The people of Philadelphia 'threw the rascals out' and put in a dedicated mayor. Washington Gladden, the 'father of the social gospel,' was assured that the general awakening was creating a moral revolution in the lives of the people. In other countries, profound impressions were made.[33]

What was the social effect outside Western Protestantism? On mission fields, the missionaries multiplied their schools and hospitals.[34] In twenty years, pupils in Christian schools in India doubled to 595,725; 90% of all nurses were Christian, mostly trained at mission hospitals. In China, missionaries pioneered secondary and higher education and laid the foundations of the medical service; the beginnings of the African educational systems and medical service were due likewise to the missionary impulse.

15

THE EXPECTATION IN INDIA

The Methodist Bishop Thoburn declared at the turn of the twentieth century his hope of general revival:[1]

> The next movement of its kind will find India prepared for it throughout all its extended borders, and the results will be such as have thus far never been seen in the mission fields of the world.

The expectation in India was not an isolated phenomenon. Indeed, it appeared to be only one manifestation of a worldwide wave of intercession for an awakening in the twentieth century. Many were the outward signs.

Towards the end of the nineteenth century, students and faculty at the Moody Bible Institute in Chicago shared a burden to pray for another great Evangelical Awakening around the world.

An 1898 Week of Prayer at the Moody Church and Moody Bible Institute was continued as a regular Saturday evening prayer meeting for worldwide revival. Attendances rose to three hundred each session; sometimes prayer continued all night.[2]

In 1899,[3] just before he died in harness, D. L. Moody opened his heart on the subject of Revival:

> Now the question is, 'Shall we have a great and mighty harvest?' . . . I would like before I go hence to see the whole church of God quickened as it was in '57 . . .

Moody was, without doubt, the most widely-accepted Christian leader of the closing century. The burden of prayer spread from Moody Bible Institute to believers around the world. There were prayer meetings in India and East Asia, in various parts of Africa, and in Latin America. More particularly, the Chicago prayer meetings were related to a chain of prayer meetings held in Melbourne and a prayer circle of multiplied thousands radiating from the Keswick Convention. All these factors influenced Indian Christians to pray for an awakening in India.

Five years before the end of the nineteenth century, a rising tide of spiritual expectation was noted in India. Books on the ministry of the Holy Spirit circulated, and the need of a pentecostal outpouring upon India was acknowledged. In Bombay, the first Saturday of each month was set aside for prayer for Bombay and for India. In other cities, there was a similar concern and at Mussoorie in the North and Ootacamund in the South, conventions of Christians were moved to study the infilling of the Holy Spirit.[4]

In 1897, the leaders of the Student Volunteers suggested 'a Day of Prayer for the Awakening of India,' which was observed in December in many parts. In August 1898, the Reverend R. J. Ward of Madras urged that another Day of Prayer be set apart, and there was such approval that the time of intercession became an annual event.[5]

R. J. Ward was one of those used to prepare India for the outpouring of blessing.[6] He was an Englishman who had been in the ministry for all of twenty-seven years when he experienced a vital change at the Keswick Convention of 1891.[7] In 1902, he joined with others in instituting a general prayer circle among missionaries of all denominations committed to praying for an outpouring of the Holy Spirit, reaching a membership of more than eight hundred in India in a few years.[8]

At the turn of the century, a company of missionaries met together at a southern hill station, Kodaikanal, and decided that the time had come to pray definitely for a mighty awakening in the Indian Church.[9] They issued a prayer circular, and sent it to Britain, America and Australia to mobilize intercession.

At the same time that R. J. Ward was moved to a life of prayer in Britain before proceeding to India, an American student, John Hyde, had a similar experience and sailed for India in 1892.[10] Until the end of the century, John Hyde engaged in prayer more and more, until it became his consuming passion. As Ward was used in the South, Hyde was used in the North, forming a prayer fellowship there to enlist both missionaries and national leaders.[11]

The future of Evangelical Christianity in those parts of Northwest India which later became Pakistan was affected by the events of the early twentieth century in the Punjab, then inhabited by Muslim, Hindu and Sikh communities.

While the 1880s were years of unprecedented growth of Chuhra churches, the 1890s showed a levelling off, due to various reasons—one being the desire of missionaries to delay acceptance to fellowship of newcomers until those already received were thoroughly trained.[12]

In February 1896, General William Booth of Salvationist fame held meetings for the deepening of the spiritual life in Amritsar, his interpreter Ihsan Ullah, a Muslim convert serving as Anglican pastor in Narowal, near Sialkot.[13] So powerful was the General's preaching that his interpreter burst into tears, but went on when Booth begged him to consider others in greater need. On Sunday, in Narowal, Ihsan Ullah shared his experience with his congregation and a local revival spread to the villages.

Until 1896, there had been 'no Pentecostal outpourings where individuals exhibited profound conviction of sin.'[14] In 1896, however, there came one of those preparatory revivals which so often has signalled a great outpouring of grace. On 24th March, the Sialkot Presbytery met at Pasrur and studied the first two chapters of Acts, earnest prayer and confession being followed by joy and praise. Similar events were reported here and there, but the management of the Christian Training Institute in Sialkot, a school for young men, closed its doors to the influence, provoking a student to pray that the forbidden place might become a channel of blessing to all of India.[15]

A prayer movement began, and gathered strength for all of seven years. The American student volunteer, John Hyde, from his arrival in India in 1892 had more and more devoted himself to intercessory prayer.[16] Praying Hyde, as he was called, with a group of friends spent days and nights in prayer for an awakening throughout India, in all its provinces.

The intercessors formed the Punjab Praise and Prayer Union. Its members were committed to prayer for personal purity and power and for a great awakening throughout India. To promote their objectives, a convention was arranged at Sialkot in the autumn of 1904. Attendances were small but the sessions were led by Hyde, Ihsan Ullah and two Church of Scotland ministers who had spent thirty days and nights in prayer prior to the convention.[17]

That the Awakenings and the Revivals of New Testament Christianity in India that followed were not isolated phenomena was recognized, for a typical missionary veteran in writing home stated:[18]

> It will be difficult to dissociate our experiences from the great spiritual movements throughout the world. Ours seem to form only a small part of a wave which at present is encircling the globe.

The recognized antecedents of Revival were first united prayer, such as the three hundred or more intercessors at the Moody Bible Institute in 1899, and the prayer for worldwide revival on the part of a band of ministers and laymen meeting each Saturday afternoon for eleven years or so in Melbourne, and the movement at the Keswick Convention in 1902 where 5000 Christians resolved to form home prayer circles for world-wide blessing, and praying bands all over India; the second was the revival of Bible study in many missions, and the third was the faith, obedience and self-sacrifice on the part of many Indians.[19]

Pandita Ramabai became burdened for India's need of revival. In 1903, she became interested in the movement of prayer in Australia which preceded the Torrey-Alexander campaigns there. In 1904, she learned of the Revival in Wales. So Pandita Ramabai commenced special prayer-circles at the beginning of 1905, and hundreds of her helpers and friends attended these sessions.[20]

The famine which distressed India in the year before the Revival redoubled the prayers of the Christians all over the country, as did the great epidemics following its misery.

It may be asked, why were such awakenings not experienced until the beginning of the twentieth century, when evangelization had begun so much earlier? A possible clue to the answer may be found in a statement made by the Rev. W. T. A. Barber of the Wesleyan Missionary Society, at the 1900 Ecumenical Missionary Conference in New York:[21]

> Now, as far as my knowledge goes, ordinarily the Holy Spirit does not move on heathen populations —at any rate, in Eastern lands — in this wondrous way. He does mightily save men in every heathen land, but a revival in the sense that we have learned to associate the term with the labour of such men as Moody does not occur among unprepared Chinese or Hindus. The remarkable thing is that such revivals do occur amidst the generations that had been leavened by the influence of Christian schools. When, a year or two ago, the Reverend Thomas Cook—one of our most successful English evangelists—conducted a special campaign in Ceylon, he found that many were brought to conversion, but, with scarcely an exception, every convert had been educated in mission High Schools.

There is a certain 'coming of age' in Revival. The 1905 Awakenings in Asia were indigenous, the period marked by a rising of Asian ministers and laymen to responsibility.

THE EXPECTATION IN INDIA 111

The first manifestation of evangelical revival in India in the early twentieth century occurred among some unwilling sojourners in the country.[22] At the turn of the century, the Anglo-Boer War had been fought. The outnumbered Boers waged war both cleverly and bravely, but finally capitulated. The British authorities shipped the prisoners-of-war to camps across the Atlantic and Indian Oceans.

At the Capetown docks,[23] a Bible Society agent stood and addressed the prisoners-of-war by means of an interpreter, offering the gift of the Scriptures in their accustomed language—'that God's Word may comfort and counsel you in this hour of need!' noting that 'both they and I wept together.'

Ds. A. P. Burger, minister of Middelburg, Transvaal, was taken prisoner in February 1902 and sent with two thousand others to camp at Shahjahanpur, United Province. He there began regular worship services and taught classes in school every day. The pattern of revival was repeated. At night, the neighbouring Moslems and Hindus listened to the singing of five hundred or so newly-revived prisoners-of-war. There were similar reports from Sialkot.

Ds. D. J. Viljoen was shipped with prisoners-of-war to India in 1901, holding shipboard service for an interested group each day.[24] The prisoners were sent to Fort Ahmednagar in the Maratha country, where a thousand men were detained behind thick walls and barbed wire.

Ds. Viljoen commenced worship services, at first enlisting prisoners with experience of lay ministry and using them for visitation, prayer meetings, catechism and church services, but not for the sacraments. Classes and young folk's meetings were also organized.[25] A small group of deeply spiritual men came together daily for prayer.

Ds. Viljoen and his helpers concentrated on evangelism. In spite of poor attendances at first, the results were encouraging, and within a few weeks, he was busy daily in services. There was a genuine revival among the Christians and many conversions of sinners occurred.[26]

Fort Ahmednagar became a place of praise and prayer, singing sweeping the camp in day-time, and the voice of prayer the stillness of the night.[27] The Christians were impressed by the need of the Hindus around them, and eighteen of them became missionaries upon release.[28] The Revival continued in the camp until the end of the war. The area round about was one of those so deeply moved by the Indian Revivals a few years later.

16

THE AWAKENING IN ASSAM

The broad valley of the Brahmaputra and the mountains on either side comprise the country of Assam on India's northeastern corner. The language of the people in the populous valley is Assamese, an Indo-Aryan tongue akin to Bengali, but the people of the central hills, such as the Khasis, speak a Mon-Khmer language, while the Nagas in the hills south of the valley speak various dialects of Tibeto-Burman origin, as do the Mizos and others in the far south.

The people of the central plateau between the Brahmaputra and Surma valleys, the Khasi and Jaintia Hills, known in general as Khasis, were formerly head-hunters, human sacrifice in connection with snake-worship persisting.

The Nagas, a group of tribes inhabiting the northern part of the hills dividing Assam from Burma, were also head-hunters. The very rugged nature of the country made each tribe distinct from the other, speaking a dialect often unintelligible to its neighbours.

In the extreme south of Assam, the Mizos inhabiting the Lushai Hills were a people noted for their warlike qualities, like the other tribes the terror of the plains inhabited by Hindus of mixed blood, immigrant and aboriginal.

There was immediate contact also between Wales and Assam, for there were many Welsh missionaries serving up in the hills of Assam.[1] A Welshman, the Reverend John Roberts of Cherrapunjee, was on furlough in Wales in 1904.

Early in 1903, a church at Mawphlang in the Khasi Hills of central Assam announced Monday evening prayer meetings to seek an outpouring of the Holy Spirit throughout Khasia and all the world. In 1904, these prayer meetings became more fervent in spirit as, by the end of the year, the news from Wales created an immediate, heart-felt hunger.[2]

The annual General Assembly of the Khasia Presbyterian Church was held at Cherrapunjee in 1905, and it proved to be a remarkable one indeed. The delegates returned to their villages with increased faith and an intensified longing for an outpouring of the Spirit.[3]

The answer to their prayers began in a matter of weeks. On the first Sunday in March, at Mawphlang, when their Bible lesson dealt with the baptism of the Holy Spirit, an unusual manifestation of feeling filled the congregation with prayer and weeping and praise.[4]

A presbytery meeting at Pariong broke the pattern of its usual procedure. When the chairman invited one or two by name to lead in prayer, others also stood up to lead the congregation in intercession.[5] It became impossible to close the usual service the following Sunday, simultaneous prayer and praise and weeping, and even fainting, affecting the congregation. These manifestations accompanied the extension of the awakening into other parts, and continued for eighteen months or so.

The Khasi tribes people being head-hunters, with human sacrifice persisting in obscure cults, it is therefore interesting to note how the impact of the Welsh Revival affected the Christian community drawn from such people.

The intense conviction of sin which began in March gave way in June to a wave of rejoicing. In a united presbytery meeting of fifteen hundred folk, the singing overwhelmed the preaching, many of the awakened people dancing for joy, their arms outstretched, their faces radiant.[6] Missionaries were astounded to see principal men and leading elders jump for joy. At first some missionaries disapproved, changing their minds as the revival transformed the Christians and won hundreds of non-Christians to the fellowship.

There were setbacks in some quarters when 'spurious signs and prophecies' appeared, but the Khasi Christians quickly learned to distinguish between the true and false, noting the way of life of those deceived by alien impulses in times of excitement.[7]

To the west of the Khasi Hills are the Garos who inhabit the hills where the Brahmaputra emerges into Bengal, an American Baptist field. By 1907, the Garos had a total of twenty-one churches with 5694 members, of whom 499 had been added by baptism.[8] Two years later, it was reported that work among the Garos was being maintained with more than ordinary aggressiveness.

In 1906, tidings of awakenings were received from the Nowgong, Golaghat, Sibsagor and North Lakhimpur fields in Assam.[9] The Baptists stated that the Holy Spirit had of late 'moved in remarkable ways' along the Brahmaputra valley in towns and villages.[10]

Nowgong was the first of these riverstations to be reached by the revival influences which had so profoundly influenced the Khasi and nearby hills.[11] December 2nd, 1906, had been set aside as a Day of Prayer for India.[12] The Sunday morning worship went as usual, but in the 2 p.m. meeting of young men, followed by the women's meeting, all of the young people continued praying. Some broke out into bitter crying. Then followed confessions of sin, while groans and cries and earnest prayers arose. This continued until eight p.m. No one seemed to think of going out to prepare their rice for the evening meal. 'Showers of blessing are still coming,' the missionaries reported in 1907.[13]

At Nowgong, all the churches joined more or less heartily in a special 'concert of prayer' for a great advance in the kingdom of Christ as well as the salvation of the lost multitude, especially in the district and province. It continued for several months and was marked by a degree of spiritual enthusiasm that was refreshing, revival spreading from the valley towns to the hills.[14]

From North Lakhimpur, the awakening began to spread into the tribal areas north of the river Brahmaputra, the missionaries reporting in 1907:[15]

> The past nine months have seen a marvelous change in the condition of our churches. The growth in Christian knowledge, the giving up of old sins and of hidden heathen practices, a reaching out after the life and love of God, and a sense of responsibility for the conversion of the heathen, have characterized almost every church in the North Lakhimpur area.

The Awakening spread to south of the river. The revival was first manifested while a Bible class was in session in Golaghat at a conference which was attended by delegates from the churches. On Saturday night, the whole congregation broke down weeping and were in great agony because of their sins; both young and old cried for mercy. On Sunday, the meetings began as early as 6 a.m. and continued until nearly midnight, with only short intervals for meals.[16]

From Golaghat and Sibsagor, the Awakening spread south and southwest into the Naga Hills. The movement among the Naga Tribes proved less spectacular than that among the Khasis. The year 1905 'had been one of reaping as well as one of steady sowing of the seed.' Results had appeared in unexpected places and places where long years of work prepared the way. Thus the Naga Christian body grew:[17]

THE AWAKENING IN ASSAM 115

We have not had an emotional revival, but the number of baptisms has been three times the average for the last five years and there has been in some directions a marked spiritual uplift... The association meeting this year was the most widely representative Christian gathering ever held in the Naga Hills.

Evangelists reported a great change in the attitude of the Angami Nagas toward the Gospel.[18] They claimed that people, listening well, were inquiring about Christ as never before.

In the year 1907, a large ingathering was reported from the Imphur field among the Nagas. The year was one of unusually large increase, and was one of more than ordinary success, for one hundred and three were baptized in a single out-station.[19] Evangelism among the Nagas went steadily forward, large additions to the churches being reported, as well as hundreds of converts who begged to be baptized.[20]

Christian influence in the Hills had become so great that in 1906 the Deputy Commissioner declared liberty of conscience for all Nagas, which act represented a deathblow to paganism among the Naga tribes.[21]

The news of the Khasi Hills Awakening was received among the Mizos (Lushai Hills tribes) far to the south, and stirred great interest in the Christian community,[22] Baptist down south and Presbyterian up north, both of Welsh origin.

Early in 1906, it was decided to send some young people to attend the Khasi Assembly held at Mairang.[23] The party of ten set out—Chawngo, Khuma, Thanga, Pawngi, Thangkungi, Vanchunga, Siniboni from North Lushai (Presbyterian); and Thangkunga, Parima, Zathanga from South Lushai (Baptist).

They walked the whole distance through mountain jungle, taking two weeks. The ministry was all given in Khasi, of which they understood not one word. But they wondered at what they saw and sensed a strange power in it all. They made their way back to Lushai feeling sadly depressed. At Chatlang, two miles from Aijal, they paused to offer prayer and felt their hearts filled with a strange joy. (The revival was regarded by some as beginning here.) But the joy died away. At Aijal, prayer meetings were held every night for a week, but 'nothing happened.'[24]

On 9th April 1906 (Monday), the three southerners decided that it was time for them to move on, for they still had four or five days' walking ahead. In a short farewell meeting, they were singing 'God be with you till we meet again!' when 'the Spirit was outpoured upon them' in a remarkable manner.

Others from nearby houses joined them, and they continued in prayer and praise, with the phenomena of revival seen for the first time in Lushai. It spread to all parts, creating extraordinary interest.[25]

The Reverend D. E. Jones prophesied at one of these prayer meetings in Aijal that revival would break out in a very large village named Phullen, several days' journey from Aijal. So a teacher originating from Phullen set out, it being expected that he would initiate a movement; but upon his arrival four days later, he found that revival had begun at the time of the prophecy being made.[26]

As a result of the Awakening, membership in the Church increased, and hundreds gave their names as inquirers, but during the revival there was not the tremendous increase that occurred in Khasia. The chief characteristic was conviction of sin among believers and adherents.[27]

Unlike the sweeping success of the Khasi work, one of the immediate results of the revival was an intense persecution of the Christians which broke out in the autumn. The growing churches in Phullen and surroundings suffered intensely. Christians were evicted at midnight from their villages and driven into the jungle. The chief and his henchmen made life miserable for believers in many villages. It was a sad time for all who professed the faith.[28]

Worse was to come. The 1907 persecution was followed by an 'anti-revival,' a resurgence of blatant heathenism that mimicked the revival in form, heathen lyrics being sung with great abandon and young people of both sexes dancing in ecstasy, followed by great feasts. It spread like wildfire, with demonstrations in every village.[29]

The Christian Church suffered a serious set-back in the anti-Revival, the leaders despairing. Paganism ran rampant in the Lushai Hills until, in 1911-12, the flowering of the bamboo brought a horde of rats. Although stores of rice had been laid up in anticipation, the rats appeared almost overnight and devoured the stores of food and the grain in the fields, leaving nothing.[30]

Famine havoc was terrible. People subsisted upon roots in the hills, and the refugees poured onto the plains, while multitudes died of starvation. Missionaries cared for the orphans. In Wales, collections were made, and Christians in Lushai shared their food ungrudgingly with hungry pagan people. The distress and the charity brought an end to the pagan revival among the Mizos.

THE AWAKENING IN ASSAM

Revival was rekindled in 1913, breaking out with great power at presbytery meetings in 1913, when the first Mizo was ordained to the pastorate.[31] In 1919, an even greater Revival broke out simultaneously in three separated places, spreading with speed even to Tipperah and Manipur States. Four thousand were converted, more than the total number of current communicants.[32] Hymn-singing accompanied by the drum swept the land in a wave of rejoicing.

One effect of these Revivals, within a generation, was to make head-hunters into a predominantly Christian people, inhabiting India's most Christian and most evangelical area, in zeal far surpassing the early evangelized fields, as well as the places which claimed a thousand years or more of a traditional Christianity.[33-38]

17

THE AWAKENING IN ANDHRA

About the beginning of the Christian era, the Andhra dynasty was ruling southern India from sea to sea, but Andhradesa, the land of the Telugus, was split up into senseless divisions during the nineteenth century. The people of Andhradesa, largely Dravidian in tongue and blood, were re-united in the mid-twentieth century thirty-two million strong.

Prayer for revival in Andhradesa began at a hill station, Kodaikanal. LaFlamme, a zealous Canadian missionary, said in 1905:[1]

> We are firmly convinced that in very little time the great Revival, of which we are now enjoying a foretaste, is coming. And we long to be in it.

The first movement of revival in Andhradesa occurred in the Akidu district in 1905, almost a year before the 1906 Awakening.[2] In September 1905, an evangelist (S. E. Morrow) went to Peddukapavaram where his ministry produced deep conviction of sin, followed by confessions.[3] At Siddapuram, villagers were so fearful that they could not sleep at nights until they had confessed openly to receive the forgiveness of God. The revival affected Atmakur in October.

Meanwhile, Atmakur was considered to be a hard field, the Madigas nowhere friendly to the Gospel, scarcely a Mala willing to listen, and Sudras with other castes making excuses. But fifteen months' drought with a famine resulting left them weeping for their children.[4]

The major Awakening in the Akidu district was yet to come, for the following year a report noted that the year past had been extraordinary——the intense heat, the awful cholera and the wonderful Revival——'things never to be forgotten.'[5]

In the greater part of Andhradesa, there was still no outbreak of Revival. An observer noted:[6]

> But this year has been full of blessing. The number of members excluded or dropped seems to have been larger than usual. But this is often a good sign . . .

the cutting off of dead wood will result in a healthier growth. It is a temporary separation which results in true repentance, reformation and restoration. One of the most encouraging things in the year's work was the unparalleled sale of Scriptures.

Ten months passed from the initial outbreak in Akidu area. A missionary, E. S. Bowden of the Godavery Delta Mission, reported revival in Chettipet.[7] It began simultaneously at Akidu[8] and Yellamanchili[9] on Sunday 11th August 1906:[10]

> The meetings last from five to ten hours and some even longer. Yet no one gets tired and the people are loth to leave even at the end of such sessions. There is no order of service, no leader, no sermon in any meeting except the divine order of the Spirit as He leads. Be it noted that there has been absolutely no human instrument in this wonderful visitation: we missionaries have taken no part in it except to pray, not even that in public at first.

It was discovered that, on the very day that revival began at Akidu and Yellamanchili, Dr. Brown, Secretary of the Foreign Mission Board, and Messrs. LaFlamme and Craig were praying with hearts burdened to tears in an upper room on Brunswick Avenue in Toronto for awakening in that portion of the Telugu field.[11]

The astounding outpouring of spiritual power came up the coast from the south as a monsoon. The historian of the Nellore Awakening, David Downie, as a young man had attended one of the great prayer meetings in the Bowery Theatre in New York during the American Awakening of 1858. It was packed from pit to top gallery.[12] Later he heard a missionary address by Alexander Duff and received a call to India, where he served in Telugu Country for forty years. He commented: 'I was in the great revival of 1858 and in many revivals since, but I never saw anything like that time . . . in Nellore.'

One evening in 1906, at Chambers Hall in Nellore, it was agreed that the Telugu church should be asked to pray every evening until the blessing of revival came. This continued for ten days until, one evening, 'the Spirit came' with power, startling the intercessors:[13]

> There was a rumbling noise like distant thunder, and a simultaneous, agonizing cry went up from the whole congregation. Some were sobbing, some crying out, and all were confessing their sins and beseeching God for mercy. This continued far into the night.[14]

All of the strange phenomena of revival were manifested before missionaries and church folk. Some of the girls went into trances and, though speaking to some unseen one, were unconscious of anything around them.[15] There were no human leaders. The Spirit of God led. Dr. Downie was one of those who learned this lesson personally:[16]

> One evening, thinking that the girls needed rest to fit them for the next day's work, I tried to close the meeting. I said: 'It is late and you need rest; we will sing the doxology and pronounce the benediction.' It was done but no one moved. Then a girl got up and said: 'Let us pray.' This was about ten o'clock and the meeting continued until after midnight. On another night, Dr. Boggs tried to close the meeting, with the same result.

Beginning thus in the Nellore church and the boarding schools of the town, the revival spirit spread to the village churches.[17] The prayer and praise meetings seemed peculiarly to reveal the leadership of the Holy Spirit.[18] The Sunday Schools also manifested revival in marked degree.

After the movement had run its course, very many 'infallible proofs' were discovered of the genuineness of the awakening. The headmistress testified that the Christian girls of the school were raised to a higher level of Christian life. Quarrels were settled, restitution was made of things stolen and wrongs done. Little possessions of great value to the owners, such as jewelry, were surrendered freely as free-will offerings to God.[19] Jewelry is of special value in India.

The unusual manifestations that had accompanied the revival in other parts of Andhra were not seen in Ramapatnam, where there was noted[20] 'a quiet, substantial work of grace, especially among the students of the Seminary and pupils of the boarding school.' The Seminary, and the nearby boarding school, were situated far from the busier centres of population.

From the beginning of the new school year in July onwards, meetings were held continuously every night with greater and deeper blessings. Prof. Jacob Heinrichs, afterwards a professor in Chicago, reported that their experiences were 'rather those of a reviving.'[21]

An American Baptist missionary, the Rev. James A. Baker, successor to the famous engineer, John Clough, recalled after forty years the impact of the 1906 Awakening at Ongole, farther north:[22]

THE AWAKENING IN ANDHRA 121

> The only outstanding revival I ever saw in India had its beginnings in 1905. Its dominant characteristic was the self-examination of the professing Christians before their God. The Telugu Christians are not given to displays of emotion in public. Their religious services tend easily to become conventionalized. Proclaiming personal religious experience comes hard to them. Bearing all this in mind, the circumstances seem truly amazing.

A missionary had sent to Ongole some Telugu leaflets in which the great revival in Wales was described, and while on tour Baker distributed these to various of the preachers without a comment.[23] The experiences narrated were foreign to them. They had never seen Christianity manifest itself in such a form, and they began to ask questions as to the meaning of it all. Some new seed was evidently germinating in their minds.

In Ongole, there had been no united prayers offered for revival, nor was there any expectation of anything unusual. One Sunday evening, when the High School students were holding their weekly English service, it became evident that some strange influence was pervading the place. Every one present felt that the Spirit of God was there. Some of the missionaries were in tears.[24] Eleven of the High School boys arose during this meeting and requested special prayers—among them a future professor of theology, Professor Ramanjulu of Ramapatnam. From that night's experience grew in the hearts of many a great desire for the outpouring of the Holy Spirit. Baker reported:[25]

> I was away from Ongole, touring the district, when the regular Wednesday evening Telugu prayer meeting changed its form and became a New Life Meeting, as they phrased it themselves. Each succeeding Wednesday the attendance grew larger, and the meeting lasted longer and was more intense.

Then came the usual April quarterly meetings for all the field workers and elders, for which the church had laid out a customary programme of lectures, papers and discussions. Dr. Boggs of Ramapatnam preached on the Sunday morning and his sermon was heard with unusual intensity of interest. The next morning early, the Lord's Supper was observed, followed by a season of prayer. Up to this time, the proceedings had been largely in the conventional order, and no one expected what was to follow! The missionary declared:[26]

122   THE AWAKENING IN ANDHRA

> Suddenly without warning the usual stoical mindedness of our Indian assembly was broken as by an earthquake. Everyone present was shaken. One of the most quiet and retiring of our workers arose, striking his breast, and cried in Telugu in a loud voice 'Perishudatma!' (Holy Spirit!) 'Perishudatma!' Many others followed. For the first time at Ongole, the Holy Spirit of God was glimpsed in the act of convicting His people of sin.[27]

Ordinarily, the workers returned to their own villages after the four weeks for which they received allowances; but this time they stayed on at their own expense for nearly two weeks more, holding meetings day and night. Before they left for their homes, many confessions had been made, old quarrels had been settled, and wrongs put right. The various schools of Ongole began to hold meetings of their own, often far into the night. The bed time hour was extended; their chapel was constantly in use by praying bands of students. Children in the boarding schools began saving rationed grain to share with unfortunates.[28]

After reaching their homes, the field workers spread the spirit of the meetings throughout many of the villages. During the hot months of April and May, while all the missionaries were away in the hills, revivals were constantly in progress over the field. In July came another of the usual 'nellasaris.' A large crowd was in attendance on Sunday morning. At three o'clock in the afternoon, a meeting was held lasting two hours. Some were powerfully affected. One member remained in church after all others had gone, pleading with God in prayer.[29]

That evening, Reverend W. Powell, a Welsh missionary who had been in the midst of the revival in Wales, told quietly in Telugu the simple story of God's dealings with the people of his native land. After this talk, there was to follow a few minutes of silent devotion, following which any one who wished might lead in prayer. All heads were bowed and there was an intense stillness. Then, in a flash, the spirit of confession broke forth and swept through the assembly. A thousand Indian Christians were in the church, the noise tremendous. Non-Christians from nearby places came running to see what was the trouble.[30]

A young American missionary who had no experience of phenomenal movements of the Spirit of God, Mr. Francis, assistant to Dr. Clough, called to Mr. Baker: 'Something must be done; the whole congregation is weeping and wailing.'

I rose, as if in a dream, but sat down again ... The
Holy Spirit, not I, was in charge of the meeting, and
the people were having it out with their consciences
and their God. It was my place to keep still. It was
impossible to talk to individuals, much less to the
audience. A voice could not be heard three feet away—
everyone seemed to be living in another world.[31]

After an hour, a few people gathered around the organ
and tried to sing, but their efforts went unnoticed. Matters
had to take their own course. In about two hours, some one
with a strong voice started a hymn, the congregation took
it up, and soon perfect decorum was restored. From that
time on, perfect order prevailed in all meetings. In the
days that followed, many excellent sermons were given...
by an Indian missionary to Africa ... a Seminary professor
... the pastor of the Nellore church[32] ... and others.
James Baker commented: [33]

Daily I studied the expressions on the faces of the worshippers. The old careless look still marked some of
them, others appeared puzzled, others haggard and
harassed as if by inward battles; each succeeding day,
more and more countenances took on a look of peace.

One morning, Bundara Abraham, the village schoolinspector, rose and said, 'Here in my hand I have a list of
fourteen sins of which I have been guilty. I have confessed
them all to God and now I am ready to confess them
before this meeting. Do you want me to read the list?'
It was put to the vote, and all agreed it was a matter
solely between Abraham and his God.[34]

From the time of giving the tracts, the revival lasted a
year and a half. Large numbers were baptized, including
forty-four students from the town schools. Its results were
felt in numberless ways, in changed lives, in a new sense
of service and responsibility. Even the quality of the congregational singing changed and became more melodious.
Nothing like this revival ever occurred at Ongole before.
'It left a lasting impression of the Spirit's power over the
hearts of men.'[35] The missionary at Eluru reported briefly:

We have been blessed with an outpouring of God's
Spirit such as I have never before witnessed in this
land or in any other. The revival came as a cleansing
fire and quickening spirit. As a result of the awakening, the church is showing a most gratifying activity
in voluntary work for the salvation of souls, and its
contributions are threefold increased.[36]

In the interior of Andhradesa, in the Kurnool district, the threatening cloud on the horizon was that of impending famine. The rains had totally failed and there was no harvest. Grain was selling at famine prices, and work was not to be had.[37]

Conditions in Kurnool, as in other places in 1906, worsened for the terrified population, for following hard upon the famine came the triple scourge of typhoid fever, smallpox and cholera. It swept over the field and took its relentless toll of human life. Stanton, the Baptist missionary, was stricken with smallpox, and his wife with a nervous break-down.[38]

In such times as cholera epidemics, people become wild with fright; and almost irresistible impulses seize the Christians to join with the heathen in the terrible orgies by which they hope to appease the blind wrath of their gods. This time, however, the Christians stood firm. Every night and morning, gathering together in the little chapels and school houses for prayer, they looked trustingly to God for deliverance. Heathen joined them, saying that only their God could save them.[39]

While conditions were at their worst, while Dr. Stanton was still recuperating from illness, suddenly and unexpectedly like the rushing of a mighty wind the revival came. A common quarterly meeting was turned into a revival lasting two weeks.[40] Without any leaders, it began in a great volume of prayer, rising higher and higher, all the people praying aloud and crying to God for mercy. All day and far into the night this work continued— 'burning, cleansing, quickening and transforming lives by the divine power.' It was a 'mighty spiritual upheaval such as had never been seen in Kurnool before.'

The fruit of the revival was seen in the lives of the people who professed the name of Christ.[41] The revival of 1906 was confined almost exclusively to the local Christians,[42] and the church at Kurnool had to wait six years before the great awakening among the heathen followed. In 1912, the outcastes of the area began to turn to Christ, more than a thousand being baptized on profession.[43]

The pattern was the same among Telugus in the Nizam's Dominions. At Secunderabad, first came 'the revival' leading to the confession of hidden sins, and then came evangelism, resulting in a number of conversions and in greater earnestness of the Christians.[44]

THE AWAKENING IN ANDHRA

The Canadian Baptists reported that when the American Baptist churches in Nellore and Ongole were visited, their hearts beat rapidly in expectation. The storm of blessing seemed nearer and nearer, like the monsoon, travelling up the coast.[45]

Revival began in the Kakanada girls school on August 14, and for days lessons and house work had to stand aside, food and rest almost forgotten while God dealt with souls. . . . then began a series of meetings lasting seven weeks in school and church or both for hours by day and night.[46]

The spiritual condition of the Kakanada church had been for some time unsatisfactory. The outlook was 'not very encouraging.' It was suddenly visited by the Holy Spirit in overwhelming power. Hearts too hard to be moved by pastoral appeals and entreaties were utterly broken. Sins long cherished were seen in the light of the Spirit of God and were loathed and discarded openly with tears and with bitter lamentations. Hidden things were through the power of the Spirit brought to the surface and confessed. Wrongs were righted. Stolen property was restored, and hearts long estranged were once more reconciled. Everything seemingly took on a very different aspect. Unconverted persons who came to watch all the proceedings were soon converted.[47] 'I have carefully made enquiry about those who confessed and were revived at the time,' wrote a missionary. 'They remained steadfast.'[48]

The revival held its 'moment of truth.' Two things were clearly revealed at Ramachandrapuram—that some people had been living in sin continuously up to the very eve of the revival—teachers and even preachers; and that many far otherwise had been living holy lives before God.[49] The light showed up things for what they really were.

At Samalkot, 'the great event of the year' reported was the revival at the Seminary.[50] Words failed to tell all unaccustomed things that were witnessed during 'those days of God's omnipotent working,' reported the Canadians; and after four or more months there were abiding spiritual fruits. Written examinations in all subjects brought the school teachers encouragement in affairs academic also, as pupils changed their habits of study.[51]

There were dramatic preludes to the Revival at Yellamanchili in 1906.[52] A great fire wiped out a whole section of town and destroyed the chapel. The Christians prayed as well as worked, and a change of wind saved the homes of the believers. During the epidemic, the sick missionaries were away in the hills and the town was engulfed in an extreme heat. Then came the Visitation of the churches. After the Awakening, in the latter part of the year, a revived band of witnesses enjoyed an extraordinary tour of evangelism round about.

Not every Christian congregation was visited by revival, as at Bimlipatnam where there was disappointment.[53] Otherwise, missionaries often wrote in triumphant vein:[54]

> The Spirit came like a flood and we had three glorious weeks, which to experience is worth a lifetime. Our meetings were comparatively quiet with an occasional outburst of joyous laughing and clapping when some victory was gained. One woman went into a trance-like state and seemed to give messages directly from God, visions of the Crucified One.

The Canadians reported frightening things. A teacher was so convicted that he jumped up and ran from the church but fell upon his face a few yards from the door. He was brought to full confession and cleansing and soon began to pray and witness. At another village, he contracted cholera and died. His brother cursed God, crying: 'God, how dare you take my brother away.' Something snapped in his mind, and he became as a raving maniac. It was days before his reason and his faith returned.[55]

A comparison of the annual statistics published by the Canadian Mission showed that the work was effective mainly among nominal Christians. The ingathering came later, the 1904 membership being 5924 and adherents 8276; the 1914 membership being 9,482 and adherents 13,909.[56]

Reports of the American Baptist Mission highlighted the Awakening: 58,898 communicants in 1904 had decreased to 54,649 in 1905, a loss of 4091; but the 54,327 communicants in 1906 increased to 56,001 in 1907, and to 56,525 in 1908.[57]

In the nearby American Lutheran missionfield at Guntur, baptized membership had risen in the decade 1890-1900 from 13,566 to 18,964; but in the revival decade it rose from 18,964 to 40,198; and in the Godavery district, baptized membership rose from 11,938 at the beginning of 1905 to 16,953 in 1910. Yet Lutheran records of the revival are scarce.[58]

The historians of Lutheranism in Andhradesa make no mention of the 1906 Awakening among Telugu churches, for whatever reason.[59] However, in Dolbeer's chapter titled 'the Upsurge: Reaping the Harvest,'[60] it is stressed that a large class of catechists was given Bible training at the time by Hermannsburg missionaries,[61] while in the Guntur Mission the staff of native workers, which had increased by 43 in the last decade of the old century, grew from 418 to 723 in revival times, a 600% acceleration.[62]

In the various local reports, one may uncover evidence of the impact of the Revival upon the Lutheran missions. Citing a fourfold increase of membership at Chirala,[63] it is noted that the Rev. E. C. Harris (appointed there in 1904) saw the local work develop 'very rapidly.' Rajahmundry reported 'steady growth' in the same period, as did other districts with but few exceptions.[64] These are evidences of an Awakening.

It was noteworthy that caste people displayed an interest in the Christian faith during the time of Revival, between 400 and 500 being baptized in the Guntur locality alone.[65]

The number of village congregations grew by about 25%, as reported by Lutheran missionaries, adding to the evidence for the conclusion that Lutheran work was just as strongly influenced by the movement which so powerfully affected the Baptists, even if the latter seemed more eager to report the phenomenal awakening to their home constituency.[66]

There was a similar ingathering in Anglican fields in Andhradesa, taking on the proportions of a mass movement in some areas; the Church Missionary Society grew steadily in numbers and strength.[67]

To the east of Hyderabad, in a neglected corner of the Nizam's Dominions, in Dornakal district, a folk movement occurred in the decade of the Andhra Awakening. It was guided by Vedanayakam Samuel Azariah, the first Indian Bishop. In 1902, Azariah had accompanied Sherwood Eddy to Jaffna in Ceylon and was impressed. In February of 1903, he helped form the Indian Missionary Society of Tirunelveli, a landmark in church and mission planting.[68]

The Anglicans of the Indian Missionary Society took over the field of the Dornakal Telugus, and within a decade, Azariah was consecrated a bishop. Baptizing three thousand a year for thirty years, Bishop Azariah followed methods developed in the earlier Tinnevelly Revival, as soon as possible appointing village workers and teachers as catechists, and then ordaining to the priesthood those who were qualified. Thus the results of the Revival in Andhra were conserved.[69]

18

THE AWAKENING IN TAMILNAD

South of Andhra, Christians in Tamilnad were moved by the Revival. Many in Madras had been praying for outpouring of the Holy Spirit, for the Madras Missionary Conference had issued a call to prayer and reported revival begun.[1]

At the close of 1905, the Rev. H. D. Goldsmith (serving the Madras Divinity School of the Church Missionary Society) reported Anglicans praying for the outpouring of the Spirit. Zion Church of the Anglican Southern Tamil Pastorate in Madras had been awaking to a real revival under its devout Indian pastor, and its fervency communicated itself to the Anglican Divinity School. The Indian pastor commented:[2]

> I am passing through a new spiritual experience. I can not explain it in words. I dread the very idea of telling anyone about the great and wonderful things that God the Holy Spirit is commencing to do through 'the Revival.'

Night and morning meetings were held in the Sathyanathan Memorial Hall. In the Northern Pastorate of the C. M. S.,[3] there were meetings attended by the same extraordinary blessing as seen in other parts of Madras.[4]

Poles apart from Anglicans were the Christian Brethren. Brethren missionaries were holding an annual conference in Coimbatore in June, 1905, and visitors from the various parts of India as well as members of the local assemblies, Indians, Eurasians and Europeans, took part.[5]

At the customary Sunday morning 'breaking of bread,' the Holy Spirit came upon two or three 'in mighty power, causing them to sob and cry out in pain for the sins of the Church.' A season of confession and humiliation followed. Wrongs were righted, questionable things judged and abandoned, and estranged brethren reunited.

This went on until four o'clock in the afternoon, when adjournment for the Sunday School and evening meeting became necessary. At the close of the evening meeting, many sinners were converted. The believers again gathered and confessions of the day continued till all had humbled themselves and were consciously right with God. Then, at three in the morning, the long delayed service of Holy Communion was completed by disciples rejoicing in forgiveness.

Soon all the missionaries and visitors returned to their stations, but the Revival continued in the local assemblies at Coimbatore and nearby. Handley Bird, who had worked twelve years in the area, wrote to his friends: 'God has come to Coimbatore and we are like them that dream. Our mouth literally is filled with laughter, our tongue with singing.'

The impact of the Revival upon the staid and cautious Brethren was recognized, for Handley Bird commented:[6]

> How we have toiled here and now the harvest is come and we are allowed to share in the joy. Nothing is more noticeable than the great grace upon all. We have marvelled at the patience and forbearance of older brethren who must have been sorely tried by the noise and simultaneous praying and manifest excitement under the stress of soul and desire.

At times, the cries of agony of soul and the sobbing of broken-hearted people were more than many could stand, with the amazing admixture of prayers for help and praises for deliverance at the same time. The missionary veteran was reminded of Ezra iii, 13:

> the people could not discern the noise of the shout of joy from the noise of the weeping of the people: for the people shouted with a loud shout, and the noise was heard afar off.

This type of meeting was not common among the Christian Brethren. Yet in the Revival of 1905 among them, there were trances and visions and other extraordinary phenomena. Florence Bird, at another station, reported:[7]

> One girl (Rupli) was in a trance, quite unconscious, the Lord speaking through her in the first person, for example, 'As I have saved My child Rupli, so will I save you.' . . . The use of the Word was wonderful! Passage after passage would be quoted, chapter after chapter asked to be read. There were confessions, weepings, songs of victory, cryings, callings on God for others. . . The agony in prayer was terrible to witness.

The unusual features of this revival among the Christian Brethren in India caused some consternation in Britain, for their missionary editor commented: 'We do not understand "prophesying" and "visions" of which we read, and prefer to say little about them.'[8] If such were experienced among the conservative Brethren, what of other denominations?

Dr. John P. Jones of Madurai (Congregational) reported:

> Formerly we were accustomed to say that the antecedents of Indians were such that we never could expect them to experience deep conviction of sin. This revival wave opened our eyes to our error in this matter, for never before were wilder scenes of agony and of despair under this deep conviction witnessed among any people than in India.
>
> At Pasumalai, our church congregation and the students of our institution were touched with the new life in a remarkable way. Meetings were held for hours at a time where the Christians wept under deep conviction of sin and where blessings untold were enjoyed by all those who entered into the fullness of the Christian life. In our theological seminary, there was hardly a student who was not quickened, and several received a blessing which will multiply a hundred-fold in the lives of the congregations to which they went forth.[9]

Various Congregationalists were moved and the London Missionary Society at Nagercoil experienced a quickening wave, the Rev. George Parker announcing that 'It is evident to all that the young men who were the terror and disgrace of the village are at any rate striving after holy living. There is also a renewed interest in Bible study.' [10]

The Danish Lutheran Mission at Tirukoilur reported a movement of the Spirit in their midst.[11] And at Chitoor, in North Arcot, among the staid Reformed people, there was a great awakening in October of 1906, the leader being Dr. Scudder. There was 'a great breaking down under conviction of sin,' with the usual accompaniments of manifestations.[12]

The result was a time of witnessing by life and word; more joy in the study of the Word and in prayer; keener sense of sin; more love for brethren; and greater sense of responsibility for the salvation of friends and townsfolk. This was said about Chitoor. It applied to countless places.

A Wesleyan Methodist missionary, the Rev. C. H. Monahan, also reported from Chitoor: [13]

> Some weeks before I went, the Holy Spirit had fallen on the people. What struck me was the fact that men who before were all too ready to spend the time in talk, seemed now to be possessed with the one desire to spend all the time of the meeting in the study of the Word of God and prayer.

He also reported upon his visit to the Tamil church in the Kolar goldfields. It was realised that the spiritual condition of the Church was the greatest hindrance to the success of the Gospel among the heathen. There was impurity and division. Great searchings of heart began among the workers causing the division, until finally a leader could bear it no longer but went to his opponent and asked forgiveness, whereupon the spirit of revival moved the place.

Other revivals in the Tamil country began in increased exercise of prayer, continued in confession of sin, and resulted in restitution and amendment of ways, followed by concern for the souls of friends and neighbours.[14]

In the far south, unprecedented progress was reported from the districts of Suviseshapuram and Dohnavur,[15] the prayer meeting being crowded, while sorrowful crying and confession of sins preceded the many conversions. A striking revival occurred in a boys' school in Surandei.[16]

Near the tip of South India there resided the saintly Amy Carmichael, an Ulsterwoman from the County Down, whose mother and pastor had been 'impressed' in the great Ulster Revival of 1859. Amy Carmichael had devoted her life to the rescue of devadasis, little temple prostitutes, and around her mission house in Dohnavur had grown up a numerous Christian colony of workers, together with boy- and girl-orphans, children and teenagers. The work therein was well-known to the Keswick constituency.

Amy Carmichael, in common with other folk in Tamilnad, had been praying with her helpers for a visitation of the Holy Spirit to all of India ever since the Welsh Revival and its overflow upon the Khasi Hills. Thus she wrote in her diary of events:[17]

> On October 22nd, to quote one of the little girls, Jesus came to Dohnavur. He was there before, but on that day He came in so vivid a fashion that we cannot wonder that it struck the child as a new Coming.

It was at the close of the morning service that the break came. Amy Carmichael, the one who was speaking, was obliged to stop, overwhelmed by sudden realization of the inner force of things. It was impossible even to pray. One of the older lads in the boys' school began to try to pray, but he broke down, then another, then all together, the older lads chiefly at first. Soon many among the younger ones began to cry bitterly and pray for forgiveness. It spread to the women. Amy Carmichael found it hard to recall all the details of that eventful day:

> It was so startling and so aweful—I can use no other word—that details escaped me. Soon the whole upper half of the church was on its face on the floor, crying to God, each boy and girl, man and woman, oblivious of all others. The sound was like the sound of waves or strong wind in the trees.

As the senior Anglican missionary, Thomas Walker, was away in North India, and Mrs. Walker was on the high seas, and Mrs. Carmichael was visiting Travancore, and the local pastor away from home, Amy Carmichael felt the burden of responsibility for the situation. She had never heard of such an outbreak as this among Tamil people. She regarded the Tamilians as stolid and unemotional. Some of the older men and women showed the greatest dismay and by earnest signs besought her to put a stop to the movement. No separate voice could be heard. An elderly woman seized her feet and by signs implored her to do something, but when she looked for guidance to God, the only reply was 'Do nothing.'

By this time, people in the lower end of the church, the careless part of the congregation, were staring at the other part, and talking and shouting excitedly, and the heathen rushed round the church and gazed in at the doors and windows. But nothing disturbed those who were praying, and that hurricane of prayer continued with one short break of a few minutes for over four hours. 'They passed like four minutes,' said Amy.[18]

Scenes such as the one described beggar all description. Readers perusing an account years afterwards may feel an aloof detachment, but in the course of such a meeting, with believers and unbelievers alike, every mouth is stopped.

Amy Carmichael continued her narrative:[19]

> For the next fortnight, life was apportioned for us much as it was for the apostles when they gave themselves continually to prayer and to the ministry of the Word.

The spiritual leaders worked like doctors in an epidemic around the clock, praying with distressed people and giving counsel from the Scriptures. The whole community of the mission complex was involved, night and day.

> Everything else had to stand aside. At first the movement was almost entirely among convert boys, schoolboys, our own children and workers, and some younger members of the congregation. But as the older ones were caught in the current, more or less, at first it was impossible to gauge its real depth.

THE AWAKENING IN TAMILNAD 133

What were the results? Looking back after nearly seven months of testing, they had enough of true results to make them sing with all their hearts. Almost all of the children were truly 'out and out' converted. Most of the workers too were thoroughly revived. The bungalow servants were greatly blessed and backsliders restored. Many of the schoolboys were converted and very few, if any, of the convert boys were unchanged. In the village, there were several notable conversions and the true Christians were quickened to walk in newness of life. Anglican parishes around were moved and the privileged diocese of Tinnevelly enjoyed yet another revival in a century of recurring awakenings.

The appetite for blessing was quickened also, for Amy Carmichael wrote:[20] 'For all this we do praise God... We have seen just enough to make us very hungry to see more.' The monsoon was followed by planting and reaping.

It was inevitable that the same movement of revival in Tamilnad should have effect in Ceylon to the south, where Tamil workers shared the island with the more numerous Singhalese, who were Buddhists.

Half a generation earlier, the Anglican evangelist, the Rev. George Grubb, had visited Ceylon in February 1888. His ministry, begun among Anglicans, was widely supported by other denominations, who seem so ready to welcome an Anglican evangelistic enterprise.

A widespread revival ensued, bringing spiritual refreshment to those already converted, followed by an awakening among the multitudes of nominal Christians, together with successful evangelism that brought many outsiders to real conversion.[21] In 1890, there came another revival in Ceylon, again the prophet of the movement being George Grubb, assisted by a Keswick team. The Anglican evangelist, son of a Tipperary landowner, exercised an equally acceptable ministry in South Africa and Australia.

In the wake of Grubb's successful evangelism, a choice British Wesleyan evangelist, Dr. Thomas Cook, visited Sri Lanka, and won to the faith some hundreds of young people, again the products of mission schools.[22]

One of Grubb's assistants, in Ceylon as well as farther afield, was Tamil David, who went on to be an outstanding evangelist in Dravidian India as well as Ceylon.[23] There were many calls for his services. Sherwood Eddy, of the Y. M. C. A., conducted a vigorous campaign in Jaffna, in northern Ceylon in 1902, assisted by V. S. Azariah.[24]

The wider and deeper tide of revival reached the shores of Ceylon in 1905,[25] stirring up Christians to prayer and thrusting forth witnesses to win their nominal Christian, Hindu and Buddhist friends to Christ.

In the first decade of the twentieth century, the numbers of Christians had risen by more than a sixth, which increase exceeded that of any other religious constituency—17.2% as compared with 15.1% of the population as a whole.[26] One tenth of the population of Ceylon was shown to be Christians in the census of 1911, but four-fifths of these were Roman Catholic by upbringing.[27]

The Anglicans were stronger than any other denomination of Protestants, with their strength concentrated in Colombo. The Methodist cause had grown to nine thousand members, with three times that number as pupils in schools.[28] Baptists were only a third as strong as Methodists, numerically.[29]

Despite the fact that evangelical Christianity had much influence in Ceylon, provoking Buddhists to organize Sunday Schools, lay preaching, hymn singing, and like activities, it was conceded that growth had been slow, and, in 1913, a spokesman for Ceylon commented sadly on 'a hundred years of very indifferent success' which made 'the Church long for a great revival of spiritual power.'[30]

19

THE AWAKENING IN KERALA

In the decade following the Great Awakening of 1873 onwards in Kerala, the Evangelicals who had sought to reform the Syrian Orthodox Church were forced out of its fellowship as a result of a civil action, losing their church buildings and all that seemed essential for a corporate existence.[1]

But the zeal of reform and power of revival combined to enable these evangelical Syrians to build up from almost nothing the Mar Thoma Syrian Church of Malabar.[2] Seventy years had passed since the original contact with the Evangelical missionaries of the Church Missionary Society. In another seventy years, the Mar Thoma Church was to grow to a quarter of a million members.[3]

In 1888, the Mar Thoma leaders harnessed the power of the Kerala Awakening to form the Mar Thoma Evangelistic Association, thoroughly a dynamic, indigenous movement. The zeal of this Association permeated the whole Church.[4]

As in the days of Arulappan, the next wave of revival came to Kerala from Tamilnad. There a native Salvation Army captain was the means of introducing a Tamil convert named V. D. David to a victorious Christian life.[5] Shortly after this, Tamil David (as he was known) accompanied the Rev. George Grubb in campaigns in Ceylon.

Tamil David travelled to Australia and Britain with the Grubb party, and spoke at the Keswick Convention. Tamil David wrote a tract that fell into the hands of a discouraged Anglican missionary in Uganda, G. L. Pilkington, who experienced such a change of heart that his ministry issued into a great revival in Uganda, 1375 adherents in 1894 becoming 12,086 in 1897,[6] the year that Pilkington was killed.

Archdeacon Oommen Mammen, of Mavelikara,[7] invited V. D. David and L. M. Wardsworth to visit Kerala in 1892. Throughout Central Travancore the meetings resulted in a great awakening with its usual accompaniment of confession of sins, with great brokenness and weeping and public witnessing of faith in Christ.[8] Tamil David affirmed that ten thousand people had been converted in three months! His greatest meeting was one of 25,000 at Maramon.[9] It was then (1895) that the Maramon Convention was founded, C. P. Philipos being the chief organizer.[10]

By then, doctrinal issues had begun to divide the converts and a Christian Brethren movement arose to challenge the Anglicans[11] and Mar Thomists.[12] While Tamil David and Wardsworth retained the respect of all evangelical folk, their subsequent visits were not so generally commended. So in 1900, Metropolitan Titus Mar Thoma invited the Reverend Thomas Walker of Tinnevelly to visit Kerala, the beginning of regular evangelistic campaigning.

It is recognized that Walker's ministry built up an expectancy of revival in Kerala after 1900.[13] The news of the 1904 Revival in Wales accelerated it immensely. In 1905,[14] the Church Missionary Society noticed a 'great spiritual thirst in Kerala,' stating that 'God was about to breathe into the dry bones new life and power.'[15]

In Trivandrum, in the south, news of the Welsh Revival created profound interest,[16] and prayer for an outpouring of the Spirit upon India obsessed the Christians, including pupils in boarding schools.

In the college town of Kottayam, Sunday 23rd July was set aside as a special day of intercession for worldwide revival,[17] prayer meetings continuing daily until a Sunday in November was given over to prayer for India.

As early as June of 1905, a Malayali Anglican, the Reverend P. J. Joshua, organized a meeting in the parish hall in Kunnankulam, where a rapt audience heard an account of the Welsh Revival.[18] From then on, prayer meetings were held daily in the town, with a deepening intensity. In Cochin, also north, prayer meetings were organized by Anglicans and others, every day of the week.[19]

It could therefore be said that the expectancy of revival in Kerala was general. It affected Anglicans, Congregationalists, and Mar Thomists and others of evangelical faith. It was not long before the prayers of the intercessors were being answered in a general awakening lasting years.

At the Tamil tip of India, a revival had already begun. A Salvationist team from Nagercoil was invited to minister for three days in Trivandrum,[20] the capital city of the state of Travancore. Response was immediate and heartening, as three hundred passed through rooms of inquiry,[21] and a wave of spiritual quickening was felt in local churches.

It spread to country congregations, in one of which there was 'a most inspiring revival' in which thirty-five young men were converted.[22] Statistics of the London Missionary Society confirm the hundreds added and remaining true at the end of the decade.[23]

The Church Missionary Society[24] designated the revival 'a remarkable spiritual work,' thousands being added to their membership within a couple of years.[25] Mar Thoma figures are harder to come by, but census returns show that their community doubled during the ten years of the early twentieth century Awakening.[26]

The Anglicans reported awakening in Mavelikara,[27] and parish after parish was affected in greater or lesser degree by the rising tide of spiritual power. From the College in Kottayam, it was reported that a rapid, almost unprecedented sale of Bibles followed a period of almost complete stagnation in the sale of Scriptures, thanks to the effect of revival movements in Kerala.[28]

Walker of Tinnevelly, quick to take advantage of the movement in Kerala, accepted invitations of the Mar Thoma Metropolitan to hold missions in their parish churches, with encouraging results.

Most remarkable was the impact of revival on the clergy and people of the Mar Thoma Church. A convert of the Awakening under Wardsworth and David, Punchamannil Mammen by name, received a call from God during the 1904 prayer times.[29] In his meetings in Kizhakkenmuthoor and Tiruvalla and Venmoney, there was much conviction of sin and weeping and repenting and confessing. The people flocked in from the other towns, and the evangelist extended work to Alleppey, Niranam and Kattunilam. In Venmoney the people skipped for joy, introducing a method of expression that caused some questioning.[30]

In the year following, Punchamannil Mammen preached in Tiruvalla, Kottayam, Kunnamkulam, Mepral, Kottarakara, and Chengannoor, visiting Malayalam-speaking churches in Madras also, with much encouragement.[31]

The 1905 awakening in Kunnamkulam in Kerala was typical of the movement among Malayalis. Kunnamkulam was a large town of 8000, all of them Syrian Christians.[32] The revival began with prayer that soon brought conviction of sin. There were demonstrated in a very practical manner genuine repentance, open confession, immediate restitution, unity and love. The outcome of the movement was seen in the ending of all personal animosities, the settling of social quarrels, and the mediation of congregational disputes, even former enemies uniting in the 'praying-and-preaching bands' that evangelized the nearby villages.

Some Anglican missionaries were critical of the informality of the movement, but readily admitted the power and sincerity of its prophets.[33]

In Kottayam,[34] a missionary teacher reported that the Travancore Awakening had affected the Anglican College, and yet another observed also that the itinerant Malayali Christian preacher—Punchamannil Mammen, doubtless—had earnestness and knew the Holy Scriptures well.[35] The 'dancing for joy' by the penitents receiving 'forgiveness' caused misgivings, as did the 'laying on of hands' by the evangelist, who trespassed on bishops' rights thus. It was agreed that 'some good has come to us all, even to the servants.'

In Tiruvalla, the resident Anglican missionary affirmed that 'a revival of true religion' had been enjoyed there and in Alleppey.[36] 'Approved' were the awakened interest in prayer meetings, witnessing to non-Christians and restoration of peace and harmony among those people guilty of quarreling and discord, but misgivings were expressed regarding the 'singing and dancing' and it was felt that some were carried away by the excitement.

The Anglicans recognized that the young preacher was armed with the authority of the Metropolitan of the Mar Thoma Church, his meetings packed by eager auditors, who confessed their faults and turned to God, evidencing changed lives, church attendance, and interest in prayer, a 'real work' of grace done despite 'temporary excitement.'

Quite a different attitude was taken by an Anglican principal at Pallam, who flatly forbade his students to attend the Mammen meetings.[37] 'A so-called revival movement caused us a good deal of trouble,' he announced. He characterized the Syrian Christian evangelist as 'an ignorant and uneducated' young man. He was outraged by the outbreak of simultaneous prayer, which he accused the evangelist of working up. Punchamannil Mammen rebuked the Englishman publicly, but prayed with his pupils.

Walker of Tinnevelly seemingly escaped the criticism of his fellow-Anglicans in Travancore.[38] He was invited to Kerala by the Mar Thoma clergy and Metropolitan, and enjoyed the support of the Anglican people.[39] Walker stated:

THE AWAKENING IN KERALA

> This closing year has been, in a very special sense, a year of grace for India... Congregation after congregation was bowed before the power of the Holy Spirit in deep conviction and confession of sin. At times the solemnity and power were almost painful, and we were often in church till midnight. The people of a 'revived congregation' would follow us to the adjacent villages to give their testimonies there, and their witness did far more than our preaching.[40]

Simultaneous audible prayer did not dismay Walker of Tinnevelly. He recognized it as an expression of conviction. Walker was a speaker at Maramon Convention in the year of the Awakening in Kerala. Wrote his colleague, R. T. Archibald, Children's Special Service Mission worker:[41]

> On the day before the last of the Maramon Convention I was speaking, and as we closed, the whole congregation of 17,000 broke out into audible prayer ... the noise increased every moment; so I turned to him for counsel. He said 'Let them go on; they will stop soon.' In five minutes, all had subsided.

Effects reported in the 1905 Revival were deep repentance, joy in the Spirit, and a desire to spread the Good News to the unconverted.[42] In some places, Christians and Hindus were taken up with visions of holy doves and sacred fire, but the Hindu converts were found standing true after fifty years.[43]

The Awakening that began in Kerala in 1905 lasted until the end of the decade. There are records of stirring, lasting revivals and of successful evangelism—throughout Travancore and Cochin.

The Mar Thoma Sunday School Samajam was founded in 1905 and in sixty years grew from fifty to 800 Sunday Schools, with 5000 teachers and 60,000 pupils. From a community total of 37,713 in the 1901 census, the Mar Thoma Church increased to 74,866 in 1911, an almost 100% gain, its 135 congregations served by more than eighty clergy. In the second decade, it increased 50%.[44]

The Mar Thoma Evangelistic Association in 1905 greatly increased its scope. Evangelists went everywhere preaching the Word, as did the national workers among Anglicans and others. Mar Thoma missionaries began to work among the Syrian Christians in North Travancore in the first decade of the twentieth century. This effort met with much opposition, but gained converts who were added directly to Mar Thoma churches.[45]

20

THE AWAKENING IN KANARA

The present-day State of Mysore in the south of the Indian Republic has a population of nine million, mostly Kanarese-speaking. Its thirty thousand square miles were not all within its princely boundaries at the beginning of the century, and the various Christian missions were then operating under different jurisdictions.

The Basel Mission made its headquarters at Mangalore, on the Kanarese coast. Not only did its missionaries inherit a revival tradition from the days of Samuel Hebich,[1] but they maintained both agricultural and industrial enterprises to provide for converts cut off from their caste affiliations.

The English Wesleyans had also operated in Kanarese country for more than half a century. Their main centre was Bangalore, a military cantonment city on the eastern side of Mysore. An influx of converts had followed a time of famine in the 1870s. Part of the field they shared with the London Missionary Society.[2]

The American Methodists entered the field much later, their South India Conference extended its operation among Kanarese and other South Indian peoples.[3] They ministered from Belgaum to Bangalore.

Christian communities in both the upland and lowland of Mysore received a stirring through the Indian Awakening of 1905-1906.[4] There were local revivals from the Kolar goldfields in the southeast to Belgaum in the northwest.[5]

News of the Welsh Revival reached the field in early 1905.[6] In Bangalore, prayer meetings increased in numbers, making the churches very expectant, promising every likelihood of a great ingathering. It was one thing to hear of such an awakening in Wales—so far beyond the imagination of a Kanarese Christian—and quite another when word came of phenomenal revival on Indian soil, first in faraway Assam, then in nearby Maharashtra, and then in other parts of Dravidian India. It was not long before prayer was answered in Kanara.

THE AWAKENING IN KANARA 141

In Bangalore, the Awakening produced praise and gladness, moving responses coming from the Christians, clear cut decisions from outsiders in crowded congregations.[7] Manifestations were the same, intense prayer, conviction of sinners and confessions of sin, followed by real conversions. The Wesleyan missionaries reported revivals in their various Indian fields in 1905 and 1906, there being marked results in the Kanarese congregations in Bangalore and Tumkur.[8] Within two years, the membership increasing by one-eighth, accessions being general, baptisms one of the largest numbers ever recorded.

The Wesleyans reported that the outstanding feature of religious life during 1905 was:[9]

> Its participation in that access of emotional and spiritual fervour which had its most remarkable manifestation in Wales. It is necessary to draw a distinction between what in this movement is emotional and what is spiritual.

The characteristics of the Awakening were 'a quickened sensitiveness to sin, a keener experience of godly sorrow for it, instant continuance in prayer, a clear grasp of forgiveness and acceptance.[10]

> In some places, in at least one station of the District, emotionalism overflowed its banks and developed into a flood of hysteria with results that we can only deplore... this outburst was closely connected with a real deepening of spiritual life for which we are most thankful.[11]

The official report affirmed that all their churches had in varying measure shared in the Revival, and it was emphasized that the movement was undoubtedly of God.

The movement continued into 1906, and Lenten and Easter services in Tumkur were overcrowded. For two or three years, the quickened life of the churches in Mysore gave ground for rejoicing, young men offering themselves at Synod meetings for evangelistic work.

At the New Year, 1905, 'a real Welsh Revival prayer meeting' was held in Bellary, in the London Missionary Society field in Kanara. An account of the Awakening in Wales was given, resulting in an intense conviction of sin which produced confession, reconciliation and restitution.

The Revival spread to the Girls' Hostel and 'for a long time the sound of midnight prayer and praise was heard.' The matron was called up in the night to pray with sin-stricken girls. This revival continued through the famine period, one of the fruits of the movement being the petition of the girls to 'sell the rice we have in the school and put us on famine rations.'

The Awakening in Belgaum started through a revival in a girls' orphanage and spread to the local churches. The influence of Pandita Ramabai's praying bands from neighbouring Mukti was of great importance, and also true of Bangalore.

One of the features of the Awakening was the prayer for the exorcism of demons. The writer has seen the glazed eyes, the sullen lethargy, the frenzied actions of the demon-possessed in India, and heard their screaming and shrieking. There was much discussion about this among missionaries of the London Society:

> There is a difference of opinion among ourselves as to the reality of the phenomena, but there is none as to the value of such power (exorcism) as an evangelistic agency.

The Congregational missionaries reported the case of a village woman, eighteen years of age, who was 'demon-possessed.' Her affliction showed itself in dull stupidity and erratic ways, as well as in distressing physical symptoms. Every means, occidental and oriental, was tried to effect her recovery, and every expense, with no avail. It seemed utterly hopeless.

The members of a prayer band prayed over her, in the name of Jesus exorcising the demon. The effect was immediate and the answer to prayer 'so marvellous that the people called it a miracle.' The villagers were so impressed that they flocked in for instruction in the faith.

Through neglect of the means of grace, the woman suffered a relapse. Ashamed, she called upon a native demon-doctor for help, but thereupon went into violent convulsive pains. The prayer band was sent for, and they again offered prayer in the name of Jesus. The woman was completely restored.[12]

Most significant was the impact upon the villagers. The whole attitude of the village changed.[13] The simple people were satisfied that the Good News of Jesus Christ was true, and they sought instruction. The revived prayer band had been used to cause an awakening among illiterate, unindoctrinated, lower-caste people, not another like revival, but a movement of a caste group in the direction of Christianity.

THE AWAKENING IN KANARA 143

As was the case in other parts of India, the revival of the Christians was followed indirectly by folk movements into the Christian community. The American Methodists, for instance, clinched contact with groups of interested low-caste folk from 1905 onwards, the resultant growth being regarded as a great triumph of the Gospel. Four thousand in 1905 had become forty thousand by 1925.

There was a spirit of expectancy among the American Methodists in the 1900s. The pioneer J. H. Garden declared in 1902 his expectation of a true revival that would bring thousands of outcaste people into the Christian faith. This proved true in the Kanarese as well as the Telugu field.

Just before the outbreak of revival among the Christians, the Belgaum operations of the London Missionary Society were taken over by zealous American Methodist missionaries in 1904. Their 200 church members were largely higher caste, to judge from reports.

There were limits of outreach, so far as the higher castes were concerned, but at their door were thousands of interested outcastes. The movement changed direction. In a few years, lower caste people in Belgaum and Bailhongal circuits were entering the Church.

There were folk movements in other mission districts also. As early as 1904, an increase of baptisms heralded the beginning of a group movement into the Methodist fellowship at Shorapur, and a Home Missionary Society was begun in the Raichur area in 1905, so that within five years energies were being harnessed to the shepherding of a group movement of lower caste people into the discipling care of the growing Church.[14]

Walker of Tinnevelly conducted a successful mission in the great contonment city, Bangalore,[15] congregations of all denominations reaping the benefit of his sane evangelism and teaching ministry.

The German Lutherans of the Basel Mission around Mangalore reaped a harvest following an awakening in 1906 upon the coast of Kanara.[16] In the opening years of the twentieth century, their enterprises and churches were Indianized more and more. There were few folk movements in that area.

Thus every part of Dravidian India shared in the Revival. Prayer bands and lay preachers arose and so strengthened the national Church. The 1905 Awakening was far stronger, in every way, in the South of India than in the North.

21

AWAKENINGS IN NORTH INDIA

Ramabai, as the daughter of a Brahmin scholar, was given a good education by her father who held the unusual notion that girls could be educated. Ramabai was influenced by Anglo-Catholic folk in India and was baptized in Wantage in England on the 29th September 1883,[1] as a young widow. Paraphrasing Hindu lyrics, she could say:[2]

> Christ have I sought;
> The price He asked I paid;
> Some cried 'Too great!'
> While others jeered 'Twas small!'
> I paid in full,
> Weighed to the utmost grain,
> My love, my life, my self,
> My soul, my all.

Pandita Ramabai returned to India with a great concern for the lot of young and neglected widows forbidden by Hindu custom to marry again.[3] Famine led her to extend her work to orphans, and soon she had a remarkable work in Maharashtra—at Mukti, 'the place of deliverance.'

Homeward from the United States in 1898, Ramabai attended the Keswick Convention in England and requested four thousand people there to pray for the evangelization of India.[4] Burdened by India's need of revival, in 1903 she became interested in the movement of prayer in Australia that preceded the Torrey-Alexander campaigns there; so she sent her daughter to Melbourne to enlist the prayers of Australians. In 1904, she learned of the Welsh Revival.[5]

Narayan Vaman Tilak, ordained in 1904, was at Mukti in Kedgaon with Ramabai in early 1905.[6] Pandita Ramabai had commenced special prayer circles at the beginning of 1905, and hundreds of her helpers and friends attended.[7]

At 3.30 a.m. on June 29, a young woman had a luminescent experience.[8] Next day, Ramabai was expounding the eighth chapter of John in a quiet way when her hearers began to pray aloud, until the volume of simultaneous prayer brought the Bible lesson to a close.[9]

Girls were stricken by conviction of sin, and the school became a vast inquiry room for the penitents. Conviction was followed by confession. Noteworthy were all the emotional accompaniments, the physical phenomena, the sensation of burning, simultaneous prayer, and speaking with tongues, and (later on) women praying with loud crying, though Ramabai conducted herself quietly.

What must have been the thoughts of a well-educated Indian lady of highest caste, influenced in her Christian ideas of propriety by Anglo-Catholics when the phenomena of an evangelical awakening burst upon her spiritual family? Said Ramabai, in Mukti prayer letters two years later: 'I looked upon these features with much concern, for some time, but did not try to interfere with God's work in any way.' [10]

Ramabai tried to lay down some rules for the work of the Lord at the beginning of the Revival: [11]

> But I soon found that I stopped the work of the Holy Spirit by interfering with it. I wanted to be proper and conduct meetings in our old civilized ways. But God would have none of it. He laid His hand upon me, put me low in the dust, and told me that I had better take my proper place, that of a worm. He said, 'My thoughts are not your thoughts, neither are your ways My ways.' I humbled myself under this severe rebuke and took my hand off the work. The Holy Spirit has full liberty . . .

Nonetheless there resulted the conversion of hundreds of women. Nicol MacNicol, Ramabai's scholarly biographer, wrote in retrospect: 'Those whose religion in 1907 seemed too emotional to endure long, twenty years later were bearing their witness steadfastly.' [12]

These results, reported Pandita Ramabai, were 'most satisfactory.' Lives were changed, rebel wills subdued, undisciplined natures were brought under a higher control, with purity instead of grossness; uprightness and honour for falsehood and deceit; gladness instead of gloom.[13]

An older girl who had 'sinned against the light' and was hardened in heart 'came under the hand of God' and was truly converted. Doing her usual work and attending school, she gave no indication of illness; but on July 5 while in a Bible class she was suddenly taken ill.[14] She was given every attention by doctors, remained conscious for an hour, telling the nurse before death came that the Lord was calling her.

The veteran world-evangelist, G. H. Lang of the Christian Brethren, wrote about his visit to Mukti:[15]

> It was a new experience to hear a thousand women and girls praying aloud at one time. The sound rose and fell like the roar of the sea or the wind in a forest. But what to a Westerner might seem like mere confusion did not so strike me, for I had before heard in Egypt a whole school of boys similarly. The mind of each was on his own recitation undisturbed by the noise around. Similarly, each woman and girl was oblivious of the rest and, when each finished praying, she arose quietly from the ground and left the hall.

Lang asked 'What is the force of Acts 4: 24?' When the disciples lifted up their voice with one accord, does it mean that the whole company was suddenly moved by the one Spirit to say unitedly the same words? 'The New Testament was not written as a description of modern conferences.'

At first Ramabai refused to permit even true friends to publish an account of the Mukti movement. She was convicted of refusing to give the glory to God so she permitted accounts to be sent to a Bombay journal and elsewhere.[16]

Then she took a band of revived workers to Poona, forty miles away, planning a series of prayer meetings to reach the Indian Church.[17] In these meetings, there was no break, but in the meetings held in schools and orphanages there came an awakening similar to that at Mukti. It was noticed that the waifs of the famine being cared for on principles of faith were the first to receive blessing. An orphanage at nearby Dhond was so moved, and another in faraway Allahabad in the plains of the Ganges.[18]

The Free Methodist Mission at Yeotmal in the eastern parts of Maratha country closed its schools in order to intercede for Revival. In the last week of August 1905, on Saturday night, 'the power of the Spirit came like lightning,' it was said by the missionaries.[19]

The Methodist churches in Bombay city next received a visitation of the revival spirit. Its manifestations there in that great city appeared in churches of the various denominations, English-speaking, Marathi and Gujerati.[20]

The Friends' Mission in Hoshangabad held four days of meetings to intercede for blessing. The visitation came as a 'rushing mighty wind,' and in moments hundreds were praying publicly and simultaneously.[21] Miss Evens, a deaf missionary, commented:[22]

Being deaf, I rarely hear a prayer, but in the rush of sound I could plainly hear those around me, and how direct and different each prayer was.

Confession of sin and restitution of wrong followed that first outpouring of the Spirit among the Quakers and their converts. The annual Mela of the Friends' Mission in the New Year of 1906 proved to be an extraordinary time of blessing, the awakening at Hoshangabad having stirred the other congregations in the Quaker field.[23]

At Khudawandpur, the news of the awakening in Poona stirred the Boys' Orphanage, a blind lad being the first converted.[24] Some there were who scoffed at the manifestations, whereupon a missionary who had prayed all night delivered a message in Marathi from Isaiah 28, 'Therefore hear the word of the Lord, you scoffers . . .' Such a conviction fell upon the hearers that an agony of soul continued for five or six days. The missionaries were moved to humble themselves before their Indian brethren. The awakening then spread to neighbouring orphanages in Bhaisdehi and Chikalda.[25]

In November 1905, a band of girls from Mukti arrived at Ratnigiri, on the Maharashtra coast.[26] They began by praying for the Ratnigiri people,[27] and soon their voices were joined by a general outbreak of prayer in the room. On December 3,[28] the day of prayer for India, the local people used the time to put their affairs right with God. Next day, a Biblewoman in agony of spirit confessed the sin of having robbed the Lord. Confessions of sin went on all the succeeding week. It ended in songs of deliverance and dancing for joy, and with a determined outreach to the unbelievers around.[29]

The Mukti bands continued to visit towns and villages in the Maratha country,[30] reporting the same extraordinary praying, conviction of sin, and confession, restitution, reconciliation and restoration—with conversions following.

In April 1906, a call came from the Church Missionary Society at Aurangabad for a praying band from Mukti to visit the congregation. Fifty preachers had gathered from eleven churches. The awakening began among the young men of the Normal School. The preachers objected to the simultaneous audible prayer and to confession of sin in public, and to the ministry of women. The summer heat had reached 109 degrees in the shade, yet the meetings went on, overcoming the handicaps.[31]

A girl on vacation at Aurangabad returned to the C. M. S. school in Bombay, where an extraordinary movement ensued. Not only were the girls revived and restored and converted to God, but phenomena followed.[32] One Christian girl had been accused of stealing. The girls in assembly were faced with the matter. No one would admit the theft. They went to prayer and independently two girls reported to their teacher that they had been 'shown' in prayer the guilty one, who first denied but then confessed her guilt.

Revival was felt in the Gujerati fields in 1906.[33] At the Dholka Orphanage of the Christian and Missionary Alliance there were cries of penitence at the Sunday prayer meeting. Missionaries were amazed to find orphan boys leading spontaneous prayer meetings, even at midnight. Protracted meetings followed, days and night, with repentance, confessions, and restitution. Sixty rupees of conscience money were restored, as well as stolen articles from blankets to pins. The head carpenter returned ten stolen rupees. Not one of the 300 boys and youths was untouched and a wave of evangelism surged from the place to villages roundabout.[34]

Of all the British missionaries in India, none possessed a richer heritage of revival than the generation once removed from the 1859 Revival in Ulster.[35] It was natural to expect an outbreak of revival in the Gujerati field of the warm-hearted Irish Presbyterians, whose converts shared their appreciation of a spiritual outpouring as the greatest of all manifestations of the presence of God.

In the areas of Muslim predominance, to the Northwest, the Punjab Praise and Prayer Union continued to expand its intercessory activities. Seldom, if ever, was there such a mobilization of prayer on any mission field in the world. Praying Hyde was by no means the only missionary who obeyed the commandment: 'Gather my saints unto me, those who have made a covenant with sacrifice.'

Their prayers were answered in a series of outpourings of the Spirit in northwestern India, beginning in 1905 at Sialkot.[36] A decided spiritual upheaval occurred in a girls' school directed by Mary Campbell, resulting in confession of sins and repentance toward God.[37] The revival spirit next touched a theological seminary, but missed the Institute— the directors still afraid of the dynamic movement.

A new principal, Dr. W. B. Anderson, called for united prayer meetings.[38] Missionaries and nationals were stirred

AWAKENINGS IN NORTH INDIA

and the results were seen in a deepening of spiritual life among the Christians, followed by a widening outreach of evangelism among the non-Christians.[39]

The Convention for the Deepening of Christian Life was held again at Sialkot in August 1905, revival already begun in other parts of India.[40] Pengwern Jones of the Welsh Khasi Hills Mission addressed the convention.[41] When time came to close this meeting, the whole congregation knelt before God. Confessions of sin were made that 'often shocked the hearers but later were found hard to remember.' Only one of Hyde's messages was given; the Spirit took over.

The issue of public confession of private sin was raised and after much prayer it was agreed that confession should be made only to God and to any brother wronged, and only publicly if the Spirit of God clearly commanded the individual, never because of pressure from others.[42]

Revival began at a Church of Scotland camp at Kathala in October, the influence of the Sialkot Convention bringing the movement to the Y.M.C.A. campers.[43] The Church of Scotland congregations doubled their membership, from approximately five thousand to ten thousand in the Punjab in the decade following, an uplift in all sectors.[44]

The Church Missionary Society reported a 'widespread spirit of prayer in the Punjab' in 1905[45] and the following year a folk movement got under way, with fifteen hundred inquirers at Narowal and round about, where Ihsan Ullah ministered.[46] The Anglican community doubled in ten years throughout the western Punjab.[47]

The Sialkot Convention of 1906 increased in size and in power. Instead of 300, there were 1300 present, besides seventy missionaries.[48] Preaching was powerful. Nominal Christians were 'born again,' and missionaries' lives were changed. All night long, the hall remained full of people— this in the Institute long forbidden to the movement. Day or night, intercession was a continuing feature. It was noticed that those who had come to mock or criticize were those who were convicted and humbled in agonies of spirit.

The Sialkot Conventions continued year by year, with an outpouring that was felt in widening circles throughout that northern sweep of India.[49] Hyde remained the intercessor-in-earnest; in 1911 he returned home to die of cancer six months later.[50] Paterson and Turner continued to pray.

The United Presbyterians ministered to ten thousand or so communicants in 1904; within ten years, they admitted more than twenty thousand to full membership.[51] The other denominations in the area also increased both communicant membership and adherency in that decade. While it is true that a folk movement was under way before the outbreak of the revival, the spiritual upheaval accelerated church growth —so much so that a 5% per annum increase became a 20% influx.

Farther east in the Punjab, tides of revival were coming in. An awakening began at Ludhiana through the influence of visitors to the Sialkot Convention. The greatest reviving occurred in the boys' school.[52]

The American Presbyterian missionaries at Ludhiana included E. P. Newton, E. M. Wherry, and J. N. Hyde, in a Prayer Circle that circularized its members to mobilise prayer for (1) special blessing on the newly-organized Conventions at Sialkot, (2) for a spirit of unity, (3) for guidance and wisdom, and (4) for Revival in India.[53]

In October, E. M. Wherry reported to headquarters in Philadelphia that 'the power of the Holy Spirit was felt by everyone,' and that the Mission was looking for 'a great revival' during the autumn and winter. By December, 'a new spirit of zeal' in the work was noted.[54]

Other districts of the American Presbyterian Mission experienced awakenings. At Fatehpur,[55] the Mission experienced a wonderful ingathering in three of its districts, and the year following a second season of refreshing was announced; and in Fatehgarh,[56] between November of 1905 and 1906 there were revival meetings held in the various churches, not only resulting in a large number declaring faith, but in 'so many receiving the Holy Spirit.'

The official reports and private letters of the missionaries seemed to take for granted that an awakening was taking place everywhere. If they held reservations in their inner circles, other than those voiced publicly, they gave no indication of them in their letters home.[57]

The mission fields of the Presbyterian Church in the United States of America (Northern Presbyterians) stretched from Peshawar on the far frontier of the North West to Allahabad in the middle of the Gangetic plain. In the 1900s, the American Presbyterians reported a great ingathering throughout their fields in North India. The congregational strengths in Fatehgarh, Etah, Mainpuri and Etawah had grown to 15,000 by 1907, of whom 11,000 had been baptized in the previous four years.[58] For example, Fatehgarh in

1904 had a fellowship of 1200 Christians; in 1909, there were 6000.

Of the folk movements in the Punjab, it was reported that the Christian constituency, which had doubled between 1891 and 1901 to 37,695, had in the revival decade more than quadrupled to a total of 163,994.[59]

Far to the north, an awakening began at Jammu in the state of Kashmir, where drinking and quarrels had utterly disgraced the local church. A spirit of prayer and strong conviction of sin appeared, and confession swept the congregation, ending the troubles of the time.[60]

At Dehra Dun,[61] influence of the Sialkot revival brought about an awakening, marked as usual by prayer, conviction of sin, confession, and concern for the salvation of friends. There was a similar movement in another hill-station, Landour, led by Indian young men, encountering opposition at first but silencing the critics by its obvious blessing; the influence continued.[62]

Partly by missionary communication, and partly by the interest of Indian Christians, the movements spread through the congregations of the north country.[63] As far north as Almora, in the foothills of the Himalayas, there were local occurrences of revival.[64] Often, the movements began in the educational institutions.

One such institutional awakening occurred in the town of Pilibhit, in the shadow of the Himalayan ranges. Mr. and Mrs. Salisbury, experienced American evangelists, held meetings for the Industrial Evangelistic Mission.[65] Revival began with the lads in training, then among the workers; conviction came to a widening circle of hearers, followed by confession, restitution and return of stolen property. The lads went in bands to neighbouring farmers whose field or orchard they had robbed and asked forgiveness, which was granted often with tears.[66] The news spread around the villages, and the people began to ask what it all meant, leading to fruitful evangelism.

The Salisburys communicated the revival to the Mussoorie branch of their Mission, with the same results beginning among the young men. Many similar institutions were likewise moved en masse.[67]

The Church Missionary Society congregation at Meerut experienced an awakening in October of 1905.[68] There had been much prayer for two years. The first sign of coming blessing came when a couple of members prayed for an infilling of the Holy Spirit. Then the Anglican missionary dealt with a couple of penitents and their wives. This was followed by 'heart-searching' prayer meetings in which confessions of sin and failure were freely made, often with tears and generally with broken voice. In ten days there were fifteen cases of conversion.

There were no unusual manifestations but the depth and reality of the Spirit's working was acknowledged by all concerned; quarrels were made up, and peace passing understanding prevailed.[69]

There was an awakening at the Reid Christian College at Lucknow at the beginning of 1906,[70] and Walker of Tinnevelly's preaching mission there brought blessing to the Anglicans and Methodists.

At Moradabad, in February of 1906, revival appeared in a Methodist School for young women and girls. The largest assembly room was opened for evening prayer. On 8th March, there was an outpouring of fervour, but Principal Means was absent and the school janitor insisted on turning the girls out of the hall at 9 p.m. They continued on the verandahs, and the movement went on in great power and with fruitful results.[71]

A same sort of movement was felt in Bareilly where the spirit of fervour began among young people, as before. It was reported that while the girls in one school were engaged in praying for the boys in another community, some of the boys were converted in bed in their dormitories.

The Methodist Bishop Warne claimed that 200 young people set themselves apart in a covenant to enter the Christian ministry, though knowing that it was not a lucrative prospect compared to others for which their education qualified them in life.[72] The Bareilly Theological Seminary was at once affected.

Everything seemed to have gone wrong at the Hindi Methodist Church in Allahabad, the workers becoming desperate.[73] The prayers of several of the multiplying praying bands were enlisted. The movement began quite suddenly in a mid-week prayer meeting, with a deep sense of conviction of sin upon all who were present. It seemed impossible to close the meeting, so the Indian pastor announced 'special meetings' which continued for many weeks, with 'conviction, confession, restitution, an earnest effort to put wrong things right, then the consciousness of pardon and unspeakable joy.' The result was that the church

AWAKENINGS IN NORTH INDIA

was completely transformed; old troubles were settled; enemies were reconciled; evangelism was extended; and workers went out to preach enthusiastically.[74]

A District Conference succeeded in spreading the movement throughout its congregations and mission stations near and far.[75] It recalled Taylor's work thirty years ago, in the same cities.

Quite a new atmosphere was reported in Agra after Walker of Tinnevelly's meetings in 1906. The ten days of ministry left an indelible mark.[76] The Anglican evangelist toured the cities of the north in 1906, 5500 miles all told,[77] reporting a floodtide of blessing. In the aftermath of revival, Thomas Walker wrote:[78]

> Special missions are being called for everywhere. Both the missionary body and the Indian Church are feeling as never before the need of power from on High.

It was in 1906 that revival was felt in many parts of Bengal.[79] In Calcutta, the Reverend D. H. Lee gathered his family, teachers and workers for a day of fasting and prayer on 9th February.[80] Five days later, the house was 'full of prayer,' many praying audibly and some sobbing aloud. A number were 'brightly converted.' After much prayer, a number of Bengali young men formed an evangelistic band and toured the villages, the first being Janjara, a village on an island where converts were won among the islanders.[81]

In October 1906, a group of sixty missionaries met at Darjeeling to hear the account given by a C.M.S. missionary, the Reverend E. T. Butler, of the awakening in the Nuddea district of Bengal.[82] He prefaced his report by saying that he and his wife were matter-of-fact people engaged in a teaching ministry. Thus, when Revival came, it took everyone by surprise. The Anglicans also burst into simultaneous praying and confession of sin. Lives were thus transformed and earnestness replaced carelessness while a number of people were converted. Butler spoke guardedly of the manifestations, but told of individuals entering a state of trance and of a meeting in which he saw and experienced pentecostal tongues of 'fire.'[83]

At Darjeeling, a Bengal Prayer Union was formed. Its members carried the revival longing far and wide in the language-area and many were the reports of local awakenings received.[84]

There was a 'visitation of the Spirit' in the Santal country in Bengal. At Mihijam, Jamtara and Karmatur, there was an outpouring that made a missionary write that it surpassed anything he had seen in eighteen years of service.[85]

The London Missionary Society reported many revivals in Bengal. Not only was there stirring in the metropolis, Calcutta, but the provincial towns such as Moorshidabad enjoyed a work of God.[86]

Dr. John P. Jones at the 1910 Conference of the Student Volunteer Movement in New York affirmed that the Revival in North India brought a mighty inflow of joy and power to the missionaries themselves, many of whom were transformed into men and women of tenfold power beyond that of their past.[87]

It of course is true that missionaries are almost everywhere and always mentioned in such reports surviving in the English language, but it is equally certain that the movement in the Aryan North was indigenous, its chief vehicles for movement and expansion being Indian students, and in many cases these students were orphans of the disastrous famine.

There was certainly a difference between the North and South of India. In Dravidian India, a numerous Christian constituency existed, and among them developed a true revival. Up North, the revival occurred in schools and conferences, to be translated into evangelism in the non-Christian community.

As in the South, the Awakening manifested itself as a 'Catharsis of the Church' throughout North India. The impact was one on believers. Following the Revival, regular evangelism and folk movements added multitudes to the Christian community in the North.

It is significant that the numbers of Indian evangelists and workers doubled in the five years, 1900-1905, and doubled again 1905-1910. Lay activity followed the outpouring of the Holy Spirit upon the body of believers.[88]

There was a Census of India taken in 1901 and another in 1911, the figures being useful for an estimate of the size of the constituency rather than actual church membership. An international review by missionaries in 1912 reported that the Christian constituency of India had increased by 69.9% as compared with 16.3% among Muslims and 4.6% among Hindus.[89] Thus, in one decade, Christians grew sixteen times as fast as the Hindu majority.[90]

22

PRE-INDEPENDENCE EVANGELISM

In the first decade of the twentieth century, the population of the Indian Empire rose from 295,000,000 to 315,000,000. During that decade, the greatest revival of New Testament Christianity in India's history had taken place. In the north, a 445% increase in the number of Christians in the Punjab was reported—from 37,000 to 165,000.[1] In the south, there was a 16% increase in the number of Christians in Madras Presidency, or double the percentage of Hindu gain.[2] The Christians increased 116% in the Bombay Presidency.[3] In the United Provinces, Christians increased 169%, and in the Central Provinces, 175%.[4] In Travancore, there was a 30% gain, compared to a Hindu growth of 12%.[5] In all India, the Christians increased 70% as compared with little more than 16% among Muslims (including the provinces which later constituted Pakistan) and less than 5% among Hindus.[6]

Undoubtedly, the Roman Catholic Church had grown in the 1900s. Their total community, including Portuguese and French possessions, numbered 1,860,876 in 1901, and 2,223,546 in 1911, a less than 20% increase.[7] The 1,636,731 baptized Protestants numbered less than the total of their longer active competitors, but their growth was much more rapid, rising 40% from 1,149,745 in 1901, not counting the children of Baptist church members nor the Mar Thomists, avowedly Evangelical. The prime factor was the Revival.[8]

During the first half of the twentieth century, India was affected by two World Wars, a rapid rise of Indian nationalism, great growth in population, social changes in caste relationship, and secularism. Protestantism retained its revival impetus, increasing two-and-a-half times in numbers in a quarter century, while Roman Catholicism doubled. The numbers of baptized Protestants actually doubled in the decade which followed the years of revival. They increased only 25% in the decade further removed from the influence of the Awakening, decline in missionary funds and personnel due to the economic and spiritual depression in the western countries being another factor. But movements continued.

As in the 1860s, the revival in the sending countries brought out a host of missionary recruits. In the decade following the years of revival, despite the shortage of manpower due to worldwide war, the Protestant staff increased from 5465 to 5682, an approximate 4% gain; and their Indian staff increased from 39,555 to 48,787, a nearly 20% gain. In the decade following, affected by the decline of revival in India and the economic and spiritual depression in the West, the missionary staff dropped to 5112, an 11% decline, while the Indian staff declined to 17,323, a two-thirds drop, though it seems unlikely that Indian workers retired from all Christian service when funds dried up, for the number of Indians being ordained increased in those years.[9]

From the 1905 Awakening in the United States, E. Stanley Jones came out to India and became the best-known in the missionary body in the pre-Independence period. Jones was not a conventional missionary, resident in a city or engaged in a particular work. By his sympathy with Indian nationalism, he made a great appeal to the Indian educated classes. He crossed the length and breadth of India, holding meetings which were sure to attract several hundreds or thousands of the upper classes. This ministry did not result in any great influx of intelligentsia into the Church, but there were definite conversions. Stanley Jones also promoted 'roundtable' conferences, inviting leaders to converse and discuss what benefit they had received from their religion, while he gave glowing testimony of his encounter with Christ. He also became a regular speaker at great conventions of Indian Christians in the various states and provinces, and he conducted ashrams in various places, where a limited number could share spiritual fellowship. Undoubtedly, unbelievers found faith in these retreats. But Stanley Jones was not of the Moody-type, winning thousands to Christ and adding them to the organized churches. Rather, he became a promoter of pro-Christian opinions among Indians, and enjoyed the friendship of Gandhi, Nehru and other national leaders.[10]

There were many evangelists of the more conventional types among the European and American missionaries in India in the pre-Independence years. Their numbers began to decrease in the years of depression, for it goes without saying that mission societies retrench evangelists and their evangelism rather than cut down educational and medical personnel and activity, for institutions once built must be sustained, even if primary purposes are sacrificed.

PRE-INDEPENDENCE EVANGELISM 157

During the times of revival in the Punjab, a young Sikh was baptized. He had seen a vision of Christ and had then resolved to follow Him. His family disowned him. Sundar Singh became a Christian sadhu, travelling from place to place in the manner of Hindu holy men.[11]

Sadhu Sundar Singh engaged in simple evangelism. At first he walked from place to place, and taught villagers the simple truth of the Gospel. He was fascinated by the Himalayas and the Tibetan borderlands. He also ministered in Western India, and journeyed south to Madras. He was held in veneration as a holy man by others besides the Christians. Sundar Singh's work was not that of a mass evangelist.[12] It was one of influence.

The Sadhu visited Burma in 1918, and journeyed by sea to Malaya. His fame had preceded him, and crowds gathered to hear him. From Singapore, he sailed for Japan, addressing small meetings in Kobe, Osaka, Kyoto and Tokyo, but making a deep impression. He landed in Shanghai, spoke at meetings here and there, visited Nanking, Hankow and Peking, then sailed from Shanghai for Madras.[13]

Sundar Singh kept in close contact with several of the leaders in the revival movement of 1905.[14] In 1920, Sundar Singh sailed for Liverpool, and began to minister in a quiet way at Selly Oak, then Oxford. His meetings in the ancient university were packed out by eager students. It was the same at Cambridge. When he preached in Westminster, the church was crowded, listeners sitting in the chancel, on the steps, in the aisles and in every space. His dress, a simple saffron robe, his hair and beard, his sandals, reminded folk of his Master. The Archbishop of Canterbury was eager to receive him. Five hundred London clergy gathered to hear him, and the Bishop of London chaired the meeting. He also visited Ireland and Scotland.[15]

Sundar Singh's tour of the United States was organized by Dr. Frank Buchman, founder of the Oxford Group, afterwards known as Moral Re-armament. His reception by Americans repeated his welcome by British crowds.[16] He sailed from San Francisco for Sydney, and again the people responded. Churches were packed to the doors. He visited New Zealand also and then sailed for Bombay.[17]

In 1922, Sundar Singh visited Switzerland, Germany, Holland, Sweden, Norway and Denmark. From 1924 until 1929, he was in India, living more quietly in the Punjab. In 1929, he revisited Tibet, and never returned.[18]

After the worldwide awakening of 1905, a new agency was introduced to India, the Pentecostal movement. According to a reliable Pentecostal authority, Donald Gee, the first speaking in tongues made public in India occurred during the visit of the Mukti Bands to Aurangabad in 1906.[19] And from there, it spread to Bombay. Both missionaries and national leaders were touched by the movement, which was at first considered unsectarian rather than denominational. There followed outbreaks of glossolalia in the Gujerat field of the Christian and Missionary Alliance.[20] Tongues-speaking also occurred in the Nilgiri Hills, Bengal, and the United Provinces, long before any Pentecostal missionaries reached India from Britain and the United States. The newly-founded Pentecostal Missionary Union sent two missionaries from Britain to India in 1909.[21] Americans arrived earlier.

Pentecostalism in the United States and United Kingdom became a missionary movement from the first decade of the twentieth century. A. G. Garr, a pioneer Pentecostal missionary from Los Angeles, conducted meetings in the Bowbazar in Calcutta, out of which came a Pentecostal congregation of Bengalis, Eurasians, and Europeans.[22] At Landour, a resort in the Himalayan foothills, a Pentecostal lady, Miss Barber, introduced many to the 'experience.'[23]

Also in 1908, T. B. Barratt of Norway shared his message at Coonoor, in the Nilgiri Hills in the South.[24] George Berg, an American Pentecostal, settled in Bangalore that year, and introduced charismatic ministry to Kerala as well as Kanara, indigenous Malayali congregations being formed in Travancore.[25] Berg's associate, Robert Cook, opened a work in Tamilnad,[26] where he baptized sixteen converts in 1913. Thus, before World War I, the Pentecostal message had been given, chiefly in Kerala, Tamilnad, Kanara and Andhra. Much of this enterprise was linked with the Assemblies of God, formed in the United States in 1914.[27]

In 1913, two Swedish ladies ministered in the suburbs of Madras.[28] A hunchback, Jacob Benjamin, took over their work and built up the Madras Pentecostal Assembly, which became the mother church of many throughout India.

While missionaries from overseas contributed to the spread of the Pentecostal movement, its greatest factor for growth was Indian Christian enthusiasm. Indigenous Indian churches were springing up, becoming self-supporting and self-propagating. Persecution was forthcoming, but this only accelerated the indigeneity of Indian Pentecostalism.

Prof. W. J. Hollenweger has commented upon the notable indigeneity of the Indian Pentecostal community of churches, as indigenous as any.[29] Several attempts were made by well-meaning leaders to bring these denominationations together in a united front, but they failed. The Indian Pentecostal explosion seemed to possess more fission than fusion.

The fragmentization of Pentecostalism occurred in many countries. The centripetal force of a common charismatic practice was balanced by the centrifugal stress of varied denominational origins. But, as other new denominations, such as the Christian and Missionary Alliance, overcame inherited doctrinal tensions by united commitments, the Pentecostal fragmentization may perhaps be attributed to tensions of leadership due to insistence upon conflicting claims to spiritual guidance, a common failing.

The Indian Assemblies of God were incorporated in 1918 at Saharanpur in North India.[30] Despite the secessions in the South, the Assemblies expanded their fields. Malayali evangelists assisted the missionaries and pioneered on their own, setting up Bible Schools in Kerala and Tamilnad. Assembly of God missionaries opened schools, orphanages and dispensaries. More than four hundred and fifty congregations were established within a couple of generations.[31]

Meanwhile, in 1913, an awakening was reported by the Church Missionary Society in Nasik and Aurangabad, and a thousand inquirers were enrolled. At the same time, in South India, the Methodist mission to the Telugus enjoyed a very rapid growth, 8000 members in 1910 becoming 12,000 in 1913. A folk movement occurred in Hyderabad, resulting in six thousand baptisms. The following year, a vast folk movement among the Mehtars (Sweepers) of the north was reported, leading to 150,000 baptisms. There was another folk movement in Gujerat.[32]

Sherwood Eddy, a Y.M.C.A. evangelist who had been busy during the years of revival with V. S. Azariah, stirred up the Indian Churches in 1915 to pray for another reviving. A week of prayer at Vellore was followed by a week of evangelism, and two-thirds of the communicant members enrolled in Bible classes. No less than 8288 Tamil workers preached in 3814 towns and villages to audiences totalling 300,000 people. Of 8503 inquirers, 6422 professed to follow Christ. There was an overflow of the blessing to Travancore State, where whole churches engaged in Sunday afternoon evangelism, the laity being especially active.[33]

The weeks of simultaneous evangelism brought together unparalleled crowds in the two southernmost areas of India and the convening of Christians in strength spread to other parts of the sub-continent. Bishop Azariah and Bishop Abraham, Tamil Anglican and Malayali Syrian, were active leaders in the movement, which used the services of the Maratha poet, Narayan Tilak, and the sadhu, Sundar Singh, as well as those of H. A. Popley and G. S. Eddy and other missionaries.[34]

The South India United Church, a union of Congregational (L.M.S. and American Board) churches with Presbyterian (Scottish) and Reformed (American) congregations that had come together in the wake of the Revival, enthusiastically embarked upon another evangelistic drive in 1917-1918. At the same time, the Anglican Dornakal Diocese promoted a very similar campaign, allotting a number of villages to each congregation for visitation evangelism. Up to a third of their communicants were actively engaged in the effort.[35]

In 1919, Bishop Abraham and a Mar Thomist evangelist, Moothampackal Kochukunju, rendered daring service to the sick and dying in a cholera epidemic in south Travancore. The evangelist moved from place to place, and large crowds flocked to hear him. In 1921, the movement provoked by Sadhu Kochukunju became community-wide, a revival of the Christians, an awakening of nominal adherents, and a folk movement of non-Christians into the Church. The movement continued for several years in Malayalam-speaking Kerala and in contiguous Tamil areas, for the sadhu was proficient in Tamil as well.[36]

A Paraya convert, Poikayil Yohannan, attracted a large following from outcaste families, but veered off into heresy. The movement flourished until 1925, but seven years later he died, and the sectarians re-joined Hinduism officially. It was quite different with the Voluntary Evangelistic Association, encouraged by Bishop Abraham. This Mar Thomist laymen's movement was dedicated to the revitalization of the parishes and the evangelization of rich and poor, high caste and outcaste. It won several hundred converts from the unbelieving multitude each year.[37]

Between 1917 and 1944, Abraham Mar Thoma served as suffragan bishop of the Mar Thoma Church in Kerala. In 1944, he succeeded to the highest office of that Church, but served as Metropolitan for only three years. By all accounts, Bishop Abraham was an evangelistic power in Kerala. On his death, E. Stanley Jones wrote: 'The bright spot in the Christian situation in India is the Mar Thoma Church.[38] And the brightest spot in that Church has been Bishop Abraham, the metropolitan . . . The greatest Christian of India is gone, but he left behind a growing, dynamic Church, manned by growing, dynamic men.' One of the two surviving bishops succeeded to the office of metran as Juhanon Mar Thoma, bringing notable administrative talents to the work, while the other, Matthews Mar Athanasius, maintained his zeal for evangelism. The churches continued to grow throughout the 1930s and 1940s.

The folk movement which followed the revival of 1905 in the territory of the American Methodists continued through the second decade of the twentieth century and into the third. In 1919, the evangelist Tamil David conducted his revival ministry among the churches.[39] In 1923, the missionaries brought together a hundred and fifty national leaders in one district, and experienced 'a marvelous outpouring' of the Holy Spirit.[40] This was followed by a great revival in the churches and an awakening in their community. Both the South India Conference and the Hyderabad Conference were continuing to enjoy a great ingathering.

In the early 1930s, there was a decline in membership. The recorders of the Hyderabad Conference deplored the lack of spiritual growth in their congregations. A survey revealed that 45% of the heads of families in one Methodist district were confessed drinkers, while 39% attended non-Christian festivals to their own detriment and to that of the Cause. Only 37% of the men and 23% of the women church members professed to know the Ten Commandments, 31% of the men and 26% of the women the Lord's Prayer, 8% of the men and 4% of the women the Apostles' Creed.

After 1935, the Christian community began to grow again. In a dozen years before Independence, the Hyderabad Conference community increased from 51,207 to 65,424, while the South India Conference community expanded to 37,705 from 23,947. The growth was attributed to successful rallies, camp meetings, itinerant evangelists' ministry and laymen's witness bands.[41]

In the Telugu country, a folk movement began among the Sudras, a caste people highly placed in society. In the 1920s, various missions[42] (Anglican, Baptist, Lutheran, Methodist) began baptizing numbers of Sudras. The influence of changed lives among lower caste people was a factor.

Although Bishop J. W. Pickett himself does not point out the connection in his classic study of folk movements toward Christianity in India, it is significant that most of these movements began within a decade of a revival-awakening in the Christian community, and in many cases the earliest converts or forerunners of these movements were actually converted in times of revival, just as the leading missionary contacts were redirected by the revival. The discouraged C. M. S. missionary, Darling, gave himself to prayer and the Mala robber Venkayya was converted thereafter — in 1859 (not 1849, as Pickett stated it), when British folk were praying for great revival—thus bringing together the key missionary and national figures in the Mala ingathering. John Clough was converted in the 1858 Awakening in Iowa, and Yerraguntla Periah converted in the same movement when it reached India, bringing together the key missionary and national figures in the Madiga influx—as noted by John Clough himself.[43]

Likewise, the 1905 Awakening was followed within the decade by vast ingatherings of non-Christians. Revived missionaries and national pastors were praying the Lord of the Harvest for direction and the same Spirit was moving uninstructed peoples to seek for the Word. Ten thousand were added to church membership in South Travancore in 1915-1917 ingatherings, bringing the total membership up to 100,000.[44] In the North India Presbyterian Mission, a total of 489 communicants and 943 baptized community in 1896 had become 4870 and 29,833 respectively in 1916—a ten-fold and thirty-fold increase.[45] In Hyderabad, a total Christian community of 716 in 1908 became 9320 in 1913 and 27,107 with 10,000 inquirers in 1916, according to the Methodists, who had a waiting list of 150,000 for baptism in all of India that year.[46] In 1922, the Church of Sweden Mission in Madura, far south, reported an ingathering of robber people, while the Swedish E. F. S. announced an awakening among the Gonds, a primitive tribe in Central India.[47] By 1915, the Chamars in the United Provinces were flocking in for baptism, 50,000 in the Meerut district. Ten years later, there were sixteen thousand inquirers, and in the twelfth year, another thousand were baptized.[48] In the Coimbatore district of Tamilnad, at Dharapuram, 'the fire began to burn' in 1913, according to English Wesleyans, becoming—surely it was reported by an Irish Methodist— a 'flood' and 'a tidal wave.'[49]

Undoubtedly, these folk movements were not revivals in the classic sense with deep conviction and true repentance and proven regeneration. But there was a connection with the revivals which immediately preceded them.

There were revival-awakenings in many parts of the world in the 1930s—in Scandinavia, for example; in China and East Africa. There were sporadic revivals in India also. The godly Free Methodists, with their strict standards of Christian conduct, were grieved in 1933 to find that in all their field around Yeotmal there had been only six baptisms. In 1934, the missionaries and national leaders began to confess their faults and failures openly, and their prayer circles increased in power and widened in scope.[50]

In December of 1934, the Rev. Eleazar S. Timothy— pastor of the Scots-built Presbyterian Church in Nagpur— realized a Divine command to return to Yeotmal where previously he had scandalized some saints by lighting up a cigarette after preaching in the Free Methodist Mission. In the meantime, he had entered into a new experience with God. Timothy preached with unction for two-and-a-half hours, his audience gripped by an unseen power. Men fell on their faces to confess their sins and to cry for mercy. A revival was under way, and the missionaries persuaded Timothy to extend his ministry.

Alas, Timothy bore a happy encumbrance in the support of a wife and eight children, so he returned to Nagpur to raise funds. The telling of his story provoked a revival in Nagpur. The pastor returned to Yeotmal. In February of 1935, there occurred an unusual moving of the Spirit upon the people, resulting in simultaneous audible prayer. The movement in church transformed the young people in school. A great concern descended upon the congregation, and it was decided to witness for Christ on the courthouse steps each afternoon at 5. Alas, the hundreds who were sincerely impressed were members of higher castes, and none dared join the church. But teams of young people went out farther and farther to distant villages. Thirty-five thousand people of Telugu speech and outcaste status were discovered. An evangelist converted from Islam gathered a congregation of Madigas in Rajur; another evangelist won a following among his fellow Pardhans; others won a hundred village groups of Mahar people, those who declined to follow Ambedkar's movement to Buddhism. None of these people were affected by news of overseas revivals. Local revivals touched them.

Farther east, an extraordinary awakening began in the Hanamakonda district of Hyderabad State in 1931. It was marked by repentance and confession.[51] A Friday morning meeting ended with 'the phenomenon common to many revival meetings' when all were praying at once, pouring out their sins before God. Not far away, in Kurnool, another revival began among the Baptists, rejoicing the heart of Dr. W. A. Stanton who had experienced the outpouring of the Spirit in the same place in 1906.[52] In 1931, five hundred confessed their faith by believers' baptism, and in 1934 the 'large ingathering' was continuing. In the Dornakal Diocese nearby, in the three years following 1931, the clergy of the Anglican Bishop Azariah baptized 35,494 converts, who included a thousand Sudra caste people. In 1935 alone, in the campaign of evangelism in May, eight thousand were baptized.[53]

In 1935, 'revival fires' were reported by the Methodists in Jubbulpore, Khandwa, Shahjahanpore, and other northern city churches, the Christians 'on fire for God.'[54] Far to the south, the English Methodists in the Coimbatore district—whose 'fire' had become a 'flood'—now noted that their Christian community of 2061 of 1913 had become 23,751 in 1936, and claimed that 'the flood has continued to rise and has approached the dimensions of a tidal wave.'[55]

In 1936, the Dornakal Anglicans visited 2457 villages and preached the Gospel to 259,000 auditors, half of all their communicants participating.[56] In 1938, twenty-four thousand Bhils, a primitive folk in Central India, were baptized.[57] In 1932, two women emerged as leaders of a revival movement in Kerala, Mrs. Aleyamma Oommen who formed a team with her children, and Miss Pennamma Sanyasini, one Anglican and the other Mar Thomist.[58]

In 1931, there was a dearth of vital religion in Nellore. An evangelistic series was arranged, and the Downie Hall was packed from top to bottom. The ensuing movement reminded the old-timers of the great revival of twenty-five years before.[59]

In 1914, the revived Churches of India decided to form a council for cooperation, at first missionary, then national. The National Christian Council maintained a vigorous work of evangelism from 1923 onwards, in 1935 issuing 'a call for prayer'[60] followed by a Five Years' Evangelistic Movement. This interdenominational organization of the Indian Protestant establishment continued to promote evangelism of a vital sort until the coming of Independence.

In Madras, the assistant headmaster of a High School, Nagabathula Daniel, experienced reviving in 1918, taking up evangelistic activity in the years that followed. In 1937, he was asked by the Student Christian Movement to minister to unemployed graduates, so he set up an ashram for them. This led to Daniel's visiting colleges and other institutions with a message suited to student needs, and to conducting retreats for both students and laymen. He encouraged the formation of local groups for fellowship and witness. In due course, the Laymen's Evangelical Fellowship was set up, the movement remaining interdenominational in scope. All over Tamilnad and Andhra, Daniel and his co-workers conducted weeks of meetings in various cities and towns, and in various places the response of both Christians and non-Christians took on the proportions of a local awakening which helped extend the believing Church.[61]

One such movement occurred in a series of revivals in Kakinada district in Andhra. Canadian missionaries invited the evangelist, Nagabathula Daniel, to preach and the Word was delivered with power. Another school-teacher, Bandela Rajaratnam, attended a prayer meeting where more than seven hundred people had gathered and Daniel spoke on 'Sin and judgment.' 'In a little while,' he recalled, 'the Spirit of God enveloped the place.' Men beat their breasts and cried for salvation. Rajaratnam found himself in great agony of conviction all day, finally capitulating to God.[62]

Rajaratnam entered full-time ministry in 1944. Great spiritual movements followed in Andhra towns, Penamalur, Mudunur, Nidamanur, Penumutcha, Pasumarru, Hindupur, and Kakinada. Bandela Rajaratnam became the outstanding evangelist in a wide-spreading awakening in Andhra. There were striking healings occurring as well as conversions, and the evangelist showed an uncanny gift of discernment.

The multiplication of Indian national evangelists continued apace, many of them independent and many Pentecostalist. In 1930, K. E. Abraham, an associate of Robert Cook—who had separated from the Assemblies of God—started an independent Pentecostal organization, with its own Bible School.[63] This indigenous Malayali movement became the Indian Pentecostal Church of God. Its Malayali Pentecostal preachers journeyed far and near, establishing churches in New Delhi, Lahore, Allahabad, Nagpur, and other cities of the North. Within a generation, the I. P. C. claimed eight hundred churches and almost eighty thousand adherents.[64]

During the 1940s, P. M. Samuel of Kerala introduced the Indian Pentecostal Church to Andhra, itinerating all over the territory from Eluru.[65] The movement resulted in the formation of three hundred assemblies, some larger and some smaller, but uniting annually for a convention attended by ten thousand ardent Pentecostals and their friends.

The Church of God mission began supporting Robert Cook and his work, building it into an Indian Church of God that spread into several language areas, more than four hundred churches being established.[66]

In Ceylon, during the years of World War I and II and the intervening depression, Protestants multiplied more rapidly than Roman Catholics, thirty thousand gaining ten thousand. But the proportion of Christians in the population remained much the same.[67]

Rama Paul, a Brahmin convert in Kerala, studied for the ministry in an Anglican school in Ceylon.[68] In 1924, he had a glossolalic experience and became a Pentecostal evangelist of renown, closely associated with another volatile Malayali, K. E. Abraham, parting from him upon grounds of doctrinal interpretation. He founded the Ceylon Pentecostal Mission, which spread to the cities of India. Rama Paul's movement operated on a 'faith basis,' even to supplying food for twenty thousand adherents attending a national convention annually in Kerala. Madras became the headquarters of the Ceylon Pentecostal Mission in India, with other bases in New Delhi, Bombay, Calcutta, and Gauhati, reporting fifty thousand adherents in their many congregations and 'faith houses,' the latter serving as Bible schools.

The Orebro Baptists, a sector of Swedish Baptists that had adopted a pentecostal emphasis, founded a mission in India which experienced a measure of revival in 1933.[69] A conference in Gorakhpur began in prayer but continued in intense conviction of sin, leading to humbling confessions. The church remained open night and day. This movement was felt in other parts of Uttar Pradesh. Other Swedes, of Pentecostal affiliation, established a Bible School in Dehra Dun, situated in the foothills, from which many evangelists went forth to towns and cities of North India.

Thus, in the 1930s and 1940s, while the ferment of Indian nationalism continued, the Indian Churches were producing indigenous Indian evangelistic movements in preparation for the day of Independence. The effectiveness of these Indian evangelists far surpassed that of the best missionaries.

PRE-INDEPENDENCE EVANGELISM 167

In 1904, in the Sialkot district of the Punjab (now part of Pakistan), at the same time that the Holy Spirit was being outpoured upon the praying people at the commencement of the great Revival, a child was born to a Hindu contractor and his wife; the boy was named Bakht Singh Chabre and raised as a Sikh. In his college days, Bakht Singh maintained a bitter spirit toward Christianity, even tearing to pieces a Bible. He performed the external ceremonials of the Sikh religion, attended its temples and chanted its prayers. But he was far from satisfied. God began to speak to him in recurring and frightening dreams.[70]

In 1919, came serious civil disturbances in the Punjab, caused by the ferment of Hindu and Muslim agitation for more self-government.[71] A mob in Amritsar murdered five Europeans, attempted to murder two English missionary ladies, set fire to an Anglican church and a mission school with pupils and teachers within, looted banks, killed three managers, attacked the railway station, telegraph station and town hall. There were similar riots in Lahore.

On 13th April, General Dyer's troops fired upon a mob rioting in Amritsar in defiance of government orders, killing 379 and wounding 1208. This inflamed racial hatred even further, and agitated the population. War broke out with Afghanistan, and Muslims in India were incited to revolt. In 1920, eighteen thousand Muslims sold their goods and set out for Afghanistan, which refused them entrance, multitudes dying in the Khyber pass.[72]

It is not surprising that Christianity suffered a setback in the 1920s.[73] The Presbyterian statistics show a decline in church membership, and other denominations in Muslim areas faced the trouble. There was serious controversy also regarding Pentecostalism, for a number of American missionaries had embraced the glossolalic viewpoint, and some were subjected to severe discipline by the majority.[74]

In 1926, Bakht Singh's father sent him to London to study mechanical engineering. He promised not to change his religion. In London, he backslid from whatever religion he possessed, and shaved off his beard. On a voyage to Canada, Bakht Singh attended a shipboard service to demonstrate to himself his toleration. While kneeling in the liturgical order of service, he was seized with a violent trembling. Back in England, he was still unattracted to church gatherings, but his taste for sin had gone. The following year, he returned to Canada (1929). In the Winnipeg Y. M. C. A. he encountered a bright Christian layman, and he began to read the New Testament. Early in 1932, he sought believers' baptism in Broadway West Baptist Church in Vancouver. Thereafter he received a call to preach.[75]

In April of 1933, Bakht Singh arrived back in Bombay. His refusal to compromise his faith turned his father and mother against him, and his wife went back to her family never to return. Bakht Singh accepted the circumstances and engaged in humble service in the streets of Bombay. But it was not long before his ministry became much in demand. Paterson, the faithful colleague of Praying Hyde, allowed him to substitute for the Bishop of Bombay at the Sialkot Convention, and when the Bishop arrived later, he insisted on Bakht Singh's sharing further ministry with him. The Church of India, Burma and Ceylon licensed him as an evangelist, but his ministry was wholly interdenominational.

Bakht Singh ministered in Karachi and Lahore, holding great revival meetings in the latter place, and at Ludhiana, Pathancot, and Martinpore. The Punjab Praise and Prayer Union Circular featured regular reports of meetings and requests for prayer signed by B. S. Chabre, and a missions review headlined a report of startling impact: 'Another Sundar Singh?' to the world.[76]

But Bakht Singh was not another Sundar Singh. He was not a mystic, though his devotion to Christ rivalled his Sikh predecessor's. He was an Indian equivalent of the greater western evangelists, as skillful as Finney and as direct as Moody. He was a first-class Bible teacher, of the order of Campbell Morgan or Graham Scroggie.

In Maharashtra, Bakht Singh's ministry in Poona raised such a demand for Bibles that local and hurriedly imported supplies were exhausted. The Poona Bible Society reported that its sale of Bibles had risen from 500 to 12,000.[77] In the United Provinces there occurred intense conviction of sin among students, teachers, workers, missionaries and even servants. Bakht Singh now embarked upon an India-wide ministry in cooperation with the Church at large.

Even during his earlier decade of ministry, Bakht Singh adopted a fearless stance in delivering his message. He was an avid reader of Scripture. Deciding that kneeling was (in the sacred narratives) the customary posture for prayer, he would invite his thousands of hearers to kneel, which they did readily, leaving some of the missionaries seated upon chairs, whereupon the evangelist would ask them if they were too proud to kneel. He preached with authority, using English interpreted into the local vernacular outside his native province.[78]

Such was his success in Tamilnad that he made his headquarters in Madras. Great crowds thronged to hear him, and, in spite of faithful criticism, churches of all the major denominations supported his campaigns. In Madras, he was supported by two brothers, great-grandsons of the saintly John Christian Arulappan, whose ministry had provoked a great revival in Tamilnad three-quarters of a century before. Dorairaj and Rajamani were to share in his next phase of ministry also.

Bakht Singh's greatest concern became the care of the converts, as he told the present writer who had begun to preach in the same decade.[79] The peculiarity of the Indian Christian churches, living in a caste system in which they form another unofficial caste, encouraged many Indians to regard the Church as their community into which they were born. The adherents won in the great folk movements also brought into the fellowship a host of uninstructed and careless people. The converts of mass evangelism needed also to be taught. Only in times of revival did the established churches appear qualified in part for that task.

Bakht Singh became an all-India evangelist, rather than a provincial preacher in the Muslim-dominated riverine land. For full seventeen years, from 1930 to 1947, there was little more than biological growth (the normal family increase) in the western Punjab. United Presbyterians, for example, increased only 3.3% in all of that period.[80]

Afghanistan remained closed to the preaching of the Good News. In Persia, the Christian communities around Lake Urumia suffered extreme persecution, many Nestorians and Armenians being slaughtered by Muslims.[81] In Iraq, formed out of Mesopotamian territories of the Turkish Empire, there was extreme persecution of native Christians, both Nestorian and Protestant as well as Roman Catholic.[82]

During World War I, unabashed genocide was inflicted upon the Armenian minority in Turkey, massacred by the thousands, families broken up and deported.[83] The ancient Gregorian Church was particularly devastated, but the Evangelical minority also suffered. Armenians in their Caucasian homeland passed under the control of the Soviet dictatorship, which soon embarked upon its anti-religious policy of suppression.[84]

23

IN THE TRAVAIL OF NATIONHOOD

Despite the close connection between Indian Churches and British Missions, Indian Christians more and more supported the movement for self-government. It is most significant that the rise of nationalism coincided with the rise of national leadership in the Churches, the revival-awakenings raising churchmen and evangelists whose own talents far surpassed those of any missionaries of other culture and language.

Concurrent with the rise of Indian nationalism, the sect of Brahmo Samaj—founded by Ram Mohun Roy, the friend and supporter of William Carey— seemed to decline, though it had adopted much of Christian thinking into its philosophy. Pratap Chunder Mazamdar, its leader in the last decade of the nineteenth century, stated sadly:[1]

> We cannot hide from ourselves the fact that our beloved church is in a course of steady decline, that the interests of the Brahmo Samaj, as a whole, show a fearful tendency to relaxation.

The Arya Samaj, founded in the last quarter of the nineteenth century, showed a very different, unfriendly attitude towards Christianity. Indian nationalists, for reasons of strengthening Indian sentiment, deplored the conversions attempted and achieved by the missionaries while extolling their social contributions. Gandhi, in spite of his friendship with C. F. Andrews and E. Stanley Jones and others, lent the weight of his influence to this opposition to proselytism, as it was called. Hindus could not or would not appreciate that the social conscience and burden of the Christians came from their evangelical convictions.

The missionaries in the nineteenth century shared the ideas and convictions of the imperial powers regarding their trusteeship of colonial territories, without indorsing the exploitations. And yet their educational system, which did not challenge colonialism, encouraged in the second or third generation its Indian graduates who did, as in Africa. It was an inevitable development.

Alexander Duff's old dream of converting India by means of progressive higher education faded. Noted was the failure of such higher educational projects to win many converts from the higher castes, not because the seed of the Word was unsuited, but because the soil was not fitted to receive it.

According to expert opinions, the real reason why converts were not being made in Christian colleges as they once were was because of movements within Hinduism itself that grafted Christian truths upon ancient Hindu philosophy and religion. The Christian colleges themselves helped occasion this new development in Hinduism.

Remolding of Hindu thought continued into the twentieth century, a good example being Sir Sarvapalli Radhakrishnan, first a student in a couple of Christian colleges in India, who became an advocate of a Hindu view of life obviously much influenced by Christian ideas and language. The capacity of Hinduism for embracing divergent ideas was demonstrated often during the rise of Indian nationalist leadership.

The missionary contribution to education continued. In the 1920s, the number of missionaries who engaged in educational work rose to five thousand, with more than 27,000 (out of 54000) national and foreign mission workers helping.

In India, there were fifteen thousand schools (recognized and unrecognized) maintained by the Protestant missions in 1927. That same year, the Government noted more than twelve thousand recognized mission schools operated by Roman Catholic and Protestant missions.

There were no Christian universities. But a considerable number of colleges, high schools, middle schools and primary schools were being operated by the missions:

Schools	Mission	& Pupils	All-India	& Pupils
collegiate	55	16,018	307	82,760
teacher	100	4,104	597	24,060
high school	291	92,031	2,515	747,527
primary	11,158	421,182	184,829	8,017,923
other	257	8,945	8,583	290,073
totals	12,282	595,725	204,163	10,086,048

Mission schools provided 6% of both the institutions and scholars in all of India, the highest proportion of students being in colleges (20%), no less than 17% in teacher training, and 12% in high schools, the lowest (5%) in primary schools, a considerable contribution.

To the missionary colleges were attributed the deepest influences upon students themselves, and the strongest corporate spirit, and the greatest ability and devotion— especially noted the greatest earnestness and most marked success in the general improvement of conditions of living among their students, moral and physical.

In 1921, a Church Missionary Society delegation came out to India and surveyed the field of education. In 1931, a Commission headed by A. D. Lindsay, Master of Balliol, made its recommendations regarding education in the new India, soon to be self-governing. The commission rejected the view that 'all religions are the same,' that everything in Christianity is already contained in Hinduism, a fallacy depending in the last resort upon an entire failure to understand the significance of a religion based upon history. The Christian colleges therefore greatly stressed the studies of history, economics and science, and felt that the climate produced by such studies was congenial to Christian faith.[2]

By 1931 there were forty-two colleges maintained in India by the Protestant mission societies, not including Roman Catholic colleges or Anglo-Indian and European student bodies. Five of them were theological colleges of degree standard, the remainder Arts colleges, of which three were women's colleges.[3]

There were more than 12,500 students therein. A quarter of all the students in Christian colleges in the Madras Presidency in the south were of Christian profession, whereas hardly more than one in twenty in the north was a Christian. In the south, there were thirteen Christian colleges serving a population of more than 52,000,000, and in all the rest of India there were only nineteen Christian colleges, though two of them had more than a thousand students each, mostly non-Christians. It was difficult to maintain the pro-Christian atmosphere of a college where 1026 of the 1063 students were non-Christians, a majority of the teaching staff likewise.

Of 833 teachers in Christian colleges, foreign and Indian, half were non-Christian, 30% or less Indian Christian.[4] The Government contributed $800,000, the overseas missionary constituency $400,000, student fees $600,000, $200,000 came from other sources, a total of $2,000,000, or $160 per student.

Far from being institutes of evangelization, these Indian Christian colleges showed their longer-range purpose by default, for there had been no more than a dozen conversions or baptisms in the three dozen colleges in ten years.

Was it the intention of the missionaries to set up educational systems for Indians? This was certainly not their primary objective. No doubt they took peculiar pride in contributing so much to the welfare of the people of their adopted land, and in observing how their charges from among the lower castes bettered themselves beyond all belief. They took it for granted that Christian education was a boon. But, in the mind of William Carey and Alexander Duff and other educational pioneers and their successors, there was not a doubt that the major objective was evangelism.

What would be the major objective of the Indian Church once Independence was achieved? The movements of the Spirit in the decades before and after suggested evangelism. Meanwhile, events marched to their fulfillment.

India recruited more than a million soldiers to serve in World War I, and more than two million in World War II. Between these two upheavals, self-government developed. In due course, independence was achieved, the hopes of the Indian leaders being clouded chiefly by the refusal of a large segment of the sub-continental population to accept a place in the new nation—and so Pakistan was founded as an Islamic state.[5]

Two Indian provinces suffered greatly in the bloodbath that followed independence and the separation of Pakistan. Partition signalled the beginning of mass migrations and hideous massacres. While Hindus and Muslims engaged in mutual slaughter in Bengal and the Punjab, the Christians were spared, and gained somewhat in the esteem of their fellow-citizens. India became first a Dominion, with a Tamil Brahmin as Viceroy, Chakravarti Rajagopalachari— with whom the present writer had much conversation of political, social and religious import; then, in 1950, the Republic of India, with another of Gandhi's collaborators as President, Rajendra Prasad—with whom also the writer enjoyed exchange of ideas of mutual interest.

Until his assassination, Mahatma Gandhi's figure loomed largest in India, and Jawaharlal Nehru served as prime minister, the real executor of power. Neither man was a Christian, yet both had tolerant attitudes to the faith. There were militant Hindus in places of leadership under whom the Christians would have suffered. It could well be said in later years that the Lord had raised up protectors for His people, still a tiny minority in the vast population. Indian secularism proved its worth against Hindu militancy.

A sincere secularist and not a militant Hindu, Nehru's attitudes were well known. In a cabinet meeting, several Hindus were denouncing Christian activities and baiting the one Christian cabinet minister in a not too subtle way when suddenly the Prime Minister said sharply, in his schoolmasterly manner, 'That's enough. I do not subscribe to any religion, but if I did, I think it would be Christianity.'

In the early years of independence, Dr. P. Sitaramayya as president of the Indian National Congress declared that although the last British soldier and many civilians had left India, 'the missionary lingers, and I hope that he will stay, for he is a desirable commodity.' [6]

With such a friendly attitude evidenced by the new rulers of India, the number of missionaries in India increased, many former American and British servicemen returning to serve in the land of their military experience. By 1952, their total strength reached 4683.[7] Hindus took fright.

In 1952, an unprecedented number of visas for incoming and returning missionaries were refused by New Delhi. Any inquiries about the matter proved less than useful. India's home minister, Dr. K. N Katju, spoke approvingly of the work carried on by missionary educational, medical and social services, but deprecated proselytization.[8]

The writer discussed this matter with several state governors as well as the President of India. All spoke so highly of missionary services, but only one showed any kind of appreciation or understanding of the motivation of the missionaries. Bishop Manikam interpreted the anti-mission sentiment as Hindu antipathy to any conversion rather than on anti-foreign national feelings. An enterprising Ukrainian would have been encouraged to convert a Tata staff-member to militant Marxism, but a zealous New Zealander trying to convert him to Christianity would have been refused a visa.

The first to feel the weight of disapproval of immigration authorities in India were the American missionaries. For a while, Commonwealth folk were excepted from restrictions upon entry, so a number of American societies enlisted Canadians to fill positions. Then they too were restricted.

In 1954, the writer addressed the Evangelical Fellowship of India at an Anglo-Indian college at Deolali, near Nasik, a sacred Hindu city where the militant Hindu Mahasabha organized a procession of protest led by a former mayor of Poona against the presence of Christian missionaries. This kind of protest was by no means uncommon.

Even more serious was the action in 1954 of the Madhya Pradesh state government which appointed a Christian Missionary Activities Commission. One met medical missionaries who told of village elders receiving loaded questionnaires from the capital asking whether local missionaries maintaining medical clinics had bottles marked 'poison.' [9]

The Report of the Commission was astounding. It charged the missionaries with making converts by undue influence and by misrepresentation. It proposed that Indian Christians were less than loyal to their country—that an Indian who shouted 'Jai Yeshu!' could not be as loyal as one who shouted 'Jai Rama!' It suggested that adherence to Christianity meant loyalty to a supranational power, 'the Universal Church.' And it declared pontifically that[10]

> As conversion muddles the convert's sense of unity and solidarity with his society, there is danger of his loyalty to his country and his state being undermined.

Shortly after this, M. E. Nyogi, the chairman of this Commission, was himself converted to Buddhism, and took the pledge in a mass ceremony with Dr. B. R. Ambedkar and 75,000 outcastes. Though the vast majority of Buddhists inhabited countries alien to Aryan India, it was not suggested that Mr. Nyogi was giving his loyalty to a supranational power, Buddhism. The Commission declared that the evangelization of India appeared to be part of a uniform world policy to revive Christendom in order to reestablish western supremacy. It was darkly hinted that Dulles was responsible.

This extraordinary report caused indignation among the millions of Indian Christians. The National Christian Council expressed its sorrow. Indian Christians were quick to point out that the Report cited the case of a British missionary sentenced to imprisonment on related charges without any mention that he had later appealed and had been acquitted. The Report recommended making any attempt to influence another person's convictions illegal and prohibited—which would have subjected the Mahatma himself to arrest.[11]

Fortunately many moderate Indians repudiated the Report, and Dr. A. Krishnaswami, a member of Parliament, found otherwise in his report to the United Nations Commission on Human Rights. But the agitation against missions went on, the State of Orissa passing a law in 1968 to award any missionary a fine of $1000 or a year in prison for converting minors, women or untouchables![12] The Church of South India protested this as a breach of citizen's rights.

On the eve of Independence, there were three-and-a-half million Protestant Christians in India, not counting Mar Thoma Church members, considered Syrian Evangelicals. Three-quarters of the Protestants had embraced the faith as a result of folk movements, in which they or their parents or grandparents had renounced a religion which served to keep them in social and spiritual backwardness.

Some missionaries had practised early baptism of these folk-movement converts, to be followed by thorough instruction, while others insisted upon prolonged instruction before baptism, for it was obvious that the Christians of depressed-classes background suffered from vices of their lot besides illiteracy. The missionaries tackled the problems.

On the credit side, there was an obvious improvement of living by the masses of converts. The Christians engaged in less demeaning occupations than hitherto dictated by local custom. Their homes and home life improved. Gambling and the use of intoxicants were reduced. Exploitation by money lenders became less frequent. An almost universal illiteracy gave way to a high percentage literacy. Not only so, but many Christians of depressed-classes origin became lawyers, ministers, physicians and teachers—professions hitherto denied to their kind.

But there was a discouraging side. There were nominal Christians who were addicted to drink and to irregular sexual practices. There were relapses to lower standards of honesty and truthfulness. There were divisions in denominations and in congregations, and a distressing readiness to settle all disputes at the courts of law. Illiteracy was comparatively easy to counter by elementary education, but the other handicaps persisted in spite of regular education. The only cure for spiritual disability was found in the preaching of the Word, and this became most effective in changing the lives of the Christians in times of spiritual revival, when the Spirit of God was outpoured upon the congregations of both faithful and unfaithful Christians.

When Independence came, there was an immediate rise in the number of Christians praying for spiritual renewal in all of India. National leaders were equally concerned with missionaries in preparing the body of believers for the new opportunities, responsibilities and trials which a restricted missionary influence and a resurgence of ancient religions would bring. Would the first decade of Independence produce the needed awakenings?

24

EVANGELICAL RESURGENCE IN INDIA

Following World War II, there was a worldwide reviving of evangelical interest and activity. It was more marked in some countries than others, in some parts of some nations than in others. An intense revival broke out in the Scottish Hebrides in 1949, but did not affect the rest of Scotland. A widespread awakening was manifested in California and the other Pacific Coast states, in Minnesota, in the Carolinas, and in other states of the U.S.A., but not in all of them; it gave birth to new organizations of evangelism, among college students and in mass meetings, the best known evangelist to emerge being Billy Graham. There were movements in the 1950s in Brazil, Argentina and Chile; in Korea and in parts of Africa; but there was little to report in Western Europe, including Great Britain and Scandinavia.

Indian Christians seemed challenged by the opportunity of the day. The leaders of one of the rapidly growing bodies in India declared in 1948:[1]

> A new day of evangelism has dawned in India. In the first place, the initial year of political freedom has severed the ties that existed in the minds of the people between Christianity and foreign power . . . though the British have withdrawn, Christ has come to stay . . .

Just before Independence, the Anglicans and Methodists in South India decided to unite with the Congregationalists, Presbyterians and Reformed already forming the South India United Church, the larger union being designated the Church of South India.[2] The new denomination, the largest of the non-Roman bodies, possessed a third of a million members communicating, and a total community of a million. The Church of South India adopted episcopal government, yet failed to please some ardent advocates of apostolic succession thereby, and it retained the office of presbyter in the order maintained by the Reformed bodies. Neither the Mar Thoma Church, nor the Lutherans, nor the Baptists entered the united body. The leadership of the Church of South India became more and more indigenous as the years went by.

While Indian Christians of several denominations were planning and consummating union, an Indian evangelist of nationwide influence was moving in an opposite direction. Bakht Singh had become famous throughout India as a fearless preacher of the Gospel, and congregations of many denominations welcomed his ministry. But (according to a biographer) the vices of popular Indian Christianity already mentioned, the lack of insistence upon the new birth as a test for fellowship, the superficiality of mass movements, and the wrong use of famine relief, were distressing the mind of the evangelist, whose concern was a restoration of all things taught in the New Testament. To the writer, Bakht Singh mentioned his great distress of heart in realising that the converts that his ministry were adding to the churches were not being cared for in proper ways.

In 1942, Bakht Singh and his colleagues, Dorairaj and Rajamani, spent many weeks in prayer culminating in an all-night of prayer on a mountainside.[3] They discussed the problems of Indian Christianity, and laid them alongside of New Testament practice. Like Watchman Nee of China, who was influenced by Exclusive Brethren and by the Honor Oak Fellowship of London, Bakht Singh committed himself to a restoration of New Testament Christianity, as he saw it, rather than an effort to revive the existing Churches. He felt that the missionary edifices in India were crumbling, and that denominationalism was not the answer, even if it reduced its varieties by union.

Once he had made up his mind, Bakht Singh set about forming assemblies of believers in various cities.[4] His prime method of recruitment has been his evangelistic campaigns. He gathered the revived folk and the converts of campaigns, wherever willing, into assemblies which operated without membership and without elections. Many of those impressed by his pre-1942 efforts rallied to him. It went without saying that the established denominations resented his ministry, not so much for its theological content as for its enlistment of their seceding members.

The first, and soon the largest, of the assemblies of the Bakht Singh constituency was founded at Madras and was named Jehovah-Shammah. It consisted of a large house and a pandal— usually constructed of less permanent materials in India—under which a thousand or more believers were regularly gathered. At times of 'holy convocation,' many thousands have gathered in the grounds of the church.

These assemblies of believers directed by Bakht Singh multiplied, the larger ones taking form in Bangalore and Hyderabad. They spread to smaller towns all over South India, and also in the North. Before a quarter of a century had passed, there were more than four hundred 'houses of prayer' in which a hundred thousand people worshipped. No official name was given to the association of assemblies, which individually chose a biblical title for local use, though generally the local people named them 'Bakht Singh's church.' The work spread to Malaysia in the east and the Persian Gulf States in the west, and north to the Tibetan border, where two-thirds of those attending in Kalimpong were found to be of Buddhist background.[5] Generally speaking, pastors of the established denominations have reacted bitterly against Bakht Singh and his work. A more moderate criticism was published by Bishop A. J. Appasamy, on the ground that in due course the Bakht Singh assemblies also will need revival just as much as do the established churches. Bakht Singh continued to be a very effective evangelist, but no longer a revivalist so far as the church-at-large was concerned.

Between the ecumenism of the Church of South India and other schemes on the one hand and the restorationism of Bakht Singh on the other, a strong evangelical movement which sought to strengthen 'the things that remain' arose in India shortly after Independence. The Evangelical Fellowship of India was founded in 1951 at Yeotmal to engage in evangelism, to promote conferences for the deepening of the spiritual life, to encourage prayer for revival throughout India. Although promoted by representatives of the National Association of Evangelicals in the U.S.A., the Evangelical Fellowship of India tended to follow more the example of the Evangelical Alliance in providing fellowship for believers individually and collectively without establishing competitive alternatives to the National Christian Council.[6]

The second E.F.I. conference was held at Akola in 1952, with Dr. Paul S. Rees as its main speaker.[7] Rees had been active in the mid-century revival movements in the United States, and in his judgment the Akola Conference was 'most extraordinary' for its amazing outreach in spite of its small numbers registered, about 120! From Dohnavur came Mr. Norman Burns, who in 1949 had visited East Africa and had seen something of the remarkable East African Revival. In the meetings that followed, the unmistakable signs of revival were manifested. The impact was felt far afield.

For instance, one of the missionaries attending the Akola convention returned to his station in Gujerat and set about translating the revival that came to his heart into action. Letters were written and conversations held to convey apologies and seek renewed fellowship.[8] The missionary staff was deeply moved. Their burden of prayer shifted to sharing the blessing with their Indian brethren. Retreats were held at Sanjan, Dhagadmar, Vapi, Pardi and Dandi Maroli, calling in the Indian preachers and Biblewomen, catechists and teachers. A spirit of confession fell first upon the missionaries and then the workers, with weeping and agonizing intercession. 'Wrongs were righted, wounds of misunderstanding healed, attitudes changed, habits conquered, and secret sins confessed and forgiven.' This was followed by a sense of forgiveness and by joyous singing.

The third E.F.I. Conference was held at Ramapatnam in Andhra.[9] It was there that a dedicated young Naga, Imchaba Bendang Wati, was recruited as national secretary of the movement. Again there was a touch of revival among the delegates attending from all parts of India. Dr. Harry J. Hager of Chicago was the main speaker. Dr. Everett Cattell reported a rising tide of revival among the missionaries in the hill stations summer conferences, with a great concern for the Indian congregations on the plains.

The fourth E.F.I. Conference was held at Deolali, near the sacred city of Nasik in Maharashtra. J. Edwin Orr was the invited speaker from overseas, and another time of spiritual renewal occurred. In the Sunday meetings, there were 'spontaneous outbursts of confession, testimony and praise welling up from all over the company . . . meal times were delayed as one after another rose to tell of what God had done for them.'[10] Again there were repercussions, yet still there was no sweeping awakening throughout India.

A Naga choir sang the hymn, 'How Great Thou Art!' at the Deolali Conference so effectively that the speaker from overseas carried its words and harmonization to California and introduced the hymn to American audiences at Forest Home in August 1954.[11] There a music publisher took it up and helped popularize the words and music throughout the world with the help of the Graham team soloist, Bev Shea. In a short space of time, the lyrics written by Stuart K. Hine to the tune composed in Sweden became a worldwide song of praise, second to none in popular demand. This blessing was conveyed through Deolali.

Orr (after a visit to Rashtrapati Bhavan)[12] proceeded to Kerala, where he was the guest of Bishop C. K. Jacob of the Church of South India. He began his evangelistic ministry at the village of Kattannam, population 3000, commencing with 150 but soon attracting a thousand nightly. Meetings were held in Manganam, in a Mar Thoma Church, then in the Cathedral at Kottayam. Orr campaigned in other towns and shared ministry with Stanley Jones at Maramon.[13]

In 1954, Orr ministered also in Connoor and Vellore in Tamilnad, then preached to packed-out audiences in Madras, concluding likewise in Calcutta. The meetings were planned for the deepening of the spiritual life, though conversions also took place in them.

The fifth E.F.I. Conference was held at Jhansi, with both missionaries and Indian pastors present from distant points. Orr brought with him a Presbyterian colleague, William A. Dunlap, whose ministry greatly moved Rev. Aziz Williams, a school principal and pastor from Jammu, Kashmir:[14]

> I had had the experience of conversion and new birth when I was 22 years old (in 1936), but at this conference I had the experience of the anointing of the Holy Spirit, and when I returned home and preached on Sunday there was a revival in the church and people started coming to the church at 4.30 a.m. for prayer. Many lives were changed.

While Dunlap ministered in the North, Orr campaigned in Kerala. Attendances at Mavelikara began with 500 and passed the 2500 mark nightly, shutting down the cinemas. There were like attendances at Mallapally, rising to 10,000 daily. Meetings were held in other towns with great response, as in Mannamaruthy and Anaprampal.[15] In the latter place, there was a movement for missionary outreach, which sent volunteers to Nepal.

There were tensions in the Mar Thoma Church at that time. In 1951, three more bishops were elected, consecrated in 1953—Alexander Mar Theophilus, Thomas Mar Athanasius, and Philipos Mar Chrysostrom.[16] There were low-church complaints of high-church conspiracy. Some sued in court to have the Metropolitan removed from office. A conference of bishops and clergy was convened with all parties participating, Orr bringing devotional messages. A letter dated 29th January 1955 from J. Edwin Orr to E. Stanley Jones gave an insight into the moving of the Holy Spirit at this critical juncture:[17]

Soon the ministers were on their feet to express longing and hunger for God, followed by confessions of need, tears, singing, praise, reconciliation. The Metropolitan and Bishops as well as the clergy wept and prayed. It was extraordinary to see these rather formal men praying several at a time simultaneously, with no sense of discord. They continued in prayer until late, and concluded with a Holy Communion shared in by all, including some who had announced their non-participation for reasons of conscience...

The layman who was suing at law refused to withdraw his suit, and in 1960 four leaders in the case were excommunicated.[18] Others joined them, and the St. Thomas Evangelical Church of India was founded. Having begun in a negative way, the movement did not prosper, suffering further divisions and secessions. The Mar Thoma Church continued on its way, evangelical and liturgical, blending the everlasting freshness of the Gospel with its age-old ecclesiastical traditions.

Orr spoke at the Maramon Convention again, sharing the main platform with J. T. Seamands, a devout Methodist from Asbury College. Vast crowds have been attending Maramon Convention annually, attendance rising to 50,000 in a dry river bed. Orr received letters from more than 5000 people who had professed conversion in his Kerala ministry.

The most effective evangelist at that time in Kerala was K. V. Cherian, a Mar Thoma layman who founded the all-Kerala Christian Fellowship. With episcopal goodwill from both the Mar Thoma Church and the Church of South India, Cherian engaged in convention ministry, evangelistic series, radio evangelism, and literature work of an interdenominational nature.[19] Cherian sometimes used his associates to relay his words at the same time in the same meeting in the same language, as loudspeakers to conserve his own strength, for he preached fervently for hours on end.

Pentecostal missionaries brought their message to the Malayalis in the 1920s, and won some converts to their view. The work soon became indigenous, but it was opposed very strongly by the older denominations as 'a noisy sect.'[20] Two Pentecostal leaders crossed from Ceylon, and divisions began in Pentecostal ranks; the Ceylon Pentecostal Mission and the India Pentecostal Church, the Church of God and the Assemblies of God shared the field, and attracted thousands to conventions, largely at Jacobite and Marthomist expense.

In 1950, the Church of South India elevated Aiyadurai Jesudasan Appasamy to the see of Coimbatore, a populous city with districts in Tamilnad. Appasamy came from a Christian family, Dewan Bahadur A. S. Appasamy—his father—having turned from Hinduism to Christ in 1871 and thirty years later retired from a practice of law to devote the rest of his life to prayer and evangelism. On the eve of the Indian Awakening of 1905, the younger Appasamy was converted through the ministry of R. T. Archibald, who had figured in that revival movement.[21]

A. J. Appasamy possessed a brilliant mind. He graduated from Madras Christian College in 1914. He won a scholarship at Hartford, and took his first post-graduate degree at Harvard University, which encouraged him to study at Oxford University for the D. Phil. degree. (He was also granted doctorates by Marburg in Germany and Serampore in India.) Appasamy became known in India as a scholar. With the reputation for scholarship rather than for zeal in evangelism, Appasamy was elevated to episcopal office and duties.

The Coimbatore Diocese was torn by faction and filled with fear, many expressing anxiety about its future. The new Bishop was driven to prayer. He had been reading an account of the 1859 Awakening in Britain, and decided that only the outpouring of the Spirit of God could meet the need of his diocese. In his inaugural sermon at Erode, Appasamy requested that the year 1951 be set aside as a year of prayer and that 1952 be used for evangelistic campaigns throughout the diocese, which included the districts of Coimbatore and Salem and the Nilgiri Hills. The Bishop noted:[22]

> The people in our three hundred congregations responded well to these proposals, and there was much earnest prayer in the year 1951 throughout many of the parishes of the area. After 1952, various unexpected things began to happen. From the ends of the earth, evangelists came to the diocese and held missions for us. . . . A revival broke out and progressed for several years.

Evangelist Nagabathula Daniel came from nearby Madras and held meetings in the churches; there was a reviving. At Alambady, where hitherto it had been difficult to get people to attend Sunday services, now they were assembling each morning before dawn for prayer. There was dissension in the town church in Erode, as in Salem and Coimbatore. A movement began among teachers and pastors, upon whom Daniel had unusual influence.[23]

In 1952, Dr. Joe Church and Mr. William Nagenda of the East African Revival movement visited India and engaged in a ministry of stirring up the Christians to revival and the many nominal Christians to vital experience. Their work among Christians in the Nilgiri Hills near Coimbatore had far reaching effects. They returned in 1954, and visited also the city of Salem, on the plains, where there had been trouble and dissension among the Christians, and between Indians and missionaries, necessitating disciplinary action. Prayer groups for early morning intercession sprang up among the church people. Missionaries were constrained to humble themselves before their Indian friends. A couple from England, the Rev. and Mrs. D. P. Collins, realized that their ministry had been almost fruitless for seventeen years on the field, and they entered into a new experience of grace, which they later described to the writer as a true conversion. The Collins couple, and others like them, became ardent evangelists in the years following. Teams of Indian and European evangelists operated here and there.[24]

Another lay evangelist was Paul T. Kadambavanam, a convert from Hinduism who became an evangelist upon his retirement as head clerk in the diocesan office in Rangoon. So successful were these lay evangelists that the diocesan authorities set up a lay order of evangelists. In 1953, there were reports of continuing revival in the Erode area. In 1954, the Rev. Cyril R. Thompson and a team of Indians conducted a Youth for Christ crusade in Coimbatore. About a thousand attended nightly, a fifth of them Hindus and Muslims. A hundred inquirers were counselled.

In the meantime, gospel teams were formed among laity and ministers, and this movement in Coimbatore diocese continued into 1955, 1956 and 1957. Bishop Appasamy was rejoicing in manifold blessings when, in 1958, he called on J. Edwin Orr to visit Salem, Erode and Coimbatore before going to the Maramon Convention.[25] Dr. Appasamy reported:

> For the first ten days, he spoke to the Christians in Coimbatore. All the fourteen churches in the city worked together closely during the meetings. The pastors as well as the people belonging to the C.S.I., Mar Thoma, Lutheran, Brethren and Pentecostal churches, attended the meetings. They were held in the garden of the Immanuel C.S.I. Church. There were large audiences every evening, ranging from one thousand to one thousand five hundred people.

The Bishop was pleasantly surprised that simple teaching held these congregations nightly. He and the other sponsors applied to the Municipality for the use of a large stadium across the street. It was granted freely, only a rupee a night being charged for lighting! Attendance rapidly rose from two thousand to five thousand. Three thousand people marched in the final procession of witness, and hundreds of Hindus attended, many coming from the city's colleges—in which Orr had addressed more than a thousand students in voluntary meetings. A couple of hundred people gave their names and addresses, requesting counselling. 'The teaching methods of Dr. Edwin Orr,' reported the scholarly Bishop, 'have appealed to some of our people who had tended to regard the revival meetings as merely emotional and not of lasting value.' He reported that the campaign had drawn far larger crowds than any other. In Salem, the largest church was filled nightly, followed by meetings in a secular hall in which the speaker was introduced by a prominent Hindu. An encouraging crowd of inquirers gathered the month following, including a number of student teachers asking for baptism. In Erode, large crowds gathered, up to a thousand, and 200 registered as inquirers. Hindus made up a high proportion of those attending.[26]

In March of 1959, A. J. Appasamy retired from his office as bishop in Coimbatore. He had served not quite a decade and most of the years were full of blessing, the reviving of the church members and the winning of outsiders to the faith. For his nearly nine years, he published his diocesan letters and reports, making available to others the way in which his prayers were answered. Then he returned to writing.

The Gospel Association of India, founded by Rajaratnam, continued its advance in Andhra.[27] In a campaign conducted in Vijayawada, the evangelist preached to five thousand one night on 'Immorality.' A man in the crowd thought that his personal life had been singled out, and resolved to kill the evangelist, who knew nothing of him personally. As he raised a rock to smash the evangelist's head, he was bitten by a scorpion—and repented to become an evangelist. In 1967, Rajaratnam was stabbed by a militant fanatic, who suffered a paralytic stroke within a day; the martyr's mantle fell upon his son, Yesupadam Bandela, helped by thirty evangelists of the Association. The movement, thoroughly indigenous— financed by national funds, staffed by national workers— met with both opposition and cooperation.

In 1956, Billy Graham accepted an invitation from the Evangelical Fellowship of India to campaign across India. Graham's Bombay rally was cancelled on account of local riots on the language issue. He made the most of greater opportunities in the South, in Tamilnad and Kerala. The attendance at Kottayam exceeded 75,000 and the response to his evangelistic appeal was 'unutterably moving.' Far south, at Palayamkottai, great crowds thronged the meetings. In Madras, the message in English was interpreted into Tamil and Telugu to vast crowds. Billy Graham spent only four weeks in India, but the tour made an impact, giving great encouragement to the Christians, and winning many nominal adherents and outsiders to full faith in Christ in this series of Christian melas.[28]

Among the many results of the Graham visit was the emergence of Dr. Akbar Abdul Haqq as an India-wide and worldwide evangelist. A doctoral graduate of Northwestern University, Haqq was a first-rate scholar. He addressed the E.F.I. Conference in Calcutta in 1957, then conducted a city-wide evangelistic campaign in Kanpur in March, the attendances growing from 700 to 2500.[29] There were 876 inquirers counselled, quite unusual for North India.

J. T. Seamands, who later returned to Asbury College in Kentucky as professor of missions, becoming Serampore's second Doctor of Theology,[30] organized in 1956 a chain of prayer for spiritual revival, for the Graham Crusade, and for India's leaders. Many churches participated in the vigil and many reaped a harvest in evangelism, as (for example) Kohlapur, where the 24-hour vigil lasted three weeks but the subsequent outreach of Augustine Salins and Seamands lasted three months, with hundreds of people coming to a vital declaration of faith. Undoubtedly, the Graham visit increased the tempo of evangelism in India, besides making Christianity front-page news in national and state press.

The Evangelical Fellowship of India continued to be the main focus of cooperative evangelism in India as well as a platform for the advocacy and expectation of revival. A very capable Naga, Imchaba Bendang Wati, became in 1957 the Executive Secretary of the movement.[31] Annual all-India Conferences were held at Deolali (1960), Calcutta, Hyderabad and Lucknow, then Madras, Deolali, Hyderabad, Bangalore, Poona, Bhubaneswar, and (in 1970) an all-India Congress on Evangelism.[32] In all these gatherings, the hope of revival as well as the need for evangelism was expressed.

A nephew of the volatile statesman, Krishna Menon, by name Paul Sudharkar, a sincere Hindu, wrote to the famed Hindu scholar, Sir Sarvepalli Radhakrishnan— afterwards President of India—and asked him to become his guru. Sir Sarvepalli replied with deep humility that he was not at all worthy to become his guru, and he suggested that Sudharkar make Jesus Christ his guru. The younger man wrote again and asked how he could make contact with Jesus Christ and was told, alas, that he was dead. In the mercy of God, Paul Sudharkar discovered that He was very much alive, so he accepted him as Saviour as well as example and teacher, and became an outstanding evangelist, ministering throughout India in cooperation with the Evangelical Fellowship of India and in wider circles.[33]

In the same constituency, other able evangelists operated, such as Subodh Sahu of Orissa and Masilamani of Andhra. Victor Manogarom gave his evangelistic talents to extended ministry for Youth for Christ, based on Madras; likewise, Gaston Singh, a Trinidadian, operated from New Delhi.[34]

The evangelical resurgence was also accelerated by the growth of evangelical colleges.[35] Frank Kline was a moving force in the establishment of Union Biblical Seminary at Yeotmal. Paul Gupta, a convert from Hinduism, built up the Hindustan Bible Institute, affiliated with Serampore, in the city of Madras. The Southern Asia Bible College was built up by the Assemblies of God, operating in Bangalore with a recognized academic curriculum. There were many others, and in them—as in other countries—revivals occurred.

At the South India Bible Institute, Bangarapet, shortly after the writer's lectures there on evangelical awakenings, a student was assigned a reading of the accounts of revivals in various parts of the world, and 'a fire was kindled in his heart.' Others joined him in fasting and in fervent prayer. 'Suddenly, deep conviction of sin fell upon the forty men-students; some confessions were made and a burden of prayer continued for over an hour.'[36]

The Evangelical Literature Fellowship, India, affiliate of E. F. I., promoted the production and circulation of Christian literature.[37] Another affiliate, the Evangelical Radio Fellowship of India, took advantage of the Far Eastern Broadcasting Company's offer of time on Manila broadcasts.[38] A department of Christian Education was set up by E. F. I., by 1970 producing study courses in a dozen languages. These activities helped fulfill the Great Commission.[39]

India's northeasterly state of Assam contained not only millions of people of Aryan speech—Assamese and Bengali—but two million tribal people of ancient Mon-Khmer and Tibeto-Burman languages and culture. Thanks to the tribal movements toward Christianity, accelerated by the revivals beginning in 1905, the tribal areas of Assam became rapidly and thoroughly Christian.

In the westerly salient of Assam between Bangladesh and Bhutan, the central hill country south of the Brahmaputra sheltered the Garo and the Khasi-Jaintia hill tribes, the former Tibeto-Burmam, the latter Mon-Khmer. For them, the Indian state of Meghalaya was set up in 1970, autonomy achieved without bloodshed. A third of the population of 840,000 were Christians, a sixth Hindus, the remainder mainly animists. The capital chosen was Shillong, a hill-station beloved of the British.

The Garos had been moved during the Assamese Revival of 1905, which affected hills and plains people alike, but between 1915 and 1920, the churches scarcely grew, gaining only four hundred members.[40] In the 1920s, there occurred a period of significant church growth, accelerated by a 'strange revival' that swept the Garo churches around Mongoldai, on the north bank of the great river, provoking a folk movement that won thousands of converts among the Kacharis, another tribal people numbering 250,000 where the Garos numbered 300,000 or so.[41]

For twenty years, until 1950, the Garo churches suffered a period of slow growth, but in the decade following, there occurred a budding of evangelism and a pruning of church discipline.[42] When the jubilee of the 1905 Revival was noted, there came an encouraging ingathering of ten thousand souls. In the 1960s, in spite of wars with China and Pakistan as well as agitation for autonomy, the churches kept growing.

East of the Garo Baptists, the tribes were Presbyterian. In 1952, a youngster named U Paila Pariat was raised up as an evangelist among the Khasis.[43] In 1955, the fiftieth anniversary of the Khasi Revival, the Synod set aside a Sunday for special prayer for another awakening. A revival began in the Mikir Hills, then swept over the Khasi and Jaintia Hills, reviving the churches and sending members out to win the lost, increasing the number of baptisms in 1956 and doubling the annual average in 1957, when 5293 were reported.[44] In this revival, there were tremblings due to conviction and dancing for joy of deliverance.

In the mid 1960s, an evangelistic campaign was conducted in Shillong, the hill capital. A spirit of prayer came down upon the people, the English Presbyterian Church being filled in early mornings with praying people, and a crowded service of intercession preceding the evening's preaching. The evangelistic meetings were held in a shamiana, but by the end of the series, when the Rev. Ian North preached, the crowds had increased to 10,000, hundreds coming forward.

Due east, in the Naga Hills, Christianization rolled on apace. The Ao Naga Baptist churches enjoyed unparalleled growth 1921-1971; Angamis garnered 'a great ingathering' from 1951 onwards; Lothas and Semas shared in a strong folk movement; and other Naga tribes showed great increase in numbers of communicants and adherents.[45]

In Kohima in 1952, a revival gave opportunity to zealous Pentecostals to develop a denomination in Nagaland. The first Nagaland 'Revival Convention' was held in Kohima's environs in 1961, and attracted six hundred. The movement grew, still very much in the shadow of the widespread work of the Naga Baptists in all the tribes. Nehuli Angami, the principal of the Kohima Bible College, emerged as a leader. This 'Revival Church' of Pentecostal origin claimed 20,000, a tiny fraction of a Baptist constituency of 247,069 in a total 409,824 population.[46]

Naga church growth occurred in spite of political strife, for civil war had erupted between Indian forces and rebels. Billy Graham and other notable evangelical leaders shared in the Ao Naga Baptist centenary celebrations in 1972, huge crowds attending the meetings.[47]

Independence for Nagaland, the objective of the dissidents, seemed an impossible dream. State autonomy, the compromise with federal authority, produced a remarkable civil government in India, a state whose inhabitants and elected legislators were predominantly Christian. Baptist polity and Baptist conviction ruled out any likelihood of a state Church, yet Naga Christianity was well established.

Nagaland was not the only tribal area to be evangelized. Between 1911 and 1931, the number of Christians among the Mizos of the Lushai Hills increased from 2,000 to almost 60,000. A Baptist Missionary Society Report in 1921 stated:[48]

> Since the first outpouring of the Holy Spirit upon the Lushai Church in 1907, every six years has witnessed a similar but increasing pentecostal experience empowering believers for joyous and fruitful service and

greatly affecting the heathen as well. Each gracious visitation has raised the Church to a higher plane of Christian experience than the one preceding it and has resulted in a large ingathering of souls.

Observant missionaries deplored the other side of the progression of revivals among Mizos. E. L. Mendus wrote of the untold blessing of revival, but sorrowed over a form of spirituality which was shallow and spurious, discarding reason and conscience for the guidance of an inner voice, always a hazardous proceeding.[49]

Strange to relate, some Lushais adapted a form of British Israel teaching, and held that the Mizos were one of the 'Lost Ten Tribes' of Israel. In the late 1950s, Pentecostal preachers gained a following among the Mizo people, and claimed a thousand tribal prophets.[50]

In the 1960s, the Garos numbered 315,586, the Khasi and Jaintai tribes, 389,969, the Nagas (twenty tribes in all) 420,230, and the Mizos of the Lushai Hills 224,180.[51]

The 1961 percentage of literacy in the state of Assam was 27.36%, but typical hill tribe literacy rate[52] was 44% —the figure for the Lushai Hills, 86% among the Christian folk there. The total number of Christians in tribal areas of Assam was 567,049, the highest total percent in India, and literates among them were 474,189.

In the tribal areas of Assam, many primary schools had been maintained by the churches which, in the Garo, Khasi, Jaintia, Naga and Lushai Hills, were by mid-century fully indigenous, self-supporting and self propagating. The hill tribes thus set forth in indisputable evidence the power of the Gospel of Christ to transform primitive peoples and to fit them for self government.

This rapid Christianizing of the hill tribes encouraged interest in self-government, for tribes people encountering communities on the plains of Assam discovered that tribal standards of education and ethics were far superior, due to success of a religious and cultural revolution. How best to satisfy the obvious desires for tribal autonomy while trying the sub-continent of India became a problem for Indian statesmanship. State governments were set up for various tribal areas, Garos and Khasis, Nagas, and Mizos, all of them tribally transformed by Christianity.

25

THE EVANGELIZATION OF SOUTHERN ASIA

The writer in the course of a lectureship in the colleges of India was amazed to find that the extraordinary awakening in Andhra in 1906 was unknown to his friends, neither bishops nor moderators nor presidents nor pastors nor evangelists having heard of it. And a perusal of the standard histories of several denominations deeply moved by the several great awakenings revealed not a word of refererence to them.

The primary task of this treatise, therefore, has been to collect and collate the facts concerning evangelical revivals in India, in (newly-independent) countries south and west, and (in lesser degree) in the Christian communities of western Asia.

Southern Asia was affected by the worldwide awakenings of Evangelical Christianity (first) following the 1790s, (second) in the 1830s and 1840s, (third) from 1858 till the end of the century, (fourth) in the 1900s, (fifth) in an upsurge in the 1920s and 'thirties, particularly in India, and (sixth) in a resurgence of evangelistic outreach following 1947.

At first, the movements were limited to the pockets of Evangelical Christianity in India; then they were felt in the ancient Christian communities to the west; then in the areas of Evangelical concentration in India, followed by folk movements; then, at the turn of the twentieth century, they were endemic in the South of India, epidemic from Northwest to Northeast, thoroughly indigenous; and, while Christians suffered genocide to the west, an upsurge of evangelism occurred in India; Independence was followed by a dynamic resurgence of Evangelical Christianity in India, less so in Ceylon and Pakistan, and less so in Western Asia.

At the turn of the nineteenth century, there occurred a thoroughgoing renewal in the dormant churches of the sending countries everywhere. 'Turn-of-the-century' revival directly affected Christian work in India by exporting thereto an encouraging number of abler pioneers of convinced evangelical conviction, who initiated a host of evangelistic and philanthropic agencies.

In India, not only did missionaries and their allies in government in Britain and in the East India Company engage in the evangelization of non-Christians and in an assault upon superstition and ignorance, but local revivals stirred up many nationals to reach the folk nearby with the Good News. The areas thus affected by awakenings maintained a numerical lead for fifty years, particularly in the extreme south of India where the most thorough movements had occurred.

Then a second wave of revival reinforced the foreign missionary invasion of all the continents, and continued its social impact upon the sending countries. Waiting missionary reinforcements found wider opening doors into sectors of India hitherto closed, thanks partly to pressures brought on the British Parliament by revived Evangelicals and their political allies.

Throughout India, the missionaries then undertook their arduous tasks of educating the ignorant, extending their projects into district after district, until the fully-fledged educational systems became part of the life of the state, the secular establishment.

Most of the converts of the missionaries came from the less privileged classes. It became very necessary for the missionaries to educate their charges, and this procedure in education proved to be extremely useful in evangelizing the higher castes also. The missionary societies operated upon 'a shoe string,' hence their constituency was very limited, though out of all proportion to their strength in greater India. Yet this subordinate interest of the missions proved to be of major import in the whole development of education to this day. The names of Alexander Duff of Calcutta and John Wilson of Bombay, John Anderson of Madras and Stephen Hislop of Nagpur, are found in secular accounts of the history of education in all-India. Ceylon and Pakistan benefitted likewise. These represented the impact of the Revivals in Britain upon Southern Asia and they paralleled a great movement in the sending countries.

During the spring of 1858, an extraordinary movement of prayer spread from New York throughout the United States. The same movement also affected the United Kingdom in 1859. Approximately ten per cent of the populations of both countries professed conversion, and repercussions in many European countries and overseas communities. The effects were felt for a generation or more.

THE EVANGELIZATION OF SOUTHERN ASIA

The mid-century awakenings were felt in Southern Asia, touching all the active Christian churches, particularly in South India. The Irish Revival of 1859 was marked by the phenomenon of physical prostration, and so was the Revival in South India (in Tamilnad and Kerala) associated with John Christian Arulappan and his followers.

The prayer movement which affected groups throughout India in 1859 and 1860 was followed by 'folk movements' of lower caste and outcaste communities into the Christian Churches. While these were not revivals, each possessed a link with the praying people of previous revivals anxious to evangelize the non-Christian majority.

The mid-Century Awakenings revived all the existing missionary societies and enabled them to enter many other fields. The practical evangelical ecumenism of the Revival was embodied in the great China Inland Mission founded by Hudson Taylor in the aftermath of the British Awakening— the first of the interdenominational 'faith missions.'

The 1858-59 Revivals in Europe and America brought missionaries to Southern Asia who developed an extensive system of medical missions, one which set the pace for the founding of clinics and hospitals all over Southern Asia and other areas. India owed as much to the pioneer medical missionaries as to pioneer educationalists, derived from the revivals in the sending countries.

The Awakenings of 1858-59 were followed up by eager missionaries engaged in evangelism, entering the opened provinces and extending stakes. Most of the work thus begun among the non-Christian peoples was elementary evangelism, but even so the greatest advances were made wherever outbreaks of the phenomena of revival occurred in the infant churches. Missionaries who had seen these phenomenal awakenings at home prayed for like 'manifestations of power' on the mission field.

Yet many missionaries who had seen the power of God in revival in the homeland waited in vain for the same in the land of their service. Theirs was the prospecting, and the ploughing, the removal of obstacles, and sometimes the planting. Others who had not seen revival phenomena at home witnessed its advent on the mission field.

In the 1870s, D. L. Moody rose to fame as a world evangelist, preaching to millions in Britain and the States. His contemporary and associate, William Taylor, preached with power in the cities of India.

The Awakening resulted in an extraordinary invasion of world universities and colleges by the Christian message and the most successful recruitment of 'university-trained' personnel in the history of higher education and evangelism. In this movement, associated with Moody, hundreds of university graduates came to Southern Asia to serve in an effective enterprise of evangelism and social service.

Thus far, no movement of Evangelical Christianity in India had been nationwide. Nor could it be said that any general movement had been mainly indigenous. The coming of a nationwide movement in the first decade of the twentieth century was part of a world pattern, for similarly indigenous awakenings occurred in East Asia and South, Central, East and West Africa, and elsewhere.

The spark that caused the conflagration originated in the Welsh Revival, an extraordinary movement which had added 100,000 to the churches in a matter of months, sweeping Britain, Scandinavia, Europe, and North America.

India's greatest evangelical awakening of all time was the nationwide movement of 1905-1906. Preparation for the 1905 Awakening was mainly missionary, but as soon as the revival broke out, the great majority of participants and the greater number of leaders were Indian.

Forty years afterwards, Dr. W. A. Stanton of Kurnool analysed the great Awakening of 1905. In every instance, so far as he knew, the human means employed by God to bring the revival were united and persistent prayer, not of the missionaries only, but of the people, not for revival in general, but for a reviving in each Christian life.

The most sensitive and sober-minded of the missionaries, who had watched this movement with most intense interest, were unanimous in regarding it as a work of God. They thought of it as related to spiritual movements in other parts of the world—as a world-wide awakening. And, in marking its Divine origin, they too agreed that the Revival had been preceded by earnest intercession. There was a singular absence of human leadership, for, as a missionary wrote: 'The empty pulpit has testified to the unseen Leader. Formerly, the people listened to us, but now they seem to be listening to Another.'[1]

The reports of the 1905 Awakenings in India showed a remarkable unanimity of assessment. Missionary reviews by the Baptists in January 1907 reported upon the Indian Awakening at the end of 1906:[2]

THE EVANGELIZATION OF SOUTHERN ASIA 195

> This has been everywhere a strictly revival movement, manifesting itself in a quickening of religious life on the part of those who professed to be already Christians. The most marked feature in all our work has been the revival which has visited our stations. Never in the history of our mission has such an awakening been witnessed. The work has been most spontaneous and profound, characterized by the same manifestations in almost every place—a deep conviction of sin, profound humiliation accompanied by prostrations, sobs and tears, public confession, restitution, and in many cases a deeper religious experience accompanied by a new infilling of the Holy Spirit and a condition of intense earnestness and joy in the Lord, and followed by prayerful and zealous efforts for the salvation of others. While these results have been mainly confined to Christians, they have also begun to extend to the outside community, and have led to some conversions. Nearly our whole mission has been brought within the sweep of this mighty spiritual upheaval. A few stations which have not experienced a revival, with the common manifestations, can yet report a reviving of the work.

Ten years or so after this Awakening, a comment from an Anglican viewpoint was published:[3]

> All over India, toward the end of 1905 and beginning of 1906, men and women read the words (of Ezekiel's prophecy upon the Dry Bones) with hearts strung to expectation. For them at least those months stand out from all other months of life. They saw a new thing then, a thing which up till then had been but a dream of desire, and they cannot be again as those who never saw. For during those wonderful months they, prophesying as they were commanded, watched the Spirit of God clothe the barest sentence with power. They saw whole churchfuls of ordinarily restrained people . . . swayed before the passing of a mighty wind.

The major characteristics of the 1905-06 Awakening in India were (first) its sudden appearance, and in a few cases, sudden disappearance; (second) its manifestation among believers; (third) the deep conviction of sin accompanying it; (fourth) the general confession of sins that followed it; (fifth) the simultaneous, audible prayer; (sixth) the laughing and singing that accompanied the realization of forgiveness and cleansing; (seventh) the visions, trances and other manifestations that concerned chiefly the sufferings of Christ on the Cross. All these were phenomenal. As general effects, the standard of expectation was raised; there was a new concept of the holiness of God; and there was a reaching out for converts.

The Welsh Revival of 1904 was marked by the confession of sin, and so too were the 1905-06 Awakenings in India, which were emotional in a much greater degree. Yet no one could say that either the emotional displays or confessions were in any way promoted. Rather they were spontaneous, instantaneous, and apparently irresistible.

Those who tried to account for the Awakening by calling it sympathetic hysteria found it hard to explain why the movement was so independent of human initiative and why solitary Christians in far-off villages cut-off from mass excitement were seized by the same spirit of grief for sin.

The Revival revealed that Indian Christians could weep over their sins. Missionaries, who had worked twenty or thirty years among some folk and had baptized adults by the thousands, had—with very rare exceptions—never seen the confessing candidates weep over their sins. But in the revival meetings, the conviction of sin was intense, shown in weeping for sin. Strange things, besides speaking in tongues, happened—men willingly paid back money that had been misappropriated, clearing off their debts, while old quarrels were settled, enemies reconciled, and even schoolboys impelled to ask forgiveness.

There was criticism of this movement. The visions and trances frequently reported proved repellent to some, and the undeniably painful exposure of sinful practices awakened disquiet. In the 1905-06 Awakening, there were criticisms of emotional extravagance and of public confession of sin, both by Evangelicals and by less evangelical churchmen, but not one word has come to the notice of this researcher of any criticism of the theology of the Revival. All mouths seemed stopped as the Spirit of God vindicated the preaching of the Cross of Christ and His power to redeem lost sinners.

News of the Awakening was received with enthusiasm in many quarters, especially by missionaries and alert native pastors who viewed with dismay the encroachments of unbelief, one such commenting: 'It is blessed to turn away from the withering effects of destructive criticism and see how the Spirit is gushing forth as Living Waters.'[4]

THE EVANGELIZATION OF SOUTHERN ASIA 197

The editor of a leading Christian periodical, the veteran Bishop Robinson whom a worldwide missionary review described as 'not an emotional man,' carried his careful enthusiasm for the Revival into his editorials. He declared that he had witnessed more striking manifestations of the transforming power of the Holy Spirit in human hearts in the six months past than in all his thirty years of service in India.[5] Nowhere were the meetings attended by serious extravagance, though whole scenes beggared description.

Of the quality of prayer, a veteran wrote in retrospect:[6]

> Every experienced missionary will know what I mean by the weariness of words among the people of this land. With a remarkable gift of language and self-expression, whether in a prayer or in a testimony, it is words, words, words. The prayers of the people from the little child to the grown-up man are composed of expressions that have long since lost life and power. We have sometimes thought that this endless flow of words was one of the greatest curses of the Indian Church ... One of the most blessed fruits of the revival was the gift of a new tongue. It can be truly said that they spoke, not in the old manner, but as 'the Spirit gave them utterance.' New words and thoughts, new ideas, new conceptions of sin and self and God—these welled up out of their hearts and fell from their lips like the refreshing dew from heaven.

The 1905-06 Revival in India left a lasting mark upon the Indian Christian Conventions, hills and plains. 'Keswick' attracted people from India who committed their lives to God, and soon emissaries of this Keswick message were carrying their good news to Indian conferences, including the Maramon Convention. Reciprocated visits to Keswick included those of Walker of Tinnevelly and Ramabai.

When the Awakening came, it showed that the didactic discourses and methods of the Keswick teachers and the prophetic utterances and modes of the Revivalists were different, but not incompatible. And when the storm of blessing passed, the gentler breezes of the convention message continued to benefit both seekers and finders in vastly augmented numbers. The Indian Conventions grew and multiplied.

The Christian and Missionary Alliance noted that, after the periods of intense prayer and agonizing conviction, the unspeakable joy had a long-lasting effect on Indian workers, and on the churches:[7]

> The revival has given a new body of native evangelists and most of our native preachers have experienced a baptism of the Holy Ghost, which has completely transformed their spirit and work.

The actual Revival lasted only a few years, but it was reported that the need of such revival remained uppermost in the minds of those who looked for the redemption of India. The Church rearmed settled in to its customary warfare against the powers of darkness. In 1909, Walker of Tinnevelly commented: [8]

> India is in an interesting transition stage; but, spiritually speaking, there seems to be a reaction at present from the promise of the widespread revival that seemed so imminent a few years ago.

Transition? Missionaries noticed that, in the 1905-06 Revival, the real independence of the national Church was stressed, for, in the aftermath of revival, new men were ready for new work in new fields, men who had formerly been agents and employees of the Missions now carrying revival-evangelism to the villages with a hope of extending self-government, self-support, and self-propagation thus.

Dayspring in the national Church seemed to be dawning in 1905, for, quoting a Canadian: 'Probably no event of the past year has been so significant as the formation of the National Missionary Society,'[9] which was started on its way in Carey's library at Serampore, with V. S. Azariah serving as its first secretary. The movement expressed a spiritual force, a revival of the evangelistic impulse.

The worldwide Awakening of 1905 preceded a disastrous World War, 1914-1918, a period of uneasy peace, a worldwide Economic Depression, and a second World War, 1939-1945, with the end of colonialism in sight. As nationalism emerged, an Indian National Christian Council developed.

Generally, a score of years pass by before the social impact of such an Evangelical Awakening can be measured. The 1920s in India were marked by an emphasis on social service. Another stirring of Revival was noticed in the mid-1930s, and yet another in the 1950s and 1960s.

The significance of the resurgence of New Testament Christianity in the 1950s lay in its demonstration that India clearly possessed an indigenous Evangelicalism. The time of foreign mission predominance had passed, never to be renewed; but missionaries were still needed to open up new areas, geographically and socially.

THE EVANGELIZATION OF SOUTHERN ASIA 199

Just as the population of India overshadowed the rest of Southern Asia, so the evangelization of India has been the most important objective of Evangelical missionaries west of Singapore. To date, the Revival of 1905-06 has been the decisive event in the process of evangelization.

The noteworthy factors in the evangelization of Southern Asia, particularly India, were (1) the missionary pioneering; (2) the Scripture translation; (3) the faithful transcultural evangelism; (4) the winning of vanguards of individuals or groups; (5) the inception of folk movements of caste or of tribal entities toward Christianity; (6) the evangelization and indoctrination of the seekers; (7) the education of the believers, their children and related communities; (8) the acceleration of folk movements under way; (9) the concern of national and missionary leaders about deplorable standards of spirituality among superficially changed church members in folk movements; (10) the outbreak of revivals of vital Christianity; (11) the indigenization of leadership; and (12) the impulsion of native evangelistic outreach, both intra-culturally and trans-culturally.[10]

It is indisputable that the evangelical missionary pioneers were thrust forth by evangelical awakenings in the sending countries—William Carey and Henry Martyn are excellent examples—and every subsequent revival sent out a quota of dedicated missionaries.

It was the evangelical awakenings which produced the Bible societies, and every revival in the sending countries and every awakening on the mission field accelerated the translation and distribution and effect of the Scriptures in the language of the people.

Typically, James Thoburn (Methodist) in North India and John Clough (Baptist) in South India were thrust forth from the 1858 Revival in the United States; and every awakening in the sending countries has produced missionaries who gladly sacrificed comfort to cross cultural lines with the saving message.

The forerunners of the Mala and Madiga folk movements to Christ were Pagolu Venkayya and Yerraguntla Periah respectively, both converted during the mid-nineteenth century awakenings in India, each contacted by a revived foreign missionary. In both cases, incipient folk movements followed these conversions, and grew steadily until they reached landslide proportions. This sequence of development can be illustrated from many instances of folk movements.

Workers converted or commissioned in times of revival engaged in ardent evangelization and faithful indoctrination of inquirers, as illustrated by such men as Rhenius and Arulappan in Tinnevelly. Examples can be multiplied from each awakening and the years following.

The early nineteenth century awakening in Scotland sent out Alexander Duff, John Wilson, Stephen Hislop and John Anderson to organize remarkable educational enterprises; the mid-nineteenth century movement sent out medical pioneers. Education exalted the lowly peoples.

Where folk movements were under way, as among the Chuhras of the Punjab, the outbreak of revival on the field accelerated the rate of increase—from 5% per annum to 20% per annum for twenty years.

In the great Hyderabad folk movement shepherded by the Methodists, it was found that in the 1930s 45% of the heads of families were addicted to alcohol, 30% of the members only knew the Ten Commandments and fewer the Lord's Prayer. Revival accelerated the movement again.

In the Northeast, the outbreak of phenomenal revival in 1905 produced extraordinary effects in the infant Khasi and Mizo churches, the outstanding event of Khasi history and a recurring event in the Lushai Hills. Much the same could be said of the Naga missions, in varying stages of development from folk movements to pioneering.

Throughout India, the revival of 1905 raised up a body of native evangelists, and Indians rose to leadership in every sector of church life. Revival had produced Indian leaders in the South in earlier generation; now the rise of Christian leaders paralleled the rise of political leaders in India.

The 1905-06 movement in particular thrust forth Indian evangelists to proclaim the Word in their own constituency, and it set in motion the efforts of Indian evangelists to reach other constituencies of different culture within India and far afield. The numbers of Indian evangelists operating within the sub-continent since Independence are beyond calculation —to survey their activities would be a major project.

In not one foregoing paragraphs could it be said that Revival was the only factor in the reported development— in each there were many factors; but the Holy Spirit of God as author of Revival is aware of all such factors, positive and negative, and so has moved in a conjunction of circumstances, including the willingness of certain groups to hear and the willingness of other folk to tell.

Notes on Chapter 1: THE SECOND GENERAL AWAKENING

1. See J. Edwin Orr, THE EAGER FEET, Chapters 1-12, for an account of the Second General Awakening and fuller documentation of the details.
2. Robert P. Evans, 'The Contribution of Foreigners to the French Protestant Reveil, 1815-1850,' Ph.D. Dissertation, University of Manchester, 1971; B. C. Poland, FRENCH PROTESTANTISM AND THE FRENCH REVOLUTION, appendices detailing French Huguenot abjurations.
3. On the Union of Prayer in the 1780s in Britain, and the Concert of Prayer in the United States in the 1790s, see J. Edwin Orr, THE EAGER FEET, pp. 14-15; pp. 52-53; also documented notes by E. A. Payne, 'The Evangelical Revival and the Beginning of the Modern Missionary Movement,' CONGREGATIONAL QUARTERLY, 1943, XXI, pp. 223ff; and by R. P. Beaver, 'The Concert of Prayer for Missions,' ECUMENICAL REVIEW, 1957-1958, X, pp. 420ff.
4. See G. M. Trevelyan, ENGLISH SOCIAL HISTORY, p. 468, for reaction in Britain.
5. James Sigston, A MEMOIR OF THE LIFE AND MINISTRY OF WILLIAM BRAMWELL, pp. 65ff.
6. D. E. Jenkins, THE LIFE OF THOMAS CHARLES OF BALA, Volume II, pp. 89-94.
7. See Alexander Haldane, THE LIVES OF ROBERT AND JAMES HALDANE; Hugh Watt, THOMAS CHALMERS AND THE DISRUPTION; John Kennedy, THE APOSTLE OF THE NORTH (Dr. John MacDonald).
8. C. H. Crookshank, HISTORY OF METHODISM IN IRELAND, Volume II, passim.
9. Heman Humphrey, REVIVAL SKETCHES, pp. 286-287.
10. See Sverre Norborg, HANS NIELSEN HAUGE.
11. See Bengt Jonzon, STUDIER I PAAVO RUOTSALAINEN.
12. Gunnar Westin, GEORGE SCOTT OCH HANS VERKSSAMHET I SVERIGE.
13. Alexander Haldane, THE LIVES OF ROBERT AND JAMES HALDANE, pp. 401ff.
14. See Paulus Scharpff, GESCHICHTE DER EVANGELISATION, pp. 114ff.
15. A. B. Strickland, THE GREAT AMERICAN REVIVAL, pp. 43ff.
16. See Heman Humphrey, REVIVAL SKETCHES; W. B. Sprague, LECTURES ON REVIVALS OF RELIGION, appendices.
17. William Speer, THE GREAT REVIVAL OF 1800, passim.
18. NEW YORK MISSIONARY MAGAZINE, 1802, p. 87.
19. See J. Edwin Orr, THE EAGER FEET, Chapter 10.
20. C. P. Shedd, TWO CENTURIES OF STUDENT CHRISTIAN MOVEMENTS, pp. 37ff.
21. See J. Edwin Orr, THE EAGER FEET, pp. 93ff.
22. Details in chapter 2: 'Quickening at the Cape,' following.
23. W. Canton, HISTORY OF THE BRITISH AND FOREIGN BIBLE SOCIETY, Volume I, pp. 1ff.
24. See J. Edwin Orr, THE EAGER FEET, Chapter 13.
25. The volume, THE EAGER FEET, Chapters 2-5, provides the details of the British response.

Notes on Chapter 2: ORGANIZING FOR ADVANCE

1 K. S. Latourette, A HISTORY OF THE EXPANSION OF CHRISTIANITY, Volume IV, pp. 34-35.   2 Volume IV, pp. 65-66.
3 W. Jones, THE RELIGIOUS TRACT SOCIETY, pp. 12ff.
4 See American Tract Society, ANNUAL REPORT, 1826.
5 G. R. Balleine, A HISTORY OF THE EVANGELICAL PARTY IN THE CHURCH OF ENGLAND, p. 133.
6 W. Canton, A HISTORY OF THE BRITISH AND FOREIGN BIBLE SOCIETY, Volume I, pp. 1ff.
7 H. O. Dwight, CENTENNIAL HISTORY OF THE AMERICAN BIBLE SOCIETY, Volume I, pp. 7ff.
8 W. Roberts, MEMOIR OF THE LIFE OF HANNAH MORE.
9 W. CORSTON, THE LIFE OF JOSEPH LANCASTER, pp. 11 & 16.
10 See J. H. Harris, ROBERT RAIKES: THE MAN AND HIS WORK; E. W. Rice, THE SUNDAY SCHOOL MOVEMENT, 1780-1917.
11 E. A. Payne, 'The Evangelical Revival and the Beginning of the Modern Missionary Movement,' CONGREGATIONAL QUARTERLY, 1943, XXI, pp. 223ff.
12 R. P. Beaver, 'The Concert of Prayer for Missions,' ECUMENICAL REVIEW, 1957-58, X, pp. 420ff.
13 E. A. Payne, THE CHURCH AWAKES, p. 31.
14 Eugene Stock, THE HISTORY OF THE CHURCH MISSIONARY SOCIETY, Volume I, p. 57.
15 See S. Pearce Carey, WILLIAM CAREY.
16 PROCEEDINGS OF THE WESLEY HISTORICAL SOCIETY, XXX, pp. 25-29.   17 S. Pearce Carey, WILLIAM CAREY, p. 83.
18 F. D. Walker, WILLIAM CAREY, MISSIONARY PIONEER.
19 William Carey, AN ENQUIRY INTO THE OBLIGATIONS OF CHRISTIANS TO USE MEANS FOR THE CONVERSION OF THE HEATHENS, Leicester, 1792.
20 R. Lovett, HISTORY OF THE LONDON MISSIONARY SOCIETY, Volume I, p. 5.
21 W. Carus, LIFE OF THE REV. CHARLES SIMEON, p. 229.
22 Findlay & Holdsworth, HISTORY OF THE WESLEYAN METHODIST MISSIONARY SOCIETY, Volume I, p. 72.
23 D. Mackichan, THE MISSIONARY IDEAL IN THE SCOTTISH CHURCHES, pp. 74, 112ff.
24 J. Edwin Orr, THE EAGER FEET, p. 91.
25 Peter Thacher, SOCIETY FOR PROPAGATING THE GOSPEL AMONG INDIANS AND OTHERS IN NORTH AMERICA.
26 J. W. Alexander, THE LIFE OF ARCHIBALD ALEXANDER, pp. 48-81.
27 C. G. Woodson, THE HISTORY OF THE NEGRO CHURCH, pp. 78ff.
28 C. H. Wesley, RICHARD ALLEN: APOSTLE OF FREEDOM.
29 See K. S. Latourette, A HISTORY OF THE EXPANSION OF CHRISTIANITY, Volume IV, pp. 335-336 for various sources.
30 This handicap is evidenced by statistics of births and marriages, regrettably even today, a century after emancipation.
31 Heman Humphrey, REVIVAL SKETCHES, pp. 286-287.
32 Ebenezer Mason, COMPLETE WORKS OF JOHN M. MASON, Volume III, pp. 270-271.
33 NEW YORK MISSIONARY MAGAZINE, January 1800, p. 9.
34 R. Pierce Beaver, PIONEERS IN MISSION, pp. 235ff.
35 John Blair Smith, THE ENLARGEMENT OF CHRIST'S KINGDOM.

36 ANNUAL BAPTIST REGISTER, III, pp. 535ff; CONNECTICUT EVANGELICAL MAGAZINE, Volume I, p. 14.
37 MASSACHUSETTS BAPTIST MISSIONARY SOCIETY, Volume I, pp. 5-12.
38 CONNECTICUT EVANGELICAL MAGAZINE, Volume I, p. 31.
39 S. B. Halliday, THE CHURCH IN AMERICA, pp. 515ff.
40 J. Tracy, HISTORY OF THE AMERICAN BOARD, pp. 24ff.
41 F. Wayland, MEMOIR OF ADONIRAM JUDSON.
42 J. M. Reid, MISSIONS AND MISSIONARY SOCIETY OF THE METHODIST EPISCOPAL CHURCH, Volume I, p. 17.
43 J. C. Emery, A CENTURY OF ENDEAVOR, pp. 29ff.
44 A. J. Brown, ONE HUNDRED YEARS, pp. 21ff.
45 George Drach, OUR CHURCH ABROAD, p. 23.
46 NEW YORK MISSIONARY MAGAZINE, Volume I, 1800, pp. 80-81.
47 THE PANOPLIST, Boston, Volume XI, January 1815, pp. 19-20.

Notes on Chapter 3: THE OPENING UP OF INDIA

1 See W. Germann, ZIEGENBALG AND PLUTSCHAU.
2 Allen & McClure, TWO HUNDRED YEARS: HISTORY OF THE S. P. C. K., 1689-1898, pp. 260ff.
3 W. Germann, MISSIONAR CHRISTIAN FRIEDRICH SCHWARTZ.
4 See J. Edwin Orr, THE EAGER FEET (Awakenings of 1792— and 1830—) & THE FERVENT PRAYER (1858-1899).
5 Charles Hole, THE EARLY HISTORY OF THE CHURCH MISSIONARY SOCIETY, p. 20.
6 George Smith, HENRY MARTYN, passim.
7 S. Pearce Carey, WILLIAM CAREY, passim.
8 See J. C. Marshman, THE LIFE AND TIMES OF CAREY, MARSHMAN AND WARD, passim.
9 Stephen C. Neill, BUILDERS OF THE INDIAN CHURCH, p. 81.
10 Carl Rhenius, MEMOIR OF THE REV. C. T. E. RHENIUS.
11 I. H. Hacker, A HUNDRED YEARS IN TRAVANCORE, 1806-1906.
12 George Gogerly, THE PIONEERS IN BENGAL, pp. 59-61.
13 Richard Lovett, A HISTORY OF THE LONDON MISSIONARY SOCIETY, Volume II, pp. 18ff.
14 K. S. Latourette, A HISTORY OF THE EXPANSION OF CHRISTIANITY, Volume II, p. 109.
15 W. E. Strong, THE STORY OF THE AMERICAN BOARD, p. 18.
16 P. Cheriyan, THE MALABAR CHRISTIANS AND THE CHURCH MISSIONARY SOCIETY.
17 Findlay & Holdsworth, THE HISTORY OF THE WESLEYAN METHODIST MISSIONARY SOCIETY, Volume V, pp. 176ff.
18 Amos Sutton, ORISSA AND ITS EVANGELIZATION, pp. 101ff.
19 BAPTIST MISSIONARY MAGAZINE, Volume XVI, p. 142; & E. R. Clough, SOCIAL CHRISTIANITY IN THE ORIENT, pp. 61ff.
20 J. A. Ewing, LANKA: THE BAPTIST MISSION TO CEYLON, pp. 16ff.
21 W. M. Harvard, THE MISSION TO CEYLON . . . FOUNDED BY THOMAS COKE, passim.
22 Eugene Stock, A HISTORY OF THE CHURCH MISSIONARY SOCIETY, Volume I, pp. 216ff.
23 H. I. Root, A CENTURY IN CEYLON, AMERICAN BOARD, 1816-1916, passim.
24 See J. Edwin Orr, THE EAGER FEET, pp. 15ff & pp. 52ff for accounts of the Concert of Prayer.

Notes on Chapter 4: THE THIRD GENERAL AWAKENING

1 See J. Edwin Orr, THE EAGER FEET, Chapters 19-24, for an account of the Third General Awakening and fuller documentation of the details.
2 Charles G. Finney, MEMOIRS OF REV. CHARLES G. FINNEY, WRITTEN BY HIMSELF.
3 W. E. Farndale, THE SECRET OF MOW COP, passim; cf. H. B. Kendall, A HISTORY OF THE PRIMITIVE METHODIST CHURCH, passim.
4 THE HOME MISSIONARY JOURNAL, 1831, p. 210.
5 AMERICAN BAPTIST MAGAZINE, 1831, p. 155.
6 See J. Edwin Orr, THE EAGER FEET, Chapter 19, 'American Outpouring in 1830.'
7 THE JOURNAL OF FRANCIS ASBURY, Volume III, pp. 210-211, edited by Elmer T. Clark.
8 G. L. Curtiss, MANUAL OF METHODIST EPISCOPAL HISTORY, pp. 148-149.
9 See H. C. Vedder, A SHORT HISTORY OF THE BAPTISTS, p. 327.
10 See J. Edwin Orr, THE EAGER FEET, Chapter 20, 'British Revival and Reaction, 1830—'
11 R. W. Church, THE OXFORD MOVEMENT: 1833-45, pp. 82ff; cf. TRACTS FOR THE TIMES.
12 James Caughey, METHODISM IN EARNEST; and SHOWERS OF BLESSING, passim.
13 Thomas Rees, HISTORY OF PROTESTANT NONCONFORMITY IN WALES, FROM ITS RISE TO THE PRESENT TIME, 1861, passim.
14 W. J. Couper, SCOTTISH REVIVALS, passim; cf. Mary Duncan, HISTORY OF REVIVALS IN THE BRITISH ISLES.
15 See J. Edwin Orr, THE EAGER FEET, on Ireland's 'Second Reformation,' pp. 152ff.
16 H. A. Ironside, A HISTORICAL SKETCH OF THE BRETHREN MOVEMENT, pp. 10ff.
17 J. Edwin Orr, THE EAGER FEET, Chapter 21, 'Scandinavian Stirrings, 1830—'
18 See A. R. Tippett, PEOPLE MOVEMENTS IN SOUTHERN POLYNESIA, passim.
19 Orramel Hinckley Gulick, THE PILGRIMS OF HAWAII: THEIR OWN STORY, pp. 315ff.
20 G. C. Henderson, FIJI AND THE FIJIANS, 1835-1856, see also Williams & Calvert, FIJI AND THE FIJIANS, passim.
21 N. Grundemann, JOHANN FRIEDRICH REIDEL, passim.
22 J. Edwin Orr, THE EAGER FEET, Chapter 23, 'Awakenings in South Africa.'
23 J. Edwin Orr, THE EAGER FEET, Chapter 24: 'Stirrings in the East.'
24 G. M. Thomssen, SAMUEL HEBICH OF INDIA, pp. 186ff.
25 See Francis Mason, THE KAREN APOSTLE: KO THAH-BYU.
26 W. W. Sweet, REVIVALISM IN AMERICA, p. 135.
27 C. G. Finney, LECTURES ON REVIVALS OF RELIGION, p. 5.
28 J. E. Hodder-Williams, LIFE OF SIR GEORGE WILLIAMS.
29 J. W. Ewing, GOODLY FELLOWSHIP: THE LIFE AND WORK OF THE WORLD'S EVANGELICAL ALLIANCE.
30 See Chapter 6: 'Social Impact of Revival,' following.

Notes on Chapter 5: WORK WIDENING AND DEEPENING

1. George Smith, THE LIFE OF ALEXANDER DUFF, p. 2; & William Paton, ALEXANDER DUFF (MISSIONARY EDUCATION)
2. See J. Edwin Orr, THE EAGER FEET, Chapter 4, 'Scottish Revivals, 1790—.'
3. George Smith, THE LIFE OF JOHN WILSON, passim.
4. George Smith, STEPHEN HISLOP, PIONEER MISSIONARY.
5. John Braidwood, TRUE YOKE-FELLOWS: THE LIFE OF JOHN ANDERSON AND ROBERT JOHNSTON, passim.
6. See J. R. Fleming, HISTORY OF THE CHURCH IN SCOTLAND, p. 50; William Paton, ALEXANDER DUFF.
7. Robert Jeffrey, THE INDIAN MISSION OF THE IRISH PRESBYTERIAN CHURCH, pp. 29ff, pp. 131ff.
8. J. H. Morris, THE STORY OF OUR FOREIGN MISSION (the Presbyterian Church of Wales), pp. 9ff.
9. Mrs. Groves, MEMOIR OF ANTHONY NORRIS GROVES: HIS LETTERS AND JOURNALS, passim.
10. See V. H. Sword, BAPTISTS IN ASSAM, pp. 41ff; E. R. Clough, SOCIAL CHRISTIANITY IN THE ORIENT, pp. 61ff.
11. Andrew Gordon, OUR INDIA MISSION: the United Presbyterian Church of North America, pp. 17ff.
12. Mrs. W. I. Chamberlain, FIFTY YEARS IN FOREIGN FIELDS, (the Reformed Church in America), pp. 24ff.
13. Clementina Butler, WILLIAM BUTLER; 37th & 39th REPORTS of the Missionary Society of the Methodist Episcopal Church.
14. Drach & Kuder, TELUGU MISSION OF THE EVANGELICAL LUTHERAN CHURCH IN NORTH AMERICA, passim.
15. Hermann Karsten, GESCHICHTE DER LEIPZIGER MISSION, Volume I, pp. 66ff.
16. Wilhelm Schlatter, GESCHICHTE DER BASLER MISSION, Volume I, pp. 1ff.
17. See Wilhelm Kruger, Dr. FRIEDRICH RIBBENTROP; Ludwig Notrott, DIE GOSSNERSCHE MISSION (KOHLS), Volume I.
18. Ronald Bryan, ALL IN A DAY'S WORK, pp. 26ff. See also PROCEEDINGS OF THE CHURCH MISSIONARY SOCIETY.
19. Stephen C. Neill, A HISTORY OF CHRISTIAN MISSIONS, p. 277.
20. J. G. Halliday, THE LIFE OF SAMUEL HEBICH BY TWO OF HIS FELLOW-LABOURERS (Gundert & Mogling).
21. G. M. Thomssen, SAMUEL HEBICH OF INDIA, pp. 187ff.
22. See J. C. Halliday, THE LIFE OF SAMUEL HEBICH OF INDIA, and Traugott Scholly, SAMUEL HEBICH, passim.
23. G. M. Thomssen, SAMUEL HEBICH OF INDIA, pp. 189ff.
24. Cf. Julius Richter, INDISCHE MISSIONSGESCHICHTE, p. 217.
25. MISSIONARY HERALD, Boston, 1837, p. 326.
26. August 1835 & March 1836, MISSIONARY HERALD.
27. MISSIONARY HERALD, 1837, p. 326 & 1838, p. 152.
28. George Smith, HISTORY OF WESLEYAN METHODISM, Volume III, p. 13; see also Moscrop & Restarick, CEYLON AND ITS METHODISTS, passim.
29. J. A. Ewing, LANKA (BAPTIST MISSIONARY SOCIETY).
30. See PROCEEDINGS OF THE CHURCH MISSIONARY SOCIETY, 1830-1840; and James Selkirk, RECOLLECTIONS OF CEYLON, with an Account of the Church Missionary Society's Operations.
31. Stephen C. Neill, A HISTORY OF CHRISTIAN MISSIONS, p. 295, & p. 559.

Notes on Chapter 6: SOCIAL IMPACT OF REVIVAL

1 JOHN WESLEY'S WORKS, (1872 Edition) Volume V, p. 296.
2 See W. M. Gewehr, THE GREAT AWAKENING IN VIRGINIA, Chapter 8.
3 W. W. Sweet, REVIVALISM IN AMERICA, p. 41.
4 T. Clarkson, ABOLITION OF THE AFRICAN SLAVE TRADE BY THE BRITISH PARLIAMENT.
5 ENCYCLOPEDIA BRITANNICA, 1970, article on Slavery.
6 John Wesley, THOUGHTS UPON SLAVERY, 1774.
7 J. C. Colquhoun, WILBERFORCE: HIS FRIENDS AND HIS TIMES.
8 G. M. Trevelyan, ENGLISH SOCIAL HISTORY, p. 495.
9 J. W. Bready, THIS FREEDOM—WHENCE? p. 44.
10 ENCYCLOPEDIA BRITANNICA, 1970, article on Slavery.
11 T. Clarkson, ABOLITION OF THE AFRICAN SLAVE TRADE BY THE BRITISH PARLIAMENT.
12 J. Harris, A CENTURY OF EMANCIPATION, pp. 3ff.
13 G. H. Barnes, THE ANTI-SLAVERY IMPULSE, passim.
14 J. Field, THE LIFE OF JOHN HOWARD, passim.
15 T. Taylor, MEMOIRS OF HOWARD, passim.
16 J. W. Bready, THIS FREEDOM—WHENCE? pp. 246ff.
17 A. R. C. Gardner, THE PLACE OF JOHN HOWARD IN PENAL REFORM, passim.
18 J. W. Bready, THIS FREEDOM—WHENCE? pp. 251ff.
19 See J. Whitney, ELIZABETH FRY, QUAKER HEROINE.
20 Fliedner's Autobiography is found only in his native German, cf. Catherine Winkworth, THE LIFE OF PASTOR FLIEDNER.
21 A. B. Wentz, FLIEDNER, THE FAITHFUL, p. 13.
22 G. Fliedner, THEODOR FLIEDNER, (3rd Edition, 1892).
23 A. B. Wentz, FLIEDNER, p. 25.
24 A. B. Wentz, FLIEDNER, p. 29.
25 Sir Edward Cook, LIFE OF FLORENCE NIGHTINGALE, passim.
26 LIFE OF FLORENCE NIGHTINGALE, Volume I, p. 479.
27 J. W. Bready, LORD SHAFTESBURY AND SOCIAL-INDUSTRIAL PROGRESS.
28 J. W. Bready, THIS FREEDOM—WHENCE? pp. 261-262.
29 E. Hodder, THE LIFE AND WORK OF THE SEVENTH EARL OF SHAFTESBURY, Volume III, p. 3.
30 THIS FREEDOM—WHENCE? pp. 264ff.   31 pp. 264-268.
32 THE SEVENTH EARL OF SHAFTESBURY, Volume III, p. 3.
33 K. S. Latourette, A HISTORY OF THE EXPANSION OF CHRISTIANITY, Volume IV, p. 155.
34 J. W. Bready, THIS FREEDOM—WHENCE? p. 265.
35 J. W. Bready, THIS FREEDOM—WHENCE? p. 266.
36 Sidney & Beatrice Webb, HISTORY OF TRADE UNIONISM, affirms the significance of the Tolpuddle 'Martyrs' in British social history and trade unionists have long revered them.
37 J. W. Bready, THIS FREEDOM—WHENCE? p. 269.
38 He had later emigrated to Canada.
39 J. W. Bready, THIS FREEDOM—WHENCE? p. 275.
40 E. D. Branch, THE SENTIMENTAL YEARS, 1836-1860.
41 W. W. Sweet, REVIVALISM IN AMERICA, p. 159.
42 G. H. Barnes, THE ANTI-SLAVERY IMPULSE, pp. 18-28.
43 W. W. Sweet, REVIVALISM IN AMERICA, p. 159.
44 K. S. Latourette, A HISTORY OF THE EXPANSION OF CHRISTIANITY, Volume IV, p. 416.

Notes on Chapter 7: SOCIAL IMPACT ON INDIA

1. Kenneth Ingham, REFORMERS IN INDIA, p. 1.
2. See J. H. Hutton, CASTE IN INDIA.
3. Joseph Schmidlin, CATHOLIC MISSION THEORY, p. 251.
4. Kenneth Ingham, REFORMERS IN INDIA, p. 23.
5. See J. C. Marshman, THE LIFE AND TIMES OF CAREY, MARSHMAN AND WARD, Volume II, p. 354.
6. Eugene Stock, THE HISTORY OF THE CHURCH MISSIONARY SOCIETY, Volume I, p. 301; see Josiah Bateman, THE LIFE OF DANIEL WILSON, Volume I, pp. 381ff.
7. Kenneth Ingham, REFORMERS IN INDIA, p. 34.
8. MISSIONARY REGISTER, 1831, pp. 31-32.
9. S. Pearce Carey, WILLIAM CAREY, fifth edition, p. 209.
10. Carey's FRIEND OF INDIA led the attack.
11. MISSIONARY REGISTER, 1824, pp. 238 & 278.
12. Kenneth Ingham, REFORMERS IN INDIA, p. 47; PARLIAMENTARY PAPERS, 1912-1813, Volume IX.
13. PARLIAMENTARY DEBATES, Volume LXII, May-July 1813.
14. also murder of parents or children, suicide or human sacrifice or torture, even if sanctioned by religion, see Boulger.
15. Kenneth Ingham, REFORMERS IN INDIA, pp. 57, 58, 59.
16. MISSIONARY REGISTER, 1823, pp. 187-190.
17. Kenneth Ingham, REFORMERS IN INDIA, p. 57.
18. MISSIONARY REGISTER, 1819, pp. 106-107.
19. Kenneth Ingham, REFORMERS IN INDIA, p. 73.
20. See J. R. Fleming, HISTORY OF THE CHURCH IN SCOTLAND, p. 50.
21. D. Mackichan, THE MISSIONARY IDEAL IN THE SCOTTISH CHURCHES, passim.
22. William Paton, ALEXANDER DUFF, p. 59.
23. D. C. Boulger, LORD WILLIAM BENTINCK.
24. George Smith, THE LIFE OF JOHN WILSON, passim.
25. George Smith, STEPHEN HISLOP, MISSIONARY PIONEER.
26. MISSIONARY REGISTER, 1824, p. 49.
27. Sir Philip Hartog, SOME ASPECTS OF INDIAN EDUCATION, PAST AND PRESENT, p. 6.
28. Philip Hartog, INDIAN EDUCATION, p. 4.
29. See H. Sharp, SELECTIONS FROM EDUCATIONAL RECORDS, Part I, 1781-1839; also Nurullah & Naik, A HISTORY OF EDUCATION IN INDIA, p. 165.
30. M. A. Sherring, THE HISTORY OF PROTESTANT MISSIONS IN INDIA, pp. 442-447.
31. M. A. Sherring, PROTESTANT MISSIONS, p. 75.
32. Philip Hartog, INDIAN EDUCATION, p. 6.
33. H. Sharp, EDUCATIONAL RECORDS, Volume II, p. 42.
34. H. Sharp, EDUCATIONAL RECORDS, Volume II, p. 44.
35. Kenneth Ingham, REFORMERS IN INDIA, p. 96.
36. Stephen C. Neill, A HISTORY OF CHRISTIAN MISSIONS, p. 209; see H. M. Zorn, BARTHOLOMAEUS ZIEGENBALG.
37. S. Pearce Carey, WILLIAM CAREY, pp. 405ff.
38. THE FRIEND OF INDIA, May 1818, p. 26.
39. Kenneth Ingham, REFORMERS IN INDIA, p. 104.
40. See J. C. Marshman, THE LIFE AND TIMES OF CAREY, MARSHMAN AND WARD, Volume II, pp. 356-357.
41. C. Manshardt, CHRISTIANITY IN A CHANGING INDIA, p. 147.

Notes on Chapter 8: THE FOURTH GENERAL AWAKENING

1. See J. Edwin Orr, THE FERVENT PRAYER, Chapters 1-12, for an account of the Fourth General Awakening with more detailed documentation.
2. CHRISTIAN ADVOCATE, New York, 5 November 1857.
3. W. C. Conant, NARRATIVE OF REMARKABLE CONVERSIONS, & T. W. Chambers, THE NOON PRAYER MEETING.
4. W. C. Conant, NARRATIVE OF REMARKABLE CONVERSIONS, p. 394. (See J. Edwin Orr, THE FERVENT PRAYER, Ch. 6).
5. JOURNAL, XLI ANNUAL CONVENTION OF THE PROTESTANT EPISCOPAL CHURCH IN THE DIOCESE OF OHIO, 1858.
6. J. Edwin Orr, THE FERVENT PRAYER, p. 42.
7. Cf. MINUTES OF THE GENERAL ASSEMBLY OF THE PRESBYTERIAN CHURCH IN THE UNITED STATES OF AMERICA, 1863-1868; and W. W. Bennett, THE GREAT REVIVAL IN THE SOUTHERN ARMIES.
8. See J. Edwin Orr, THE FERVENT PRAYER, Chapters 24 & 25.
9. J. Edwin Orr, THE FERVENT PRAYER, Chapters 7-12.
10. 'Christian Action,' see J. Edwin Orr, THE FERVENT PRAYER, Chapter 18.
11. Besides the standard biographies of D. L. Moody, see J. Edwin Orr, THE FERVENT PRAYER, 'The Evangelistic Extension.'
12. 'Appreciation and Depreciation,' Chapter 12, J. Edwin Orr.
13. J. E. Hodder-Williams, THE LIFE OF SIR GEORGE WILLIAMS, pp. 187, 203.
14. See J. Edwin Orr, THE FERVENT PRAYER, pp. 132-133.
15. W. R. Moody, THE LIFE OF DWIGHT L. MOODY; J. F. Findlay, DWIGHT L. MOODY, and other biographies.
16. See G. M. Stephenson, THE RELIGIOUS ASPECTS OF SWEDISH IMMIGRATION; also J. Edwin Orr, THE FERVENT PRAYER, pp. 83ff.
17. See Paulus Scharpff, GESCHICHTE DER EVANGELISATION, pp. 249ff.
18. J. H. Lohrenz, THE MENNONITE BRETHREN CHURCH, pp. 27ff. and R. S. Latimer, LIBERTY OF CONSCIENCE UNDER THREE TSARS, pp. 71-76.
19. See C. P. Shedd, TWO CENTURIES OF STUDENT CHRISTIAN MOVEMENTS, pp. 110ff.
20. See J. Edwin Orr, THE FERVENT PRAYER, Chapter 20.
21. S. B. Halliday, THE CHURCH IN AMERICA, pp. 347ff.
22. 'The Evangelization of Africa,' Chapter 11, following.
23. See J. Edwin Orr, THE FERVENT PRAYER, Chapter 19.
24. Chapter 24, J. Edwin Orr, THE FERVENT PRAYER.
25. T. L. Smith, REVIVALISM AND SOCIAL REFORM, p. 148.
26. Chapter 25, J. Edwin Orr, THE FERVENT PRAYER.
27. D. Carswell, BROTHER SCOTS, pp. 155ff; J. W. Bready, THIS FREEDOM—WHENCE ? pp. 277-282.
28. It was Dr. Max A. C. Warren, canon of Westminster Abbey, who drew the author's attention to the fact that his Oxford dissertation on the 1859 Revival in Britain demonstrated that a worldwide revival had occurred that caused no denominational cleavages.
29. Out of the 1859 Revival came the interdenominational missionary conference of 1860; then 1878, 1888, 1900 and 1910, for until 1910 the 'ecumenical movement' was directed by and supported by an Evangelical constituency.

Notes on Chapter 9: AWAKENINGS IN INDIA, 1860—

1 See Eugene Stock, HISTORY OF THE CHURCH MISSIONARY SOCIETY, Volume II, p. 34; MISSIONARY HERALD, 1867, p. 73.
2 1867, pp. 43, 79, 145; & AMERICAN BOARD, 1861, pp. 54ff.
3 D. A. Stoddard, NARRATIVE OF THE LATE REVIVAL AMONG THE NESTORIANS, & AMERICAN BOARD, 1859, pp. 80ff.
4 Stephen C. Neill, HISTORY OF CHRISTIAN MISSIONS, p. 279.
5 T. R. E. Holmes, A HISTORY OF THE INDIAN MUTINY.
6 C. H. Swavely, THE LUTHERAN ENTERPRISE IN SOUTH INDIA, p. 55. 7 THE REVIVAL, 3 December 1859.
8 E. B. Bromley, THEY WERE MEN SENT FROM GOD, p. 163; & George Smith, THE LIFE OF ALEXANDER DUFF, p. 302.
9 THE REVIVAL, 31 December 1859.
10 R. E. Speer, GEORGE BOWEN OF BOMBAY, pp. 232-233.
11 See H. Morris, THE LIFE OF CHARLES GRANT.
12 THE REVIVAL, 22 September 1860.
13 F. S. Downs, THE MIGHTY WORKS OF GOD, pp. 55-56.
14 G. H. Lang, THE HISTORY AND DIARIES OF AN INDIAN CHRISTIAN, J. C. AROOLAPPEN, pp. 9ff.
15 G. H. Lang, J. C. AROOLAPPEN, p. 140. 16 p. 141.
17 G. H. Lang, J. C. AROOLAPPEN, p. 148. 18 p. 143.
19 Eugene Stock, A HISTORY OF THE CHURCH MISSIONARY SOCIETY, Volume II, p. 189.
20 INDIAN WATCHMAN, October 1960.
21 CHURCH MISSIONARY INTELLIGENCER, August 1860.
22 CHURCH MISSIONARY RECORD, August 1860.
23 BOMBAY GUARDIAN, 8 October 1860.
24 G. H. Lang, J. C. AROOLAPPEN, p. 184.
25 G. H. Lang, J. C. AROOLAPPEN, p. 185.
26 J. W. Pickett, CHRISTIAN MASS MOVEMENTS, p. 41.
27 Eugene Stock, CHURCH MISSIONARY SOCIETY, pp. 179ff.
28 W. S. Hunt, THE ANGLICAN CHURCH IN TRAVANCORE AND COCHIN, Volume II, p. 160.
29 P. Cheriyan, THE MALABAR CHRISTIANS AND THE CHURCH MISSIONARY SOCIETY, pp. 287ff.
30 P. Cheriyan, THE MALABAR CHRISTIANS, pp. 287.
31 W. S. Hunt, THE ANGLICAN CHURCH, p. 157.
32 W. S. Hunt, THE ANGLICAN CHURCH, p. 154.
33 MISSIONARY CONFERENCE ON SOUTH INDIA, p. 164.
34 W. S. Hunt, THE ANGLICAN CHURCH, p. 154.
35 W. S. Hunt, THE ANGLICAN CHURCH, p. 156.
36 Eugene Stock, CHURCH MISSIONARY SOCIETY, pp. 179ff.
37 W. S. Hunt, THE ANGLICAN CHURCH, p. 157.
38 The implication is simultaneous prayer.
39 W. S. Hunt, THE ANGLICAN CHURCH, p. 157.
40 Eugene Stock, CHURCH MISSIONARY SOCIETY, pp. 179ff.
41 Eugene Stock, CHURCH MISSIONARY SOCIETY, pp. 179ff.
42 W. S. Hunt, THE ANGLICAN CHURCH, p. 158.
43 Eugene Stock, CHURCH MISSIONARY SOCIETY, pp. 179ff.
44 MISSIONARY CONFERENCE ON SOUTH INDIA, p. 167.
45 W. S. Hunt, THE ANGLICAN CHURCH, p. 160.
46 See K. K. Kuruvilla, REVIVALS IN KERALA (Malayalam)— Notes in English supplied by K. V. Cherian.
47 A. W. Carmichael, WALKER OF TINNEVELLY, p. 231.
48 W. S. Hunt, THE ANGLICAN CHURCH, p. 152.

Notes on Chapter 10: MOVEMENTS AFTER REVIVAL

1 John R. Mott estimated that 80% of the 1,800,000 Protestants in India in 1914 were products of folk movements, see J. W. Pickett, p. 5.
2 J. W. Pickett, CHRISTIAN MASS MOVEMENTS, pp. 45ff.
3 J. N. Hollister, CENTENARY OF THE METHODIST CHURCH IN SOUTHERN ASIA, p. 45.   4 J. W. Pickett, p. 47.
5 See Findlay & Holdsworth, THE HISTORY OF THE WESLEYAN METHODIST MISSIONARY SOCIETY, Volume V, p. 370.
6 A. H. Newman, A CENTURY OF BAPTIST ACHIEVEMENT, p. 187.
7 E. B. Bromley, THEY WERE MEN SENT FROM GOD, p. 163.
8 Cf. G. H. Lang, JOHN CHRISTIAN AROOLAPPEN, pp. 138-207.
9 E. B. Bromley, p. 164.
10 F. F. Gledstone, THE CHURCH MISSIONARY SOCIETY TELUGU MISSION, pp. 19ff.   11 Pagolu Venkayya.
12 F. F. Gledstone, pp. 19ff.   13 Cf. PROCEEDINGS.
14 E. R. Clough, SOCIAL CHRISTIANITY IN THE ORIENT, p. 92.
15 E. R. Clough, p. 92.   16 E. B. Bromley, p. 161.
17 E. B. Bromley, p. 161.   18 E. B. Bromley, p. 161.
19 E. R. Clough, p. 98.   20 E. R. Clough, p. 98.
21 E. R. Clough, SOCIAL CHRISTIANITY IN THE ORIENT, p. 137.
22 The folk movement gained momentum long before the great famine, cf. E. R. Clough, p. 92.   23 E. R. Clough, p. 275.
24 See David Downie, THE LONE STAR MISSION, pp. 88ff.
25 E. R. Clough, SOCIAL CHRISTIANITY IN THE ORIENT, p. 362.
26 C. H. Swavely, THE LUTHERAN ENTERPRISE IN SOUTH INDIA, pp. 19-20.   27 Ludwig Notrott, DIE GOSSNERSCHE MISSION.
28 C. H. Swavely, THE LUTHERAN ENTERPRISE, pp. 55-56.
29 See Julius Richter, INDISCHE MISSIONSGESCHICHTE, pp. 305ff.
30 M. A. Pedersen, IN THE LAND OF THE SANTALS.
31 J. N. Hollister, CENTENARY IN SOUTHERN ASIA, p. xxv.
32 See F. F. Oldham, THOBURN—CALLED OF GOD.
33 J. M. Thoburn, MY MISSIONARY APPRENTICESHIP.
34 K. S. Latourette, A HISTORY OF THE EXPANSION OF CHRISTIANITY, Volume IV, p. 191.
35 William Taylor, THE STORY OF MY LIFE, pp. 73-75, 218-228.
36 William Taylor, FOUR YEARS' CAMPAIGN IN INDIA, passim.
37 J. M. Thoburn, ISABELLA THOBURN, p. 99.
38 William Taylor, FOUR YEARS' CAMPAIGN IN INDIA, passim.
39 J. M. Thoburn, ISABELLA THOBURN, p. 100.
40 William Taylor, FOUR YEARS' CAMPAIGN IN INDIA, pp. 303ff.
41 J. M. Thoburn, ISABELLA THOBURN, p. 105.
42 J. N. Hollister, CENTENARY IN SOUTHERN ASIA, p. 112.
43 E. G. K. Hewat, CHRIST AND WESTERN INDIA, p. 231.
44 J. N. Hollister, CENTENARY IN SOUTHERN ASIA, p. 115.
45 William Taylor, FOUR YEARS' CAMPAIGN IN INDIA, p. 344.
46 J. N. Hollister, CENTENARY IN SOUTHERN ASIA, p. 123.
47 William Taylor, FOUR YEARS' CAMPAIGN IN INDIA, p. 355.
48 B. T. Badley, VISIONS AND VICTORIES IN HINDUSTAN, p. 298.
49 J. N. Hollister, CENTENARY IN SOUTHERN ASIA, p. 120.
50 R. E. Speer, GEORGE BOWEN OF BOMBAY, pp. 260ff.
51 J. M. Thoburn, ISABELLA THOBURN, p. 106.
52 Cf. MISSIONARY HERALD, December 1859 & January 1862, & Eugene Stock, THE HISTORY OF THE CHURCH MISSIONARY SOCIETY, Volume II, p. 288.   53 Volume II, pp. 206ff.
54 J. L. Barton, DAYBREAK IN TURKEY, pp. 174-175.

Notes on Chapter 11: CHRISTIAN ACTION

1 The American population had already passed that of Great Britain: United States (1860) 30,000,000; United Kingdom (1861) 27,000,000 in approximate population.
2 See Warren A. Candler, GREAT REVIVALS AND THE GREAT REPUBLIC, pp. 215-216 & L. W. Bacon, A HISTORY OF AMERICAN CHRISTIANITY, regarding the United States; and J. Edwin Orr, THE SECOND EVANGELICAL AWAKENING IN BRITAIN, p. 207 & Appendices A-E regarding denominations in the United Kingdom.
3 W. A. Candler, GREAT REVIVALS AND THE GREAT REPUBLIC, pp. 222-223.
4 See F. G. Beardsley, A HISTORY OF AMERICAN REVIVALS, pp. 230 & 237.
5 In the United States and in the United Kingdom, laymen initiated the first united prayer meetings; in India, civil servants and military men promoted prayer meetings among Europeans and their Indian associates; Indian lay workers and missionaries were responsible for meetings of prayer among the churches.
6 Cf. G. E. Morgan, R. C. MORGAN: HIS LIFE AND TIMES, pp. 159-160.
7 See J. Edwin Orr, THE SECOND EVANGELICAL AWAKENING IN BRITAIN, p. 251.
8 See W. W. Sweet, REVIVALISM IN AMERICA, p. 160; cf. C. H. Hopkins, A HISTORY OF THE YOUNG MEN'S CHRISTIAN ASSOCIATIONS IN NORTH AMERICA, passim.
9 R. C. Morgan, one of the most influential laymen in Britain, and an able editor, immediately saw the possibilities of expansion of the Y.M.C.A. See THE REVIVAL, 6 August 1859.
10 J. E. Hodder-Williams, LIFE OF SIR GEORGE WILLIAMS, pp. 187, 203.
11 For a treatment of the revival activities of William Booth, see J. Edwin Orr, THE SECOND EVANGELICAL AWAKENING IN BRITAIN, pp. 215ff.
12 The East London Special Services Committee, organizing public meeting, THE REVIVAL, 2 February 1861.
13 See Robert Sandall, HISTORY OF THE SALVATION ARMY, Volume I, pp. 22, 41-44.
14 Cf. Obituary notice in THE CHRISTIAN, 11 February 1909, and P. C. Headley, THE HARVEST OF THE HOLY SPIRIT ILLUSTRATED IN THE EVANGELISTIC LABORS OF REV. EDWARD PAYSON HAMMOND, passim.
15 Cf. Edwin W. Rice, THE SUNDAY SCHOOL MOVEMENT, 1780-1917; & Arlo A. Brown, A HISTORY OF RELIGIOUS EDUCATION IN RECENT TIMES, passim.
16 Cf. THE REVIVAL, 27 August 1859 & Appendix D, J. Edwin Orr, THE SECOND EVANGELICAL AWAKENING IN BRITAIN, pp. 273-275.
17 William Canton, THE HISTORY OF THE BRITISH AND FOREIGN BIBLE SOCIETY, Volume III, p. 74.
18 Volume III, p. 55.
19 Volume III, p. 16.
20 See J. Edwin Orr, THE SECOND EVANGELICAL AWAKENING IN BRITAIN, Chapter 10, 'Societies and the Revival'; see also A. M. Chirgwin, THE BIBLE IN WORLD EVANGELISM, passim.

Notes on Chapter 12: MOODY AND THE STUDENTS

1   W. R. Moody, THE LIFE OF DWIGHT L. MOODY, a standard text, and a recent work, J. F. Findlay, DWIGHT L. MOODY, provide the best earliest and latest findings on Moody, though a vast bibliography of volumes on the evangelist is available.
2   J. C. Pollock, MOODY: A BIBLIOGRAPHICAL PORTRAIT, p. 14.
3   Moody wrote home to tell of his involvement in the 1858 Revival in Chicago. Earlier authors, in spite of the fact that Moody had dated his letter January 6, 1857, assumed that he was referring to the Awakening in Chicago in the New Year of 1858, but later authors (a century afterward, such as Findlay, p. 63 & Pollock, p. 19) have suggested that he was referring to an earlier local excitement. The obvious explanation is that Moody (like many another) used the date 1857 inadvertently in early January 1858; no awakening in January 1857 was reported. Cf. W. R. Moody, THE LIFE OF DWIGHT L. MOODY, p. 47.
4   W. R. Moody, THE LIFE OF DWIGHT L. MOODY, pp. 55ff.
5   F. G. Beardsley, HISTORY OF AMERICAN REVIVALS, p. 237.
6   W. R. Moody, THE LIFE OF DWIGHT L. MOODY, pp. 131ff.
7   See J. McPherson, HENRY MOORHOUSE, pp. 48 & 66; cf. G. C. Needham, RECOLLECTIONS OF HENRY MOORHOUSE, passim.
8   W. R. Moody, THE LIFE OF DWIGHT L. MOODY, p. 149.
9   See THE CHRISTIAN, 3 June 1909, on Henry Varley; and Henry Varley, Jr., HENRY VARLEY'S LIFE STORY; W. R. Moody, THE LIFE OF DWIGHT L. MOODY, p. 134ff.
10 R. Braithwaite, THE REV. WILLIAM PENNEFATHER: LIFE AND LETTERS.
11 W. R. Moody, THE LIFE OF DWIGHT L. MOODY, pp. 152ff.
12 EDINBURGH COURANT, December 1873; THE CHRISTIAN (January and February 1874 issues).
13 W. R. Moody, THE LIFE OF DWIGHT L. MOODY, pp. 197ff.
14 See DUBLIN EVENING NEWS, November 1874.
15 W. R. Moody, THE LIFE OF DWIGHT L. MOODY, pp. 215ff, pp. 223ff.
16 F. Engels, SOCIALISM, UTOPIAN & SCIENTIFIC, introduction. Engels defended Marxism.
17 See NEW YORK TIMES, 4 February 1876.
18 W. R. Moody, THE LIFE OF DWIGHT L. MOODY, pp. 291ff.
19 See THE CHRISTIAN, 6 July 1882.
20 J. C. Pollock, MOODY: A BIOGRAPHICAL PORTRAIT, p. 241.
21 W. R. Moody, THE LIFE OF DWIGHT L. MOODY, pp. 297ff.
22 MISSIONARY REVIEW OF THE WORLD, May 1895.
23 W. R. Moody, THE LIFE OF DWIGHT L. MOODY, pp. 409ff.
24 See KANSAS CITY STAR, 11 & 18 November 1899.
25 W. W. Sweet, REVIVALISM IN AMERICA, p. 169.
26 J. du Plessis, THE LIFE OF ANDREW MURRAY, p. 322.
27 W. E. Boardman, THE HIGHER CHRISTIAN LIFE, Boston, 1858; London, 1860; see M. M. Boardman, THE LIFE AND LABOURS OF THE REV. W. E. BOARDMAN, New York, 1887.
28 W. B. Sloan, THESE SIXTY YEARS, p. 10.
29 J. C. Pollock, THE KESWICK STORY, pp. 30ff.
30 W. B. Sloan, THESE SIXTY YEARS, p. 19.
31 J. H. Battersby, MEMOIR OF T. D. HARFORD-BATTERSBY, (Vicar of Keswick, a founder of the Keswick Convention).

32 W. B. Sloan, THESE SIXTY YEARS, indexed references on the visiting and regular speakers at Keswick.
33 J. du Plessis, THE LIFE OF ANDREW MURRAY, passim. Cf. W. M. Douglas, ANDREW MURRAY AND HIS MESSAGE.
34 W. Y. Fullerton, THE LIFE OF F. B. MEYER, passim.
35 A. M. Hay, CHARLES INWOOD, HIS MINISTRY AND ITS SECRET, passim.
36 See C. F. Harford-Battersby, PILKINGTON OF UGANDA, chapter XII.
37 Donald Fraser, WINNING A PRIMITIVE PEOPLE, p. 279.
38 J. C. Pollock, MOODY, A BIOGRAPHICAL PORTRAIT, p. 228. & passim; cf. J. C. Pollock, A CAMBRIDGE MOVEMENT, passim.
39 W. R. Moody, THE LIFE OF DWIGHT L. MOODY, pp. 350ff.
40 THE CHRISTIAN, 23 November 1882.
41 Wilfred Grenfell, A LABRADOR DOCTOR, (Autobiography).
42 J. C. Pollock, A CAMBRIDGE MOVEMENT, passim.
43 C. P. Shedd, TWO CENTURIES OF STUDENT CHRISTIAN MOVEMENTS, pp. 110-111.
44 L. D. Wishard, 'The Beginning of the Students' Era in Christian History,' pp. 52-53.
45 COLLEGE BULLETIN, New York, April 1880.
46 L. D. Wishard, 'The Beginning of the Students' Era in Christian History,' p. 129.
47 L. D. Wishard, 'The Beginning of the Students' Era in Christian History,' p. 138.
48 See Basil Mathews, JOHN R. MOTT: WORLD CITIZEN, & John R. Mott, HISTORY OF THE STUDENT VOLUNTEER MOVEMENT, passim.
49 C. P. Shedd, TWO CENTURIES OF STUDENT CHRISTIAN MOVEMENTS, pp. 248ff.
50 REPORT OF THE FIRST INTERNATIONAL CONVENTION OF THE STUDENT VOLUNTEER MOVEMENT, pp. 161-163. The S. V. M. conventions were held quadrennially.
51 C. P. Shedd, TWO CENTURIES OF STUDENT CHRISTIAN MOVEMENTS, pp. 259ff, cf. SPRINGFIELD REPUBLICAN, 2nd August 1886; & J. R. Mott, HISTORY OF THE STUDENT VOLUNTEER MOVEMENT, p. 12.
52 C. P. Shedd, TWO CENTURIES OF STUDENT CHRISTIAN MOVEMENTS, p. 267; THE INTERCOLLEGIAN, May 1887; W. R. Moody, THE LIFE OF DWIGHT L. MOODY, p. 358.
53 G. A. Smith, THE LIFE OF HENRY DRUMMOND, pp. 370ff.
54 C. P. Shedd, TWO CENTURIES OF STUDENT CHRISTIAN MOVEMENTS, p. 275; J. H. Oldham, STUDENT CHRISTIAN MOVEMENT OF GREAT BRITAIN AND IRELAND, p. 13.
55 C. K. Ober, LUTHER D. WISHARD, pp. 122ff.
56 Cf. THE INTERCOLLEGIAN, December 1889; SPRINGFIELD UNION, 7 July 1892; & J. H. Oldham, STUDENT CHRISTIAN MOVEMENT OF GREAT BRITAIN AND IRELAND, pp. 14ff.
57 J. H. Oldham, STUDENT CHRISTIAN MOVEMENT OF GREAT BRITAIN AND IRELAND, pp. 21ff.
58 K. S. Latourette, HISTORY OF THE EXPANSION OF CHRISTIANITY, Volume IV, pp. 97-98.
59 See S. B. Halliday, THE CHURCH IN AMERICA AND ITS BAPTISMS OF FIRE, pp. 347ff; cf. R. P. Anderson, THE STORY OF CHRISTIAN ENDEAVOR, passim.

Notes on Chapter 13: CONTINUED SOCIAL IMPACT

1 Gilbert Seldes, THE STAMMERING CENTURY, p. 141.
2 L. A. Weigle, AMERICAN IDEALISM, p. 188.
3 T. L. Smith, REVIVALISM & SOCIAL REFORM, Chaps. XII-XIII.
4 G. M. Trevelyan, ENGLISH SOCIAL HISTORY, pp. 492ff.
5 THE CHRISTIAN, 3 June 1909.
6 W. Canton, HISTORY OF THE BRITISH AND FOREIGN BIBLE SOCIETY, Volume III, pp. 1-2.
7 J. W. Bready, LORD SHAFTESBURY, pp. 313, 318, 326, 333.
8 K. S. Latourette, THE NINETEENTH CENTURY IN EUROPE, Vol. II, p. 376; & J. W. Bready, LORD SHAFTESBURY, p. 402.
9 See THE REVIVAL, 27 August 1859, on education.
10 K. S. Latourette, NINETEENTH CENTURY IN EUROPE, Volume II, pp. 355ff.   11 J. W. Bready, DR. BARNARDO, p. 50.
12 THE CHRISTIAN, 22 April 1886, on Quarrier's Homes; & G. E. Morgan, R. C. MORGAN, pp. 144, 156, on Fegan's Homes.
13 Young and Ashton, BRITISH SOCIAL WORK, p. 41.
14 ENCYCLOPEDIA BRITANNICA, 1960, 'Probation.'
15 Young and Ashton, BRITISH SOCIAL WORK, pp. 159, 165, 174.
16 Josephine Butler, REMINISCENCES OF A GREAT CRUSADE.
17 William Weir, ULSTER AWAKENING, pp. 151, 190, 196.
18 G. E. Morgan, R. C. MORGAN, p. 145; cf. THE REVIVAL, 1860ff
19 Young and Ashton, BRITISH SOCIAL WORK, pp. 205ff.
20 G. E. Morgan, R. C. MORGAN, pp. 298ff; Millicent Fawcett, JOSEPHINE BUTLER, passim.
21 Young and Ashton, BRITISH SOCIAL WORK, pp. 209ff, 221.
22 Charles Dickens, ALL THE YEAR ROUND, 5 November 1859.
23 Cf. Registrar-General, QUARTERLY RETURNS OF BIRTHS, DEATHS AND MARRIAGES, 1858-65; MONTHLY RETURNS of Eight Principal Towns of Scotland.
24 See C. P. Shedd, HISTORY OF THE WORLD'S ALLIANCE OF YOUNG MEN'S CHRISTIAN ASSOCIATIONS, pp. 82ff.
25 M. T. Boardman, UNDER THE RED CROSS FLAG, p. 32.
26 See M. Gumpert, DUNANT: STORY OF THE RED CROSS.
27 B. & S. Epstein, HENRI DUNANT, p. 22.
28 T. L. Smith, REVIVALISM AND SOCIAL REFORM, p. 148.
29 A. F. C. Bourdillon, VOLUNTARY SOCIAL SERVICES, p. 45.
30 Julius Richter, A HISTORY OF MISSIONS IN INDIA, pp. 346ff.
31 Lal Behari Day, RECOLLECTIONS OF ALEXANDER DUFF.
32 Mrs. Chamberlain, FIFTY YEARS IN FOREIGN FIELDS, p. 24.
33 M. A. Sherring, THE INDIAN CHURCH, p. 218.
34 Julius Richter, A HISTORY OF MISSIONS IN INDIA, pp. 347ff.
35 Mrs. R. Hoskins, CLARA SWAIN: MEDICAL MISSIONARY.
36 See Charles Reynolds, PUNJAB PIONEER: DR. EDITH BROWN; William Wanless, AN AMERICAN DOCTOR IN INDIA; & M. P. Jeffrey, DR. IDA: INDIA. (The writer visited the last-named.)
37 Christian Medical Association, THE INNS OF HEALING, p. 144.
38 C. B. Firth, AN INTRODUCTION TO INDIAN CHURCH HISTORY, p. 203.   39 Sam Higginbotham, THE GOSPEL AND THE PLOW.
40 W. S. Hunt, ANGLICAN CHURCH IN TRAVANCORE, pp. 154ff.
41 A. D. Lindsay, CHRISTIAN HIGHER EDUCATION IN INDIA, p. 298.
42 Nurullah & Naik, HIGHER EDUCATION IN INDIA, pp. 881ff.
43 This is a factor not often considered.
44 J. Spargo, KARL MARX: HIS LIFE AND WORK.
45 Friederich Engels, SOCIALISM, UTOPIAN AND SCIENTIFIC.

Notes on Chapter 14: THE FIFTH GENERAL AWAKENING

1. See J. Edwin Orr, THE FLAMING TONGUE, Chapters 1-25, for an account of the Fifth General Awakening and fuller documentation of the details.
2. On 1st July 1916, the Ulster Division was decimated in the battle of the Somme.
3. F. C. Ottman, J. Wilbur Chapman, p. 272.
4. MISSIONARY REVIEW OF THE WORLD, 1903, pp. 20ff.
5. For an account of the prisoner-of-war awakenings, see Chapter 15, 'The Mission of Peace,' pp. 121ff.
6. J. Edwin Orr, THE FLAMING TONGUE, Chapter 23, 'Taikyo Dendo in Japan.'
7. MISSIONARY REVIEW OF THE WORLD, 1903, pp. 20ff.
8. On the ministry of Gipsy Rodney Smith, see Chapter 15, 'The Mission of Peace' in South Africa, pp. 125-129.
9. J. Edwin Orr, THE FLAMING TONGUE, Chapters 1-3.
10. J. Vyrnwy Morgan, THE WELSH RELIGIOUS REVIVAL: A RETROSPECT AND A CRITICISM, pp. 248ff.
11. Keir Hardie, converted in the Fourth General Awakening, active as a Christian throughout his trade union career, died in 1915.
12. THE RECORD, 16 June 1905; THE WITNESS, 17 February 1905; and other British journals reported Anglican support.
13. J. Edwin Orr, THE FLAMING TONGUE, Chapter 4, 'Irish and Scottish Awakenings.'
14. 'Awakening in Scandinavia,' THE FLAMING TONGUE, Chapter 7.
15. J. Edwin Orr, THE FLAMING TONGUE, Chapter 8, European continental reports.
16. STATESMAN'S YEARBOOK, 1905 & 1909 figures.
17. J. Edwin Orr, THE FLAMING TONGUE, Chapters 9-12, giving North American accounts.
18. 'The 1905 American Awakening,' pp. 74-75; 'Impact on Church and State,' pp. 93-94; in THE FLAMING TONGUE.
19. THE FLAMING TONGUE, pp. 76-79; and passim.
20. 'The 1905 American Awakening,' pp. 79-80.
21. J. Edwin Orr, THE FLAMING TONGUE, p. 80.
22. STATESMAN'S YEARBOOK, 1905 & 1911 data.
23. 'The Mission of Peace,' p. 133, following.
24. J. Edwin Orr, THE FLAMING TONGUE, Chapters 17-20, giving an account of Awakenings in India.
25. 92nd ANNUAL REPORT, American Baptist Missionary Union, pp. 99 & 119; cf. 93rd ANNUAL REPORT.
26. 'The Korean Pentecost,' Chapter 22, THE FLAMING TONGUE.
27. CHINA MISSION YEAR BOOK, 1915.
28. ATLAS OF PROTESTANT MISSIONS, 1903; and WORLD ATLAS OF CHRISTIAN MISSIONS, 1911.
29. J. Edwin Orr, THE FLAMING TONGUE, Chapter 13, 'Latin American Quickening.'
30. 'The African Awakenings,' Chapter 16, following.
31. J. Edwin Orr, THE FLAMING TONGUE, Chapter 24, 'The Pentecostal Aftermath.'
32. WESLEYAN METHODIST MAGAZINE, 1905, p. 65; CHRISTIAN ADVOCATE, 6 January 1906.
33. J. Edwin Orr, THE FLAMING TONGUE, pp. 97ff.
34. K. S. Latourette, A HISTORY OF THE EXPANSION OF CHRISTIANITY, Volume IV, Chapter 11.

Notes on Chapter 15: THE EXPECTATION IN INDIA

1 J. M. Thoburn, ISABELLA THOBURN, p. 106.
2 G. T. B. Davis, TORREY AND ALEXANDER, p. 48.
3 THE CHRISTIAN, London, 26 April 1906.
4 H. S. Dyer, REVIVAL IN INDIA, p. 28.
5 'The Prayer Circular,' Madras; see H. S. Dyer, REVIVAL IN INDIA, p. 29.   6 H. S. Dyer, REVIVAL IN INDIA, p. 29.
7 q. R. J. Ward.   8 H. S. Dyer, REVIVAL IN INDIA, p. 29.
9 Student Volunteer Movement, STUDENTS AND THE MODERN MISSIONARY CRUSADE, p. 367.
10 See G. Hyde Bone & M. Hyde Hall, LIFE AND LETTERS OF PRAYING HYDE, pp. 9ff.
11 E. G. Carre, PRAYING HYDE, (F. A. McGaw), pp. 10ff.
12 F. E. Stock, 'People Movements in the Punjab,' M. A. Thesis, School of World Mission, Pasadena, pp. 102ff.
13 F. E. Stock, pp. 129ff.
14 Robert Stewart, LIFE AND WORK IN INDIA, pp. 249ff.
15 Basil Miller, PRAYING HYDE, p. 48.
16 E. G. Carre, PRAYING HYDE, (F. A. McGaw), p. 12.
17 F. A. McGaw, in E. G. Carre, PRAYING HYDE, p. 13.
18 BAPTIST MISSIONARY REVIEW, February 1907, p. 55.
19 Cf. G. T. B. Davis, p. 48; MISSIONARY REVIEW, 1903, p. 20; and BAPTIST MISSIONARY REVIEW, February 1907, p. 55; R. A. Torrey reported much prayer for a great revival in India, a very widespread expectation, JAPAN EVANGELIST, May 1903.
20 Nicol MacNicol, PANDITA RAMABAI, p. 117.
21 ECUMENICAL MISSIONARY CONFERENCE, New York, 1900, Volume II, p. 116.
22 M. W. Retief, HERLEWINGS IN ONS GESKIEDENIS, p. 89.
23 William Canton, A HISTORY OF THE BRITISH AND FOREIGN BIBLE SOCIETY, Volume III, pp. 294-295.
24 DE KERKBODE, Cape Town, 24 April 1902, p. 182.
25 M. W. Retief, HERLEWINGS IN ONS GESKIEDENIS, p. 89.
26 DE KERKBODE, Cape Town, 24 April 1902, p. 182.
27 DE KERKBODE, 1902, pp. 41, 377 and 385ff.
28 G. B. A. Gerdener, RECENT DEVELOPMENTS IN THE SOUTH AFRICAN MISSION FIELD, p. 15.

Notes on Chapter 16: THE AWAKENING IN ASSAM

1 J. Meirion Lloyd, ON EVERY HIGH HILL, p. 52.
2 Mrs. John Roberts, THE REVIVAL IN THE KHASIA HILLS, passim; & H. S. Dyer, REVIVAL IN INDIA, Chapter X.
3 J. Pengwern Jones, INDIA AWAKE! p. 22.
4 Mrs. John Roberts, Y DIWYGIAD AR FRYNIAU KHASSIA, p. 7.
5 H. S. Dyer, REVIVAL IN INDIA, pp. 31ff.
6 J. Pengwern Jones, INDIA AWAKE! pp. 56-57.
7 Mrs. John Roberts, THE REVIVAL IN THE KHASIA HILLS, & RECORD OF CHRISTIAN WORK, 1907, p. 508. In 1905, 5100 Khasis were received into membership; in 1906, 2771, bringing the total to 28,000 out of a population of quarter of a million.
8 AMERICAN BAPTIST MISSIONARY UNION, 1907 Report.
9 AMERICAN BAPTIST MISSIONARY UNION, 1906 Report.
10 1906 Report, AMERICAN BAPTIST MISSIONARY UNION.
11 AMERICAN BAPTIST MISSIONARY UNION, 1906 Report, p. 88.

12 1906 Report, AMERICAN BAPTIST MISSIONARY UNION, p. 92.
13 BAPTIST MISSIONARY REVIEW, January 1907.
14 AMERICAN BAPTIST MISSIONARY UNION, 1905 Report, p. 165.
15 1906 Report, AMERICAN BAPTIST MISSIONARY UNION, p. 100.
16 AMERICAN BAPTIST MISSIONARY UNION, 1906 Report, p. 101: (cf. Report of C. L. Swanson, Golaghat, 1906: 'the meetings can hardly be described... pleading... weeping... wonderful... impressive...' also Report of A. J. Tuttle, Gauhati: 'more encouraging this year than any time previous.' Archives of the American Baptist Foreign Mission Society, Valley Forge.
17 See AMERICAN BAPTIST MISSIONARY UNION, 1905 Report, pp. 157ff.   18 1905 Report, p. 157ff.
19 1905 Report, p. 69.   20 1905 Report, p. 77.
21 V. H. Sword, BAPTISTS IN ASSAM, p. 11.
22 See J. H. Morris, THE STORY OF OUR FOREIGN MISSION, (Presbyterian Church of Wales), & Herbert Anderson, AMONG THE LUSHAIS, Baptist Missionary Society.
23 J. Meirion Lloyd, ON EVERY HIGH HILL, p. 52.
24 G. R. Lewis, THE LUSHAI HILLS; cf. J. Meirion Lloyd, ON EVERY HIGH HILL, p. 52.
25 J. Meirion Lloyd, p. 53.   26 J. Meirion Lloyd, p. 54.
27 Sidney Evans & Gomer Roberts, CYFROL GOFFA DIWYGIAD, 1904-1905.
28 J. Meirion Lloyd, ON EVERY HIGH HILL, p. 64.
29 The pagans adopted revival procedures, such as singing, hand-clapping, skipping for joy; see J. Meirion Lloyd, p. 55.
30 J. Meirion Lloyd, ON EVERY HIGH HILL, p. 64.
31 Evans & Roberts, CYFROL GOFFA DIWYGIAD, pp. 104 & 107.
32 J. Meirion Lloyd, ON EVERY HIGH HILL, p. 55.
33 M. M. Thomas & R. W. Taylor, TRIBAL AWAKENING, p. 29, Appendix: Naga Tribes.
34 Appendix: Khasia and Jaintia Tribes, p. 23.
35 Appendix: Mizo Tribes (Lushai Hills), p. 24.
36 M. M. Thomas & R. W. Taylor, TRIBAL AWAKENING, p. 61.
37 TRIBAL AWAKENING, p. 226.
38 TRIBAL AWAKENING, p. 228.

Notes on Chapter 17: THE AWAKENING IN ANDHRA

1 J. A. Craig, FORTY YEARS AMONG THE TELUGUS, p. 149.
2 BAPTIST MISSIONARY REVIEW, February 1907, p. 58.
3 CANADIAN BAPTIST TELUGU MISSIONS, 1905 REPORT, p. 2.
4 BAPTIST MISSIONARY REVIEW, February 1907, pp. 227ff.
5 CANADIAN BAPTIST TELUGU MISSIONS, 1906 REPORT, p. 1.
6 CANADIAN BAPTIST TELUGU MISSIONS, 1905 REPORT, p. v.
7 J. A. Craig, FORTY YEARS AMONG THE TELUGUS, p. 150.
8 J. A. Craig, p. 152.   9 J. A. Craig, p. 171.
10 J. A. Craig, p. 152.   11 J. A. Craig, p. 158; cf. CANADIAN BAPTIST TELUGU MISSIONS (1906 Report).
12 See David Downie, FROM MILL TO MISSIONFIELD.
13 David Downie, pp. 50ff.   14 David Downie, pp. 50ff. cf. AMERICAN BAPTIST MISSIONARY UNION, 1905 Report.
15 David Downie, FROM MILL TO MISSIONFIELD, pp. 50ff.
16 David Downie's Reports (23 April 1906 and 18 March 1907) in the Archives of the American Baptist Foreign Mission Society.
17 David Downie, FROM MILL TO MISSIONFIELD, pp. 50ff.

18 AMERICAN BAPTIST MISSIONARY UNION, 1907 Report, p. 114.
19 David Downie, FROM MILL TO MISSIONFIELD, pp. 50ff.
20 AMERICAN BAPTIST MISSIONARY UNION, 1907 Report.
21 Archives, American Baptist Foreign Mission Society, 1906 MS Report of Jacob Heinrichs.
22 J. A. Baker, CONTENDING THE GRADE, p. 103.
23 AMERICAN BAPTIST MISSIONARY UNION, 1905 Report.
24 J. A. Baker, CONTENDING THE GRADE, p. 104.
25 AMERICAN BAPTIST MISSIONARY UNION, 1906 Report.
26 MS Letter of J. A. Baker, 18 April 1906, Archives of American Baptist Foreign Mission Society, Valley Forge.
27 J. A. Baker, CONTENDING THE GRADE, p. 103.
28 AMERICAN BAPTIST MISSIONARY UNION, 1906 Report.
29 J. A. Baker, CONTENDING THE GRADE, p. 105.
30 AMERICAN BAPTIST MISSIONARY UNION, 1906 Report.
31 J. A. Baker, CONTENDING THE GRADE, p. 105.
32 AMERICAN BAPTIST MISSIONARY UNION, 1906 Report.
33 J. A. Baker, CONTENDING THE GRADE, p. 106.
34 AMERICAN BAPTIST MISSIONARY UNION, 1906 Report.
35 See Field Report, Ongole 1906, in the Archives of the American Baptist Foreign Mission and Letter of J.A. Baker, 18 April 1906, citing a total of 245 new believers baptized that month.
36 See AMERICAN BAPTIST MISSIONARY UNION, 1906 Report, p. 114.
37 W. A. Stanton, THE AWAKENING OF INDIA, p. 60.
38 See AMERICAN BAPTIST MISSIONARY UNION, 1906 Report, pp. 115ff.; & MS Letter of W. A. Stanton, 21 March 1907, in the Archives of the American Baptist Foreign Mission Society, Valley Forge.
39 W. A. Stanton, THE AWAKENING OF INDIA, p. 62.
40 W. A. Stanton, p. 63.   41 W. A. Stanton, p. 69.
42 W. A. Stanton, p. 87.   43 W. A. Stanton, p. 96.
44 See AMERICAN BAPTIST MISSIONARY UNION, 1906 Report, p. 115.
45 Canadian Baptist Telugu Missions, REPORT for 1906, p. 61.
46 1906 Report, p. 17.   47 1906 Report, p. 10.
48 1906 Report, p. 7.   49 1906 Report, p. 32.
50 1906 Report, p. 37.   51 1906 Report, p. 38.
52 1906 Report, p. 52.   53 1906 Report, p. 62.
54 1906 Report, p. 66.   55 1906 Report, p. 3.
56 Canadian Baptist Telugu Missions, Kakanada, REPORTS for 1904-1914.
57 BAPTIST MISSIONARY REVIEW, February 1907, p. 74.
58 See C. H. Swavely, ONE HUNDRED YEARS IN THE ANDHRA COUNTRY, p. 19; cf. Drach & Kuder, TELUGU MISSION OF THE LUTHERAN CHURCH, p. 355.
59 M. L. Dolbeer, Junior, HISTORY OF LUTHERANISM IN THE ANDHRADESA, 1959.   60 See Dolbeer, Chapter V.
61 M. L. Dolbeer, p. 292.   62 M. L. Dolbeer, p. 261.
63 M. L. Dolbeer, p. 266.   64 M. L. Dolbeer, p. 288.
65 M. L. Dolbeer, p. 265.   66 M. L. Dolbeer, p. 265.
67 See PROCEEDINGS OF THE CHURCH MISSIONARY SOCIETY, 1907-1908, pp. 164-165; see also Carol Graham, AZARIAH OF DORNAKAL, p. 42.
68 Carol Graham, AZARIAH OF DORNAKAL, p. 31-32.
69 Carol Graham, AZARIAH OF DORNAKAL, p. 42.

Notes on Chapter 18: THE AWAKENING IN TAMILNAD

1 See PROCEEDINGS OF THE CHURCH MISSIONARY SOCIETY, 1905-1906, p. 222.
2 H. S. Dyer, REVIVAL IN INDIA, p. 147.   3 p. 148.
4 See PROCEEDINGS, 1905-1906, pp. 162-163.
5 H. S. Dyer, REVIVAL IN INDIA, p. 113.   6 p. 114.
7 H. S. Dyer, REVIVAL IN INDIA, p. 116.   8 W. E. Vine.
9 Student Volunteer Movement, STUDENTS AND THE PRESENT MISSIONARY CRISIS, p. 257.
10 MISSIONARY REVIEW OF THE WORLD, 1906.
11 H. S. Dyer, REVIVAL IN INDIA, p. 64.   12 p. 150.
13 H. S. Dyer, REVIVAL IN INDIA, pp. 150-151.
14 STUDENTS AND THE PRESENT MISSIONARY CRISIS, p. 257.
15 See PROCEEDINGS OF THE CHURCH MISSIONARY SOCIETY, 1905-1906, p. 240.   16 p. 241.
17 Frank Houghton, AMY CARMICHAEL OF DOHNAVUR, pp. 146ff.
18 Amy Carmichael left voluminous documentation.
19 Frank Houghton, AMY CARMICHAEL OF DOHNAVUR, pp. 146ff.
20 See also A. W. Carmichael, WALKER OF TINNEVELLY.
21 Eugene Stock, THE HISTORY OF THE CHURCH MISSIONARY SOCIETY, Volume III, pp. 544ff; MISSIONARY REVIEW OF THE WORLD, 1889; CHURCH MISSIONARY INTELLIGENCER (July 1888); & E. C. Millard, WHAT HATH GOD WROUGHT.
22 ECUMENICAL MISSIONARY CONFERENCE, New York, 1900, Volume II, p. 116.
23 Y. Samuel, DAVID—AMBASSADOR FROM INDIA, pp. 5ff.
24 Cf. Sherwood Eddy, A PILGRIMAGE OF IDEAS.
25 P. O. Philip, REPORT ON A SURVEY OF INDIA, BURMA & CEYLON, p. 3.
26 Eugene Stock, THE HISTORY OF THE CHURCH MISSIONARY SOCIETY, Volume III, p. 257.   27 Census of Ceylon, 1911.
28 Findlay & Holdsworth, THE HISTORY OF THE WESLEYAN METHODIST MISSIONARY SOCIETY, Volume V, pp. 52 & 107.
29 J. A. Ewing, LANKA: THE BAPTIST MISSION IN CEYLON.
30 INTERNATIONAL REVIEW OF MISSIONS, 1914, pp. 43 & 487.

Notes on Chapter 19: THE AWAKENING IN KERALA

1 E. M. Philip, THE INDIAN CHURCH OF ST. THOMAS, p. 251.
2 L. W. Brown, INDIAN CHRISTIANS OF ST. THOMAS, p. 146.
3 CHRISTIAN HANDBOOK OF INDIA, 1954-1955, p. 173.
4 John Mackenzie, THE CHRISTIAN TASK IN INDIA, p. 210.
5 Y. Samuel, DAVID—AMBASSADOR FROM INDIA, p. 15.
6 N. C. Sargant, DISPERSION OF THE TAMIL CHURCH, p. 74.
7 K. K. Kuruvilla, REVIVAL IN KERALA, pp. 48-51.
8 K. K. Kuruvilla, notes translated by K. V. Cherian.
9 Y. Samuel, DAVID—AMBASSADOR FROM INDIA, p. 20.
10 K. K. Kuruvilla, notes.   11 K. K. Kuruvilla, notes.
12 K. K. Kuruvilla, p. 90.   13 K. K. Kuruvilla, p. 54.
14 See PROCEEDINGS OF THE CHURCH MISSIONARY SOCIETY, 1905-1906, p. 246.
15 MISSIONARY REVIEW OF THE WORLD, 1906, p. 162.
16 LONDON MISSIONARY SOCIETY CHRONICLE, 1905, p. 317.
17 Letter of the Rev. T. K. Benjamin, Kottayam, 31 January 1906, Archives of the Church Missionary Society, London.

18   Letter of the Rev. P. J. Joshua, Kunnankulam, 13 December 1905.
19   Letter of the Rev. K. P. Varkey, Cochin, 30 December 1905.
20   CHRONICLE OF THE LONDON MISSIONARY SOCIETY, 1905, p. 339.
21   REPORT OF THE LONDON MISSIONARY SOCIETY, 1906, p. 124.
22   CHRONICLE OF THE LONDON MISSIONARY SOCIETY, p. 317.
23   cf. REPORTS of the London Missionary Society, 1904 and 1909, Trivandrum figures.
24   Letter of the Rev. J. H. Bishop, Trichur, 13 January 1906.
25   See PROCEEDINGS OF THE CHURCH MISSIONARY SOCIETY, 1905-1906, 1908-1909.
26   A. J. Thottungal, 'History and Growth of the Mar Thoma Church,' M.A. Thesis, School of World Mission, Pasadena, p. 100.
27   Letter of the Rev. J. H. Bishop, Trichur, 13 January, 1906.
28   Letter of the Rev. J. Booth, Kottayam, 27 November 1906.
29   Letter of 27 November 1906.   30   Letter of 27 November 1906.
31   Letter of the Rev. J. Booth, Kottayam, 27 November 1906.
32   MISSIONARY REVIEW OF THE WORLD, 1906, p. 162.
33   See PROCEEDINGS OF THE CHURCH MISSIONARY SOCIETY, 1905-1906.
34   Letter of the Rev. F. N. Askwith, Kottayam, 10 January 1908.
35   Letter of Miss I. A. Baker, Kottayam, 26 November 1907.
36   Letter of the Rev. C. A. Neve, Tiruvalla, 12 December 1907.
37   Letter of the Rev. W. A. Stephens, Pallam, 7 January 1908.
38   Letter of the Rev. F. Bower, Kunnamkulam, 29 November 1907.
39   Letter of the Rev. W. S. Hunt, Trichur, 27 November 1907.
40   Letter of the Rev. T. Walker, Tinnevelly, 29 November 1906.
41   A. W. Carmichael, WALKER OF TINNEVELLY, p. 391.
42   K. K. Kuruvilla, REVIVAL IN KERALA, pp. 61-66, quoting V. P. Mammen.
43   K. K. Kuruvilla, REVIVAL IN KERALA, pp. 61-66.
44   A. J. Thottungal, 'History and Growth of the Mar Thoma Church,' M.A. Thesis, School of World Mission, Pasadena, p. 100.
45   See also C. B. Firth, INDIAN CHURCH HISTORY, pp. 172ff.

Notes on Chapter 20: THE AWAKENING IN KANARA

1   G. M. Thomssen, SAMUEL HEBICH OF INDIA.
2   Findlay & Holdsworth, THE HISTORY OF THE WESLEYAN METHODIST MISSIONARY SOCIETY, Volume V, pp. 262-310.
3   J. M. Thoburn, INDIA AND MALAYSIA, pp. 297ff.
4   The hill country, the valleys and plains were all affected.
5   MISSIONARY REVIEW OF THE WORLD, 1906, p. 542.
6   Letter of R. A. Stott, Tumkur, 15 December 1905, Archives of the Methodist Missionary Society, London.
7   Letter of E. V. Paget, Bangalore, Methodist Archives.
8   See 91st, 92nd and 93rd Reports of the Wesleyan Methodist Missionary Society, 1904-1907, London.
9   92nd Report, Wesleyan Missionary Society, 1906, p. 81.
10 Letter of W. E. Tomlinson, Tumkur, 18 April 1906.
11 94th Report, Wesleyan Missionary Society, 1908, p. 79.
12 93rd Report, p. 88.
13 92nd Report, p. 88.
14 JOURNALS of the Wesleyan Methodist Missionary Society, 1905ff.
15 See A. W. Carmichael, WALKER OF TINNEVELLY.
16 Julius Richter, INDISCHE MISSIONSGESCHICHTE, passim.

Notes on Chapter 21: AWAKENINGS IN NORTH INDIA

1 Nicol MacNicol, PANDITA RAMABAI, p. 64.
2 Nicol MacNicol, PANDITA RAMABAI, p. 61.
3 There were 24,000,000 widows in India, every fifth female in the whole population. MISSIONARY REVIEW, 1904, p. 274.
4 H. S. Dyer, REVIVAL IN INDIA, p. 41.
5 Nicol MacNicol, PANDITA RAMABAI, p. 117.
6 J. C. Winslow, NARAYAN VAMAN TILAK, p. 35.
7 Cf. Nicol MacNicol, PANDITA RAMABAI, & MISSIONARY REVIEW OF THE WORLD, 1906, p. 552.
8 H. S. Dyer, REVIVAL IN INDIA, p. 44.
9 H. S. Dyer, REVIVAL IN INDIA, p. 44.
10 H. S. Dyer, PANDITA RAMABAI, p. 11.
11 H. S. Dyer, REVIVAL IN INDIA, p. 55.
12 Nicol MacNicol, PANDITA RAMABAI, p. 118.
13 Nicol MacNicol, PANDITA RAMABAI, p. 117.
14 H. S. Dyer, REVIVAL IN INDIA, p. 47.
15 G. H. Lang, AN ORDERED LIFE, p. 134.
16 H. S. Dyer, REVIVAL IN INDIA, p. 48.   17 p. 49.
18 H. S. Dyer, REVIVAL IN INDIA, p. 53.   19 p. 61.
20 H. S. Dyer, REVIVAL IN INDIA, p. 62.   21 p. 63.
22 H. S. Dyer, REVIVAL IN INDIA, p. 63.   22 p. 63.
24 H. S. Dyer, REVIVAL IN INDIA, p. 67.   25 p. 68.
26 MISSIONARY REVIEW OF THE WORLD, 1906, p. 162.
27 H. S. Dyer, REVIVAL IN INDIA, p. 72.
28 Reports of the Missionary and Benevolent Boards to the General Assembly of the Presbyterian Church in the United States of America, 1905, Letter of A. L. Wiley, Ratnigiri, p. 206.
29 Letter of A. L. Wiley, Ratnigiri, p. 206.
30 MISSIONARY REVIEW OF THE WORLD, 1906, p. 169.
31 H. S. Dyer, REVIVAL IN INDIA, pp. 89ff.
32 H. S. Dyer, REVIVAL IN INDIA, p. 93.
33 MISSIONARY REVIEW OF THE WORLD, 1906, p. 169.
34 H. S. Dyer, REVIVAL IN INDIA, pp. 103ff.
35 Student Volunteer Movement, STUDENTS AND THE MISSIONARY CRUSADE, pp. 380ff.
36 H. S. Dyer, REVIVAL IN INDIA, pp. 97ff.
37 Basil Miller, PRAYING HYDE, pp. 47-48.
38 Basil Miller, PRAYING HYDE, p. 48.
39 H. S. Dyer, REVIVAL IN INDIA, pp. 97ff.
40 See E. D. Anderson, IN THE SHADOW OF THE HIMALAYAS, pp. 203ff.
41 Basil Miller, PRAYING HYDE, p. 63.
42 J. Pengwern Jones, in E. G. Carre, PRAYING HYDE, pp. 97ff.
43 H. S. Dyer, REVIVAL IN INDIA, p. 98.
44 See F. E. Stock, PEOPLE MOVEMENTS IN THE PUNJAB, Church of Scotland Mission graphs and statistics.
45 See PROCEEDINGS OF THE CHURCH MISSIONARY SOCIETY, 1905-1906, p. 188.
46 See PROCEEDINGS OF THE CHURCH MISSIONARY SOCIETY, 1907-1908, p. 147.
47 See F. E. Stock, PEOPLE MOVEMENTS IN THE PUNJAB, Church of England graphs and statistics.
48 H. S. Dyer, REVIVAL IN INDIA, p. 99.
49 E. G. Carre, PRAYING HYDE, pp. 32ff; 37ff.

50 Minute of Record, General Assembly of the Presbyterian Church of India, Allahabad, 31st December 1913, giving 12th February 1912 at Northampton, Massachusetts as date and place of death of John Nelson Hyde, buried at Carthage, Illinois, 20th February.
51 See F. E. Stock, PEOPLE MOVEMENTS IN THE PUNJAB, passim.
52 H. S. Dyer, REVIVAL IN INDIA, p. 101.
53 Archives of the General Assembly of the Presbyterian Church in the United States of America, Philadelphia, Pennsylvania.
54 Archives of the General Assembly of the Presbyterian Church in the United States of America, microfilm report 267, letters of E. M. Wherry, 5 October, 7 December 1905.
55 Reports of the Missionary and Benevolent Boards to the General Assembly of the Presbyterian Church in the United States of America, 1906, p. 177.
56 Microfilm report 266, Letter of C. H. Mattison, 4 December 1905, Archives, Philadelphia, Pennsylvania.
57 Archives of the General Assembly of the Presbyterian Church in the United States of America, Philadelphia, Pennsylvania.
58 ASSEMBLY HERALD, Philadelphia, April 1907.
59 INTERNATIONAL REVIEW OF MISSIONS, 1913, p. 442.
60 Report of the Rev. J. N. Hyde, REVIVAL IN INDIA, p. 102.
61 H. S. Dyer, REVIVAL IN INDIA, p. 101.
62 H. S. Dyer, REVIVAL IN INDIA, p. 102.
63 Missionaries' correspondence seemed to play a major part in the communication of news of revival from Indian church to church.
64 Almora, capital town of Kumaon district, United Provinces.
65 H. S. Dyer, REVIVAL IN INDIA, p. 59.
66 H. S. Dyer, REVIVAL IN INDIA, p. 59.
67 H. S. Dyer, REVIVAL IN INDIA, p. 60.
68 See PROCEEDINGS OF THE CHURCH MISSIONARY SOCIETY, 1905-1906, p. 171; cf. REVIVAL IN INDIA, p. 62.
69 H. S. Dyer, REVIVAL IN INDIA, p. 62.
70 H. S. Dyer, REVIVAL IN INDIA, p. 124 & 64.
71 H. S. Dyer, REVIVAL IN INDIA, p. 125.   72 p. 125.
73 H. S. Dyer, REVIVAL IN INDIA, p. 126.   74 p. 126.
75 MISSIONARY REVIEW OF THE WORLD, 1907, p. 564.
76 See PROCEEDINGS OF THE CHURCH MISSIONARY SOCIETY, 1905-1906, p. 164.
77 A. W. Carmichael, WALKER OF TINNEVELLY, p. 369.
78 A. W. Carmichael, WALKER OF TINNEVELLY, p. 356.
79 MISSIONARY REVIEW OF THE WORLD, 1907, p. 563; and BAPTIST MISSIONARY REVIEW, February 1907.
80 H. S. Dyer, REVIVAL IN INDIA, pp. 119ff.
81 H. S. Dyer, REVIVAL IN INDIA, p. 122.
82 H. S. Dyer, REVIVAL IN INDIA, p. 122.   83 p. 123.
84 H. S. Dyer, REVIVAL IN INDIA, p. 124.   85 p. 124.
86 H. S. Dyer, REVIVAL IN INDIA, p. 124.
87 Student Volunteer Movement, STUDENTS AND THE PRESENT MISSIONARY CRISIS, p. 257.
88 See ALLIANCE WEEKLY, 1907, p. 234.
89 INTERNATIONAL REVIEW OF MISSIONS, 1912, p. 28.
90 THE YEAR BOOK OF MISSIONS IN INDIA (1912) conceded to Roman Catholics a 25% growth (279,251) during the revival decade, to Syrians (including Mar Thoma) 27% and to Protestants 42.5% (488,982).

Notes on Chapter 22: PRE-INDEPENDENCE EVANGELISM

1 INTERNATIONAL REVIEW OF MISSIONS, 1912, p. 442.
2 MISSIONARY REVIEW OF THE WORLD, 1912, pp. 85-86.
3 See YEAR BOOK OF MISSIONS IN INDIA, 1912.
4 MISSIONARY REVIEW OF THE WORLD, 1912, pp. 85-86.
5 See YEAR BOOK OF MISSIONS IN INDIA, 1912.
6 INTERNATIONAL REVIEW OF MISSIONS, 1912, p. 28.
7 CATHOLIC DIRECTORY OF INDIA, 1913, p. 435.
8 See YEAR BOOK OF MISSIONS IN INDIA, 1912.
9 See Beach & St. John for WORLD STATISTICS OF FOREIGN MISSIONS, p. 59; Beach & Fahs, WORLD MISSIONARY ATLAS, p. 76; J. I. Parker, DIRECTORY OF WORLD MISSIONS, p. 18.
10 Personal knowledge; cf. E. Stanley Jones, THE CHRIST OF THE INDIAN ROAD; A SONG OF ASCENTS, etc.
11 A. J. Appasamy, SUNDAR SINGH, pp. 27ff.
12 see C. F. Andrews, SADHU SUNDAR SINGH, passim.
13 A. J. Appasamy, SUNDAY SINGH, pp. 113ff.
14 Dr. E. M. Wherry, for example.
15 A. J. Appasamy, SUNDAR SINGH, p. 129ff.
16 See NEW YORK SUN, 11 June 1920.
17 A. J. Appasamy, SUNDAR SINGH, pp. 147ff.
18 See T. E. Riddle, VISION AND CALL, for an account of the search for the missing Sundar Singh.
19 Donald Gee, THE PENTECOSTAL MOVEMENT, p. 28.
20 ALLIANCE WEEKLY, 16 June 1908.
21 See Donald Gee, THE PENTECOSTAL MOVEMENT, p. 47; & Nils Bloch-Hoell, THE PENTECOSTAL MOVEMENT, p. 68.
22 N. K. Dutt, PENTECOSTAL WORK IN EASTERN INDIA, p. 1.
23 Stanley Frodsham, WITH SIGNS FOLLOWING, p. 114.
24 Ivan R. Mark, 'The Origin and Development of the Charismatic Movement in India,' M.Th. Thesis, Howard University, 1973.
25 Kuruvilla Report, cited by Ivan R. Mark.
26 C. W. Conn, WHERE THE SAINTS HAVE TROD, p. 219.
27 P. D. Johnson, THE PROMISE FULFILLED, p. 84.
28 Eric Andreasson, PENTECOST IN SOUTH INDIA, p. 1.
29 W. J. Hollenweger, THE PENTECOSTALS, p. 67.
30 J. T. Nicholl, PENTECOSTALISM, p. 175.
31 P. D. Johnson, THE PROMISE FULFILLED, p. 127.
32 MISSIONARY REVIEW OF THE WORLD, 1913, pp. 622 & 470; 1914, pp. 84 & 231.
33 MISSIONARY REVIEW OF THE WORLD, 1916, p. 83.
34 Bengt Sundkler, THE CHURCH IN SOUTH INDIA, p. 83; see CHURCH MISSIONARY REVIEW, June 1914.
35 MISSIONARY REVIEW OF THE WORLD, 1918, p. 388.
36 George Samuel & K. C. Daniel, 'Awakenings in South India since 1914,' unpublished paper, School of World Mission, Pasadena.
37 See A. J. Thottungal, 'Revival and Church Growth in Kerala,' unpublished paper, School of World Mission, Pasadena.
38 E. Stanley Jones, in CHRISTIAN CENTURY, 1947, p. 1146.
39 See J. T. Seamands, 'A Church Growth Study of the Methodist Church in the South India and Hyderabad Conferences,' D.Theol. Dissertation, Senate of Serampore College, p. 67.
40 Hyderabad Conference Minutes.   41 J. T. Seamands, pp. 90ff.
42 See J. W. Pickett, CHRISTIAN MASS MOVEMENTS IN INDIA, 'The Sudra Movement in the Telugu Country.'

43 See F. F. Gledstone, THE CHURCH MISSIONARY SOCIETY IN THE TELUGU COUNTRY, pp. 19ff; and E. R. Clough, SOCIAL CHRISTIANITY IN THE ORIENT, p. 92.
44 INTERNATIONAL REVIEW OF MISSIONS, 1918, p. 480.
45 See Archives of the Presbyterian Church in the U.S.A., 1919-20; & INTERNATIONAL REVIEW OF MISSIONS, 1919, p. 195.
46 INTERNATIONAL REVIEW OF MISSIONS, 1917, p. 195.
47 See SVENSK MISSION OCH INDISK KYRKA (Sandgren), and INTERNATIONAL REVIEW OF MISSIONS, 1923, p. 220.
48 See MISSIONARY REVIEW OF THE WORLD, 1926, p. 301; & 1928, p. 317.
49 INTERNATIONAL REVIEW OF MISSIONS, 1937, p. 35.
50 R. N. Davis, Editor, THE CHALLENGE OF CENTRAL INDIA, pp. 180ff.
51 MISSIONARY REVIEW OF THE WORLD, 1931, p. 249.
52 Report of A. W. Stanton, 1933, in the Archives, American Baptist Foreign Mission Society, Valley Forge, Pennsylvania.
53 MISSIONARY REVIEW OF THE WORLD, 1935, p. 90.
54 Report in MISSIONARY REVIEW, 1936, p. 266.
55 INTERNATIONAL REVIEW OF MISSIONS, 1937, p. 35.
56 Eyre Chatterton, A HISTORY OF THE CHURCH OF ENGLAND IN INDIA, pp. 324ff; INTERNATIONAL REVIEW, 1937, p. 36.
57 INTERNATIONAL REVIEW OF MISSIONS, 1938, p. 36.
58 See A. J. Thottungal, 'Revival and Church Growth in Kerala.'
59 MISSIONARY REVIEW OF THE WORLD, 1931, pp. 54 & 154.
60 INTERNATIONAL REVIEW OF MISSIONS, 1937, p. 36; and MISSIONARY REVIEW OF THE WORLD, 1935, p. 247.
61 Prayer letters of Dr. Howard Guinness, 1937; personal knowledge.
62 Yesupadam Bandela, 'A Revival in Andhra,' unpublished paper, School of World mission, Pasadena.
63 John Thannickal, 'The Origin of the Pentecostal Movement in South India,' unpublished paper, School of World Mission, Pasadena.
64 T. S. Abraham, THE PENTECOSTAL MOVEMENT, p. 1.
65 P. M. Samuel, cited by Ivan R. Mark, p. 108.
66 P. D. Johnson, THE PROMISE FULFILLED, p. 126.
67 See J. I. Parker, INTERPRETATIVE SURVEY OF THE WORLD MISSION OF THE CHRISTIAN CHURCH, p. 18.
68 Samuel Paul, 'A Short Summary of the Life of Pastor Paul,' cited by Ivan R. Mark, pp. 116ff.
69 T. B. Rehnstrom, A MISSIONARY ENTERPRISE, p. 47.
70 Daniel Smith, BAKHT SINGH OF INDIA, pp. 31-32.
71 Indian and British versions of the agitation differ somewhat.
72 This was one of the incidents of the Khalifat Controversy.
73 F. E. Stock, PEOPLE MOVEMENTS IN THE PUNJAB, pp. 168ff.
74 F. E. Stock, pp. 169ff.   75 Personal knowledge.
76 Eleanore Llewellyn, 'Bakht Singh of India,' UNFORGETTABLE DISCIPLES, Presbyterian Church in the U. S. A., 1942.
77 MISSIONARY REVIEW OF THE WORLD, 1938, pp. 151-152.
78 Reminiscences of Dr. Donald A. McGavran.
79 Conversation with Bakht Singh.   80 F. E. Stock, p. 172.
81 Paul Shimmon, MASSACRES OF SYRIAN CHRISTIANS IN N.W. PERSIA AND KURDISTAN, passim.
82 See W. W. Rockwell, PITIFUL PLIGHT OF THE ASSYRIAN CHRISTIANS, passim.
83 J. O. Peters, TESTS AND TRIUMPHS OF ARMENIANS, pp. 45ff.
84 Information given the writer during a visit to Soviet Armenia.

Notes on Chapter 23: IN THE TRAVAIL OF NATIONHOOD

1. P. C. Mazamdar, THE INTERPRETER, Calcutta, 1889.
2. See PROCEEDINGS OF THE CHURCH MISSIONARY SOCIETY, 1922; & A. D. Lindsay, REPORT OF THE COMMISSION ON CHRISTIAN HIGHER EDUCATION IN INDIA, 1931.
3. A. D. Lindsay, REPORT, pp. 12ff.
4. A. D. Lindsay, REPORT, pp. 373-374.
5. Hector Bolitho, JINNAH, CREATOR OF PAKISTAN.
6. See NATIONAL CHRISTIAN COUNCIL REVIEW, 1949, Volume LXIX, p. 151.
7. Five years later, the total had risen to 5656 for the Republic of India only, WORLD CHRISTIAN HANDBOOK, 1957, pp. 38, 57.
8. MADRAS MAIL, 1st May 1953.
9. Personal knowledge, visiting India in 1954.
10. See CHRISTIAN MISSIONARY ACTIVITIES INQUIRY REPORT, Madhya Pradesh, 1954, Volume I, p. 125.
11. National Christian Council of India, 13th Triennal Session, held at Allahabad, 1954.
12. CHRISTIANITY TODAY, 1st March 1968, p. 51.

Notes on Chapter 24: EVANGELICAL RESURGENCE IN INDIA

1. South India Conference Minutes, 1948, pp. 73-74.
2. Bengt Sundkler, THE CHURCH OF SOUTH INDIA.
3. See R. R. Rajamani, MONSOON DAYBREAK, edited by Angus I. Kinnear, pp. 85ff.
4. George Samuel & K. C. Daniel, 'Awakenings in South India since 1914,' unpublished paper, School of World Mission, Pasadena.
5. Conversation with Bakht Singh, 1970.
6. R. J. McMahon, TO GOD BE THE GLORY, An Account of the Evangelical Fellowship of India's First Twenty Years.
7. R. J. McMahon, TO GOD BE THE GLORY, pp. 13ff.
8. Floyd Banker, GOD CAME TO GUJERAT, passim.
9. R. J. McMahon, TO GOD BE THE GLORY, pp. 17-18.
10. Another speaker was Mr. Norman P. Grubb, (p. 20)
11. A. J. Appasamy, WRITE THE VISION, p. 169.
12. Unpublished papers.
13. Maramon Convention, largest of its kind in the world.
14. R. J. McMahon, TO GOD BE THE GLORY, p. 21.
15. Unpublished papers.
16. See A. J. Thottungal, 'Revival and Church Growth in Kerala,' unpublished paper, School of World Mission, Pasadena.
17. Unpublished letters.
18. Mr. K. N. Daniel was a very sincere Evangelical Christian who seemed unconcerned about going to law before unbelievers.
19. George Samuel & K. C. Daniel, 'Awakenings in South India since 1914,' unpublished paper, School of World Mission, Pasadena.
20. John Thannickal, 'The Origin of the Pentecostal Movement in South India,' unpublished paper, School of World Mission.
21. A. J. Appasamy, A BISHOP'S STORY, Chapter II.
22. A. J. Appasamy, WRITE THE VISION, p. 8.
23. A. J. Appasamy, A BISHOP'S STORY, pp. 85ff.
24. A. J. Appasamy, A SPIRITUAL AWAKENING IN SOUTH INDIA, Calcutta, undated.
25. A. J. Appasamy, WRITE THE VISION, p. 203.

26 A. J. Appasamy, THE REVIVAL MINISTRY OF DR. EDWIN ORR IN THE COIMBATORE DIOCESE, passim.
27 See Yesupadam Bandela, 'Revival in Andhra, 1940,' unpublished paper, School of World Mission, Pasadena.
28 R. J. McMahon, TO GOD BE THE GLORY, pp. 23ff.
29 On Dr. Haqq's campaign, see McMahon, pp. 28ff.
30 R. J. McMahon, TO GOD BE THE GLORY, p. 27.
31 The writer has shared fellowship with Dr. Ben Wati in Asia, Europe and America. See R. J. McMahon, p. 31.
32 R. J. McMahon, TO GOD BE THE GLORY, pp. 38ff.
33 A Malayali, Paul Sudhakar exercised an all-India ministry.
34 Personal knowledge of these and many other Indian evangelists.
35 Many of these institutions are affiliated with the Senate of Serampore College, possessing a Danish university charter.
36 J. Edwin Orr, CAMPUS AFLAME, p. 181.
37 Bharat Khristya Sahitya Sangh, McMahon, pp. 32-34.
38 R. J. McMahon, TO GOD BE THE GLORY, pp. 34-35.
39 C.E.E.F.I., McMahon, pp. 35-36.
40 See K. Imotemjem Aier, 'The Growth of the Baptist Churches of Meghalaya in North East India, M.A. Thesis, School of World Mission, Pasadena.
41 ANNUAL REPORT OF THE AMERICAN BAPTIST FOREIGN MISSION SOCIETY, 1926, pp. 103, 232-233; 1927, pp. 244-245; 1928, 1929, 1930, passim.
42 K. Imotemjem Aier, Chapter VI.
43 Rieweh Robert Cunville, 'A Study of the Growth of the Presbyterian Church in the Khasi and Jaintia Hills,' M.A, Thesis, School of World Mission, Pasadena.
44 EVANGELICAL FELLOWSHIP, XVII, 1, p. 30; 2, p. 40.
45 See P. T. Philip, 'The Growth of the Baptist Churches of Tribal Nagaland,' M. A. thesis, School of World Mission, Pasadena.
46 See Nehuli Angami, REVIVAL FIRES IN NAGALAND, passim.
47 CHRISTIANITY TODAY.
48 Baptist Missionary Society REPORT, 1921.
49 E. L. Mendus, THE DIARY OF A JUNGLE MISSIONARY, p. 82.
50 GLAD TIDINGS, July 1961, J. Meirion Lloyd, 'The Mizo District.'
51 M. M. Thomas & R. W. Taylor, TRIBAL AWAKENING, pp. 19ff.
52 TRIBAL AWAKENING, p. 61.

Notes on Chapter 25: AWAKENINGS IN SOUTHERN ASIA

1 See W. A. Stanton, FORTY YEARS AMONG THE TELUGUS, pp. 64 & 67.
2 BAPTIST MISSIONARY REVIEW, Editorial, January 1907.
3 A. W. Carmichael, WALKER OF TINNEVELLY, p. 355.
4 MISSIONARY REVIEW OF THE WORLD, 1906, p. 298.
5 MISSIONARY REVIEW OF THE WORLD, 1906, p. 234.
6 W. A. Stanton, p. 68.
7 ALLIANCE WEEKLY, 1907, p. 234.
8 A. W. Carmichael, WALKER OF TINNEVELLY, p. 389.
9 Canadian Baptist Telugu Missions REPORT, 1905.
10 These conclusions are derived principally from India.

SELECT BIBLIOGRAPHY

Diaries, Documents, Journals, Letters, Minutes & Reports

American Baptist Foreign Mission Society, Valley Forge, Pennsylvania.
American Board of Commissioners for Foreign Missions, Boston.
American Lutheran Church, Dubuque, Iowa.
Baptist Missionary Society, London.
Baptist Theological Seminary, Ramapatnam, Andhra.
Christian and Missionary Alliance, New York.
Church Missionary Society, London.
Church of Scotland, Edinburgh.
London Missionary Society, London.
India Office, London.
Methodist Missionary Society, London.
Presbyterian Church in Ireland, Belfast.
Presbyterian Church of Wales, Aberystwyth.
Serampore College, Serampore, Calcutta.
United Methodist Church, Nashville.
United Presbyterian Church, Philadelphia.

Periodicals

ALLIANCE WEEKLY, New York.
AMERICAN BAPTIST MISSIONARY UNION REPORTS, Boston.
ASSEMBLY HERALD, Philadelphia.
BAPTIST MISSIONARY HERALD, Boston.
BAPTIST MISSIONARY MAGAZINE, Boston.
BAPTIST MISSIONARY REVIEW, Guntur.
BOMBAY GUARDIAN, Bombay.
CANADIAN BAPTIST TELUGU MISSIONS REPORTS, Madras.
THE CHRISTIAN, London.
CHRISTIANITY TODAY, Washington, D.C.
CHRONICLE OF THE LONDON MISSIONARY SOCIETY, London.
CHURCH MISSIONARY INTELLIGENCER, London.
CHURCH MISSIONARY RECORD, Madras.
THE FRIEND OF INDIA, Serampore.
INDIAN WATCHMAN, Madras.
INTERNATIONAL REVIEW OF MISSIONS, London.
JAPAN EVANGELIST, Tokyo.
JOURNAL, SOUTH INDIA METHODIST CONFERENCE, Madras.
JOURNAL, METHODIST EPISCOPAL CHURCH, Nashville.
DE KERKBODE, Cape Town.
MADRAS MAIL, Madras.
MISSIONARY HERALD, Boston.
MISSIONARY REGISTER, London.
MISSIONARY REVIEW OF THE WORLD, New York.
PROCEEDINGS OF THE CHURCH MISSIONARY SOCIETY, London.
REPORTS OF THE MISSIONARY AND BENEVOLENT BOARDS OF PRESBYTERIAN CHURCH IN THE U.S.A., Philadelphia.
THE REVIVAL, London.
THE STATESMAN'S YEAR BOOKS, London.

Published Books

Abraham, T. S., THE PENTECOSTAL MOVEMENT, Kumbanad, 1969.
Anderson, E. D., IN THE SHADOW OF THE HIMALAYAS, Philadelphia, 1942.
Anderson, Herbert, AMONG THE LUSHAIS, London, 1930.
Anderson, Rufus, HISTORY OF THE MISSION OF THE AMERICAN BOARD TO THE ORIENTAL CHURCHES, Boston, 1872.
Andreasson, Eric, PENTECOST IN SOUTH INDIA, Dehra Dun, 1972.
Angami, Nehuli, REVIVAL FIRES IN NAGALAND, Dallas, undated.
Appasamy, A. J., SUNDAR SINGH: A BIOGRAPHY, London, 1958.
Appasamy, A. J., A BISHOP'S STORY, Madras, 1969.
Appasamy, A. J., A SPIRITUAL AWAKENING IN SOUTH INDIA, Calcutta, 1954.
Appasamy, A. J., THE REVIVAL MINISTRY OF DR. EDWIN ORR IN THE COIMBATORE DIOCESE, Mysore, 1958.
Appasamy, A. J., WRITE THE VISION! London, 1964.
Baago, Kaj, HISTORY OF THE NATIONAL CHRISTIAN COUNCIL OF INDIA, Nagpur, 1965.
Baker, J. A., CONTENDING THE GRADE, Asheville, 1947.
Banker, Floyd, GOD CAME TO GUJERAT, Surat, 1953.
Barton, J. L., DAYBREAK IN TURKEY, Boston, 1908.
Bateman, Josiah, THE LIFE OF DANIEL WILSON, Boston, 1860.
Beach & St. John, WORLD STATISTICS OF CHRISTIAN MISSIONS, New York, 1916.
Bone, G. Hyde, & M. Hyde Hall, THE LIFE AND LETTERS OF PRAYING HYDE, Springfield, Illinois, undated.
Boulger, D. C., LORD WILLIAM BENTINCK, Oxford, 1897.
Braidwood, John, LIFE AND LABOURS OF JOHN ANDERSON & ROBERT JOHNSON, MADRAS, London, 1862.
Braisted, P. J., INDIAN NATIONALISM AND THE CHRISTIAN COLLEGES, New York, 1935.
Bromley, E. B., THEY WERE MEN SENT FROM GOD, Bangalore, 1937.
Brown, L. W., THE INDIAN CHRISTIANS OF SAINT THOMAS, Cambridge, 1956.
Bryan, Ronald, ALL IN A DAY'S WORK, London, 1954.
Butler, Clementina, WILLIAM BUTLER, THE FOUNDER OF TWO (METHODIST) MISSIONS, New York, 1902.
Carey, S. Pearce, WILLIAM CAREY, London, 1924.
Carmichael, A. W., WALKER OF TINNEVELLY, London, 1916.
Carre, E. G., with F. A. McGaw, Pengwern Jones and R. McCheyne Paterson, PRAYING HYDE: the Official Life, London, undated.
Chamberlain, Mrs. W. I., FIFTY YEARS IN FOREIGN FIELDS, New York, 1925.
Chatterton, Eyre, A HISTORY OF THE CHURCH OF ENGLAND IN INDIA, London, 1924.
Cheriyan, P., THE MALABAR CHRISTIANS AND THE CHURCH MISSIONARY SOCIETY, Kottayam, 1935.
CHRISTIAN ENDEAVOUR MANUAL, Agra, 1909.
CHRISTIAN HANDBOOK OF INDIA, Delhi, 1954-55.
Christian Medical Association of India, TALES FROM THE INNS OF HEALING, Nagpur, 1942.
Clough, E. R., SOCIAL CHRISTIANITY IN THE ORIENT, New York, 1914.
Conn, C. W., WHERE THE SAINTS HAVE TROD, Cleveland, 1955.

Clough, J. E., FROM DARKNESS TO LIGHT, Philadelphia, 1882.
Davis, R. N., Editor, THE CHALLENGE OF CENTRAL INDIA, Winona Lake, Indiana, 1954.
Day, Lal Behari, RECOLLECTIONS OF ALEXANDER DUFF AND THE MISSION COLLEGE AT CALCUTTA, London, 1879.
Dolbeer, Martin L., A HISTORY OF LUTHERANISM IN THE ANDHRADESA, New York, 1959.
Downie, David, FROM MILL TO MISSION FIELD, Philadelphia, 1928.
Downie, David, THE LONE STAR: HISTORY OF THE TELUGU MISSION, Philadelphia, 1893.
Downs, F. S., THE MIGHTY WORKS OF GOD: BAPTIST CHURCHES IN NORTHEAST INDIA, Gauhati, 1971.
Drach & Kuder, THE TELUGU MISSION OF THE EVANGELICAL LUTHERAN CHURCH, Philadelphia, 1914.
Du Plessis, J., THE LIFE OF ANDREW MURRAY, London, 1919.
Dutt, N. K., PENTECOSTAL WORK IN EASTERN INDIA, Calcutta.
Dyer, Helen S., PANDITA RAMABAI, London, undated.
Dyer, Helen S., REVIVAL IN INDIA, London, 1907.
ECUMENICAL MISSIONARY CONFERENCE, New York, 1900.
Eddy, G. Sherwood, INDIA AWAKENING, New York, 1911.
Eddy, G. Sherwood, A PILGRIMAGE OF IDEAS, New York, 1934.
Ewing, J. A., LANKA: THE RESPLENDENT ISLE, the Story of the Baptist Mission in Ceylon, London, 1920.
Findlay, G. G. & W. W. Holdsworth, HISTORY OF THE WESLEYAN METHODIST MISSIONARY SOCIETY, 5 Volumes, London, 1921-4.
Firth, C. B., AN INTRODUCTION TO INDIAN CHURCH HISTORY, Madras, 1961.
Fleming, J. R., A HISTORY OF THE CHURCH IN SCOTLAND, 1875-1929, Edinburgh, 1933.
Gerdener, G. B. A., RECENT DEVELOPMENTS IN THE SOUTH AFRICAN MISSION FIELD, London, 1958.
Germann, Walter, MISSIONAR CHRISTIAN FRIEDRICH SCHWARTZ, Erlangen, 1870.
Germann, Walter, ZIEGENBALG UND PLUTSCHAU, Erlangen, 1868.
Gledstone, F. F., THE CHURCH MISSIONARY SOCIETY TELUGU MISSION, Mysore, 1942.
Glover, R. H., THE PROGRESS OF WORLD WIDE MISSIONS, New York, 1925.
Gogerly, George, THE PIONEERS: EARLY CHRISTIAN MISSIONS IN BENGAL, London, undated.
Gordon, Andrew, OUR INDIA MISSION: United Presbyterian Church of North America, Philadelphia, 1888.
Graham, Carol, AZARIAH OF DORNAKAL, London, 1946.
Groves, Mrs., ANTHONY NORRIS GROVES: HIS LETTERS AND JOURNALS, London, 1856.
Hacker, I. H., A HUNDRED YEARS IN TRAVANCORE, 1806-1906, London, 1908.
Halliday, J. G., THE LIFE OF SAMUEL HEBICH, by Two of His Fellow-Labourers (Gundert & Mogling), London, 1876.
Hartog, Sir Philip, SOME ASPECTS OF INDIAN EDUCATION, PAST AND PRESENT, London, 1939.
Harvard, W. M., A NARRATIVE OF THE MISSION TO CEYLON AND INDIA FOUNDED BY THOMAS COKE, London, 1823.
Hess, G. R., SAM HIGGINBOTHAM OF ALLAHABAD, New York, 1967.

Hewat, E. G. K., CHRIST AND WESTERN INDIA, Bombay, 1950.
Higginbotham, Sam, THE GOSPEL AND THE PLOW, New York, 1921.
Hole, Charles, EARLY HISTORY OF THE CHURCH MISSIONARY SOCIETY, London, 1896.
Hollenweger, W. J., THE PENTECOSTALS, London, 1972.
Hollister, J. N., THE CENTENARY OF THE METHODIST CHURCH IN SOUTHERN ASIA, Lucknow, 1956.
Holmes, T. R. E., A HISTORY OF THE INDIAN MUTINY, London, 1913.
Hoskins, Mrs. Robert, CLARA A. SWAIN, M.D., FIRST MEDICAL MISSIONARY TO THE WOMEN OF THE ORIENT, Boston, 1912.
Houghton, Frank, AMY CARMICHAEL OF DOHNAVUR, London, 1954.
Hunt, W. S., THE ANGLICAN CHURCH IN TRAVANCORE AND COCHIN, Kottayam, 1933.
Hutton, J. H., CASTE IN INDIA, Bombay, 1951.
Ingham, Kenneth, REFORMERS IN INDIA, 1793-1833, London, 1956.
Jackson, John, A HISTORY OF THE MISSION TO LEPERS IN INDIA, London, 1910.
Jeffrey, M. P., DR. IDA: INDIA, THE LIFE STORY OF IDA S. SCUDDER, New York, 1938.
Jeffrey, Robert, INDIAN MISSION OF THE IRISH PRESBYTERIAN CHURCH, London, 1890.
Johnson, P. D., THE PROMISE FULFILLED, Trivandrum, 1968.
Jones, E. Stanley, THE CHRIST OF THE INDIAN ROAD, New York, 1925.
Jones, E. Stanley, A SONG OF ASCENTS, Nashville, 1968.
Jones, J. Pengwern, INDIA AWAKE! Calcutta, 1906.
Jones, R. B., RENT HEAVENS, London, 1930.
Karsten, Herman, GESCHICHTE DER EVANGELISHE-LUTHERISCH MISSION IN LEIPZIG, Leipzig, 1893.
Kruger, Wilhelm, DR. FRIEDRICH RIBBENTROP, Bremen, 1873.
Kuruvilla, K. K., REVIVALS IN KERALA, Kottayam, 1950.
Lang, G. H., AN ORDERED LIFE, Autobiography, London, 1919.
Lang, G. H., HISTORY AND DIARIES OF AN INDIAN CHRISTIAN: J. C. AROOLAPPEN, London, 1939.
Latourette, K. S., A HISTORY OF THE EXPANSION OF CHRISTIANITY, New York, 1941-44.
Lindsay, A. D., CHRISTIAN HIGHER EDUCATION IN INDIA, Oxford, 1931.
Lewis, G. R., THE LUSHAI HILLS, London, 1907.
Lloyd, J. Meirion, ON EVERY HIGH HILL, London, 1950.
Lovett, Richard, HISTORY OF THE LONDON MISSIONARY SOCIETY, 1795-1895, London, 1899, 2 Volumes.
McConaughy, David, PIONEERING WITH CHRIST, New York, 1941.
MacDonald, J. Ramsay, THE AWAKENING OF INDIA, London, 1910.
McGaw, Francis A., PRAYING HYDE, Chicago, 1933.
Mackenzie, F. A., BOOTH-TUCKER, SADHU AND SAINT, London, 1930.
Mackenzie, John, THE CHRISTIAN TASK IN INDIA, London, 1920.
McMahon, R. J., TO GOD BE THE GLORY, Evangelical Fellowship of India's First Twenty Years, 195-1971, New Delhi, 1970.
MacNicol, Nicol, PANDITA RAMABAI, Calcutta, 1926.
Manshardt, Clifford, CHRISTIANITY IN A CHANGING INDIA, Calcutta, 1933.

Marshman, J. C., THE LIFE AND TIMES OF CAREY, MARSHMAN AND WARD, London, 1859.
Mendus, E. L., THE DIARY OF A JUNGLE MISSIONARY, Liverpool, 1956.
Miller, Basil, PRAYING HYDE, Grand Rapids, 1943.
Morris, Henry, THE LIFE OF CHARLES GRANT, London, 1904.
Morris, J. H., THE STORY OF OUR FOREIGN MISSION (Presbyterian Church of Wales), Liverpool, 1930.
Moscrop, Thos. & A. E. Restarick, CEYLON AND ITS METHODISTS, London, undated.
Neill, Stephen C., BUILDERS OF THE INDIAN CHURCH, London, 1934.
Neill, Stephen C., A HISTORY OF CHRISTIAN MISSIONS, London, 1964.
Newman, A. H., Editor, A CENTURY OF BAPTIST ACHIEVEMENT, Philadelphia, 1901.
Nicholl, J. T., PENTECOSTALISM, New York, 1966.
Notrott, Ludwig, DIE GOSSNERSCHE MISSION UNTER DEN KOLS, Halle, 1874, 2 Volumes.
Nurullah & Naik, A HISTORY OF EDUCATION IN INDIA, Bombay, 1951.
Oldham, F. F., THOBURN—CALLED OF GOD, New York, 1918.
Orr, J. Edwin, CAMPUS AFLAME, Glendale, California, 1971.
Orr, J. Edwin, THE EAGER FEET, Chicago, 1975.
Orr, J. Edwin, THE FERVENT PRAYER, Chicago, 1974.
Orr, J. Edwin, THE FLAMING TONGUE, Chicago, 1973.
Orr, J. Edwin, THE LIGHT OF THE NATIONS, Exeter, 1965.
Orr, J. Edwin, THE SECOND EVANGELICAL AWAKENING IN BRITAIN, London, 1949.
Parker, J. I., INTERPRETATIVE SURVEY OF THE WORLD MISSION OF THE CHRISTIAN CHURCH, New York, 1928.
Paton, William, ALEXANDER DUFF, PIONEER OF MISSIONARY EDUCATION, London, 1923.
Pederson, M. A., IN THE LAND OF THE SANTALS, New York, 1929.
Peters, J. W., TESTS AND TRIUMPHS OF ARMENIANS IN TURKEY AND MACEDONIA, Grand Rapids, 1940.
Philip, E. M., THE INDIAN CHURCH OF ST. THOMAS, Nagercoil, 1950.
Philip, P. O., REPORT ON A SURVEY OF INDIGENOUS CHRISTIAN EFFORTS IN INDIA, BURMA AND CEYLON, Poona, 1928.
Pickett, J. Wascom, CHRISTIAN MASS MOVEMENTS IN INDIA, Cincinnati, 1933.
Rajamani, R. R., (edited by Angus I. Kinnear), MONSOON DAYBREAK, Fort Washington, Pennsylvania, 1971.
Rehnstrom, T. B., A MISSIONARY ENTERPRISE, Gorakhpur, n.d.
Retief, M. W., HERLEWINGS IN ONS GESKIEDENIS, Cape Town, 1951.
Reynolds, Charles, PUNJAB PIONEER: DR. EDITH BROWN, New York, 1969.
Rhenius, Carl, MEMOIR OF THE REV. C. T. E. RHENIUS, London, 1841.
Richter, Julius, A HISTORY OF MISSIONS IN INDIA, London, 1909.
Richter, Julius, INDISCHE MISSIONSGESCHICHTE, Gutersloh, 1924.
Riddle, T. E., VISION AND CALL, (Sundar Singh), Dunedin, 1950.
Roberts, Mrs., THE REVIVAL IN THE KHASIA HILLS, London, 1909.

Rockwell, W. W., THE PITIFUL PLIGHT OF THE ASSYRIAN CHRISTIANS IN PERSIA AND KURDISTAN, New York, 1916.
Root, Helen I., A CENTURY IN CEYLON: THE AMERICAN BOARD, 1816-1916, Colombo, 1916.
Samuel, Y., DAVID—AN AMBASSADOR FROM INDIA, Madras, 1950.
Sargant, N. C., THE DISPERSION OF THE TAMIL CHURCH, Madras, 1940.
Schlatter, Wilhelm, GESCHICHTE DER BASLER MISSION, 1815-1915, Basel, 1916.
Schmidlin, Joseph, CATHOLIC MISSION THEORY, Techny, 1933.
Scholly, Traugott, SAMUEL HEBICH, Basel, 1911.
Selkirk, James, RECOLLECTIONS OF CEYLON: CHURCH MISSIONARY SOCIETY'S OPERATIONS, London, 1844.
Sharp, H., SELECTIONS FROM EDUCATIONAL RECORDS, 1781-1839, London, 1920.
Sherring, M. A., A HISTORY OF PROTESTANT MISSIONS IN INDIA, London, 1884.
Sherring, M. A., THE INDIAN CHURCH DURING THE GREAT REBELLION, London, 1859.
Shimmin, Paul, MASSACRES OF SYRIAN CHRISTIANS IN N.W. PERSIA AND KURDISTAN, London, 1915.
Smith, Dan, BAKHT SINGH OF INDIA, Washington, D.C., 1959.
Smith, George, HISTORY OF WESLEYAN METHODISM, London, 1862, 2nd Edition, 3 Volumes.
Smith, George, HENRY MARTYN, London, 1892.
Smith, George, THE LIFE OF ALEXANDER DUFF, London, 1892.
Smith, George, THE LIFE OF JOHN WILSON, London, 1879.
Smith, George, STEPHEN HISLOP, PIONEER MISSIONARY . . . IN CENTRAL INDIA, London, 1879.
Speer, R. E., GEORGE BOWEN OF BOMBAY, New York, 1938.
Stanton, W. A., THE AWAKENING OF INDIA, Portland, Me., 1910.
Stewart, Robert, LIFE AND WORK IN INDIA, Philadelphia, 1896.
Stock, Eugene, A HISTORY OF THE CHURCH MISSIONARY SOCIETY, London, 1899-1916.
Stoddard, D. A., NARRATIVE OF THE LATE REVIVAL AMONG THE NESTORIANS, Boston, 1847.
Strong, W. E., THE STORY OF THE AMERICAN BOARD, Boston, 1910.
Sundkler, Bengt, THE CHURCH OF SOUTH INDIA, London, 1954.
Sutton, Amos, ORISSA AND ITS EVANGELIZATION, Derby, 1850.
Swavely, C. H., THE LUTHERAN ENTERPRISE IN SOUTH INDIA, Madras, 1952.
Swavely, C. H., ONE HUNDRED YEARS IN THE ANDHRA COUNTRY, Madras, 1942.
Sword, V. H., BAPTISTS IN ASSAM, 1836-1936, Chicago, 1935.
Taylor, William, FOUR YEARS' CAMPAIGN IN INDIA, London, 1876.
Thoburn, J. M., INDIA AND MALAYSIA, Cincinnati, 1896.
Thoburn, J. M., ISABELLA THOBURN, New York, 1903.
Thoburn, J. M., MY MISSIONARY APPRENTICESHIP, New York, 1884.
Thomas & Taylor, TRIBAL AWAKENING, Bangalore, 1965.
Thomssen, G. M., SAMUEL HEBICH OF INDIA, Cuttack, 1905.
Wanless, William, AN AMERICAN DOCTOR AT WORK IN INDIA, New York, 1932.
Winslow, J. C., NARAYAN VAMAN TILAK, Calcutta, 1930.
Zorn, H. M., BARTOLOMAEUS ZIEGENBALG, St. Louis, 1933.

GENERAL BIBLIOGRAPHY

Alexander, J. W., THE LIFE OF ARCHIBALD ALEXANDER, New York, 1854.
Appasamy, A. J., WRITE THE VISION! London, 1964.
Baillie, J., THE REVIVAL: or What I Saw in Ireland; London, 1860.
Balleine, G. R., A HISTORY OF THE EVANGELICAL PARTY IN THE CHURCH OF ENGLAND, London, 1908.
Barbour, G. F., LIFE OF ALEXANDER WHYTE, London, 1923.
Barclay, W., HISTORY OF METHODIST MISSIONS, New York, 1949.
Barnes, Gilbert Hobbs, THE ANTI-SLAVERY IMPULSE, 1830-1844, New York, 1933.
Beardsley, F. G., A HISTORY OF AMERICAN REVIVALS, New York, 1912.
Bennett, W. W., THE GREAT REVIVAL IN THE SOUTHERN ARMIES, Philadelphia, 1877.
Bloch-Hoell, N., THE PENTECOSTAL MOVEMENT, Oslo, 1964.
Boardman, M. M., THE LIFE AND LABOURS OF THE REV. W. E. BOARDMAN, New York, 1887.
Boardman, M. T., UNDER THE RED CROSS FLAG, Philadelphia, 1915.
Boardman, W. E., THE HIGHER CHRISTIAN LIFE, Boston, 1858.
Bois, Henri, LE REVEIL AU PAYS DE GALLES, Toulouse, 1905.
Bourdillon, A. F. C., VOLUNTARY SOCIAL SERVICES, London, 1945.
Braithwaite, R., THE REV. WILLIAM PENNEFATHER: LIFE AND LETTERS, London, 1878.
Branch, E. D., THE SENTIMENTAL YEARS, 1836-1860, New York, 1934.
Bready, J. Wesley, THIS FREEDOM—WHENCE? London, 1942.
Brown, Arthur Judson, ONE HUNDRED YEARS: A HISTORY OF THE FOREIGN MISSIONARY WORK OF THE PRESBYTERIAN CHURCH IN THE U. S. A., New York, 1937.
Butler, J., PERSONAL REMINISCENCES OF A GREAT CRUSADE, London, 1913.
Candler, W. A., GREAT REVIVALS AND THE GREAT REPUBLIC, Nashville, 1904.
Canton, William, A HISTORY OF THE BRITISH AND FOREIGN BIBLE SOCIETY, London, 5 Volumes, 1904-1910.
Carey, S. Pearce, WILLIAM CAREY, FELLOW OF THE LINNAEAN SOCIETY, New York, 1923.
Carey, William, AN ENQUIRY INTO THE OBLIGATION OF CHRISTIANS TO USE MEANS FOR THE CONVERSION OF THE HEATHENS, Leicester, 1792.
Carus, William, MEMOIRS OF THE LIFE OF THE REV. CHARLES SIMEON, London, 1847.
Caughey, James, METHODISM IN EARNEST, Richmond, 1852.
Caughey, James, SHOWERS OF BLESSING, Boston, 1857.
Chambers, T. W., THE NOON PRAYER MEETING, New York, 1858.
Church, R. W., THE OXFORD MOVEMENT, 1833-1845, London, 1891.
Clark, Elmer T., editor, JOURNAL AND LETTERS OF FRANCIS ASBURY, Nashville, 3 Volumes, 1958.
Clarkson, Thomas, THE RISE, PROGRESS AND ACCOMPLISHMENT OF THE ABOLITION OF THE AFRICAN SLAVE TRADE BY THE BRITISH PARLIAMENT, London, 1808.

Colquhoun, John Campbell, WILBERFORCE: HIS FRIENDS AND HIS TIMES, London, 1867.
Conant, W. C., NARRATIVE OF REMARKABLE CONVERSIONS, New York, 1858.
Cook, Sir Edward, THE LIFE OF FLORENCE NIGHTINGALE, London, 2 Volumes, 1913.
Couper, W. J., SCOTTISH REVIVALS, Dundee, 1918.
Craig, J. A., FORTY YEARS AMONG THE TELUGUS, Toronto, 1912.
Crookshank, C. H., HISTORY OF METHODISM IN IRELAND, London, 3 Volumes, 1888.
Davis, G. T. B., TORREY AND ALEXANDER, New York, 1905.
Dickens, Charles, ALL THE YEAR ROUND, London, 1859.
Drach, George, editor, OUR CHURCH ABROAD: THE FOREIGN MISSIONS OF THE LUTHERAN CHURCH IN AMERICA, Philadelphia, 1926.
Dwight, H. O., CENTENNIAL HISTORY OF THE AMERICAN BIBLE SOCIETY, New York, 1916.
Dyer, H. S., REVIVAL IN INDIA, London, 1907.
Ellis, W. T., BILLY SUNDAY, New York, 1936.
Emery, Julia C., A CENTURY OF ENDEAVOR, 1821-1921: A RECORD OF THE MISSIONARY SOCIETY OF THE PROTESTANT EPISCOPAL CHURCH, New York, 1921.
Fairholme, E. G., & Wellesley Pain, A CENTURY OF WORK FOR ANIMALS: THE R. S. P. C. A., 1824-1924, London, 1924.
Farndale, W. E., THE SECRET OF MOW COP, London, 1950.
Fawcett, Millicent, JOSEPHINE BUTLER, London, 1927.
Findlay, J. F., DWIGHT L. MOODY, Chicago, 1969.
Findlay, G. G., & Holdsworth, W. W., THE HISTORY OF THE WESLEYAN METHODIST MISSIONARY SOCIETY, London, 5 Volumes, 1921-1924.
Finney, Charles G., LECTURES ON REVIVALS OF RELIGION, New York, 1835, (Edinburgh, 1928).
Finney, Charles G., MEMOIRS OF REV. CHARLES G. FINNEY, New York, 1876.
Frodsham, S. H., WITH SIGNS FOLLOWING, Springfield, Mo., 1946.
Fullerton, W. Y., THE LIFE OF F. B. MEYER, London, 1929.
Gardner, A. R. C., THE PLACE OF JOHN HOWARD IN PENAL REFORM, London, 1926.
Garrard, M. N., MRS. PENN-LEWIS, London, undated.
Gee, Donald, THE PENTECOSTAL MOVEMENT, London, 1949.
Goforth, Jonathan, "BY MY SPIRIT," London, undated.
Gulick, O. H., THE PILGRIMS OF HAWAII, New York, 1918.
Haldane, Alexander, THE LIVES OF ROBERT HALDANE OF AIRTHREY AND OF HIS BROTHER, JAMES ALEXANDER HALDANE, Edinburgh, 1852 (5th edition, 1855.)
Halliday, S. B. & D. S. Gregory, THE CHURCH IN AMERICA AND ITS BAPTISMS OF FIRE, New York, 1896.
Harford-Battersby, J., MEMOIR OF T. D. HARFORD-BATTERSBY, London, 1890.
Harris, John, A CENTURY OF EMANCIPATION, London, 1933.
Headley, P. C., E. PAYSON HAMMOND, London, 1885.
Henderson, G. C., FIJI AND THE FIJIANS, 1835-1856, Sydney, 1931.
Hodder, Edwin, THE LIFE AND WORK OF THE SEVENTH EARL OF SHAFTESBURY, London, 1887.
Hodder-Williams, J. E., THE LIFE OF SIR GEORGE WILLIAMS, London, 1906.

Humphrey, Heman, REVIVAL SKETCHES, New York, 1859.
Ironside, H. A., A HISTORICAL SKETCH OF THE BRETHREN MOVEMENT, Grand Rapids, 1942.
Jeffrey, M. P., DR. IDA: INDIA, New York, 1938.
Jenkins, D. E., THE LIFE OF THOMAS CHARLES OF BALA, Denbigh, 1908.
Jones, J. W., CHRIST IN THE CAMP, Richmond, 1887.
Jones, R. B., RENT HEAVENS, London, 1909.
Jonzon, Bengt, STUDIER I PAAVO RUOTSULAINENS FROMHET, Stockholm, 1935.
Kemp, Winifred, JOSEPH W. KEMP, London, 1934.
Kennedy, John, THE APOSTLE OF THE NORTH, LIFE AND LABOURS OF THE REV. DR. MACDONALD, London, 1867.
Latimer, R. S., UNDER THREE TSARS: LIBERTY OF CONSCIENCE IN RUSSIA, 1856-1909, London, 1909.
Lloyd, J. Meirion, ON EVERY HIGH HILL, London, 1950.
Lyall, James, THE RECENT GREAT REVIVAL IN AUSTRALIA AND NEW ZEALAND, Edinburgh, 1905.
Mackichan, D., THE MISSIONARY IDEAL IN THE SCOTTISH CHURCHES, London, 1927.
MacPherson, J., HARRY MOORHOUSE: THE ENGLISH EVANGELIST, London, 1920.
Mason, Ebenezer, THE COMPLETE WORKS OF JOHN M. MASON, New York, 4 Volumes, 1849.
Mason, Francis, KAREN APOSTLE: KO THAH-BYU, Boston, 1843.
Mathews, Basil, JOHN R. MOTT, World Citizen, New York, 1934.
Miller, Basil, PRAYING HYDE, Grand Rapids, 1943.
Moody, W. R., THE LIFE OF DWIGHT L. MOODY, New York, 1900.
Morgan, G. E., R. C. MORGAN, HIS LIFE AND TIMES, London, 1909.
Morgan, J. V., THE WELSH RELIGIOUS REVIVAL, London, 1909.
Norborg, Sverre, HANS NIELSEN HAUGE, 1771-1804, Oslo, 1966.
Orr, J. Edwin, THE EAGER FEET, (Evangelical Awakenings 1792— & 1830— Worldwide), Chicago, 1975.
Orr, J. Edwin, THE FERVENT PRAYER, (Evangelical Awakenings 1858-1899 Worldwide), Chicago, 1974.
Orr, J. Edwin, THE FLAMING TONGUE, (Evangelical Awakenings 1900— Worldwide), Chicago, 1973.
Orr, J. Edwin, THE LIGHT OF THE NATIONS, Evangelical Renewal and Advance in the Nineteenth Century, Exeter, 1965.
Orr, J. Edwin, THE SECOND EVANGELICAL AWAKENING IN BRITAIN, (the 1859 Revival), London, 1949.
Ottman, F. C., J. WILBUR CHAPMAN, New York, 1920.
Phillips, D. M., EVAN ROBERTS, Welsh Revivalist, London, 1923.
Pollock, J. C., MOODY: A BIOGRAPHICAL PORTRAIT, London, 1963.
Ramsay, J. C., JOHN WILBUR CHAPMAN, New York, 1962.
Rees, Thomas, HISTORY OF PROTESTANT NONCONFORMITY IN WALES, London, 1861.
Reid, J. M., MISSIONS AND MISSIONARY SOCIETY: METHODIST EPISCOPAL CHURCH, New York, 3 Volumes, 1895-1896.
Reynolds, Charles, PUNJAB PIONEER, the Life of Dr. Edith Brown; New York, 1969.
Rice, Edwin Wilbur, THE SUNDAY SCHOOL MOVEMENT AND AMERICAN SUNDAY SCHOOL UNION, Philadelphia, 1927.
Richter, Julius, INDISCHE MISSIONSGESCHICHTE, Gütersloh, 1924.
Sandall, Robert, THE HISTORY OF THE SALVATION ARMY, Volume I, London, 1947.

Scharpff, Paulus, GESCHICHTE DER EVANGELISATION, Giessen, 1964.
Seldes, Gilbert, THE STAMMERING CENTURY, New York, 1928.
Shedd, C. P., HISTORY OF THE WORLD'S ALLIANCE OF YOUNG MEN'S CHRISTIAN ASSOCIATIONS, London, 1955.
Shedd, Clarence P., TWO CENTURIES OF STUDENT CHRISTIAN MOVEMENTS, New York, 1934.
Sherring, M. A., THE INDIAN CHURCH DURING THE GREAT REBELLION, London, 1859.
Sigston, James, A MEMOIR OF THE LIFE AND MINISTRY OF WILLIAM BRAMWELL, London, 1820.
Sloan, W. B., THESE SIXTY YEARS: THE KESWICK CONVENTION, London, 1935.
Smith, G. A., THE LIFE OF HENRY DRUMMOND, New York, 1898.
Smith, T. L., REVIVALISM AND SOCIAL REFORM, New York, 1957.
Speer, William, THE GREAT REVIVAL OF 1800, Philadelphia, 1872.
Sprague, William B., LECTURES ON REVIVALS OF RELIGION, New York, 1833.
Stephenson, George M., THE RELIGIOUS ASPECTS OF SWEDISH IMMIGRATION, Minneapolis, 1932.
Stewart, I. R., A SPLENDID OPTIMIST, Edinburgh, 1952.
Strickland, A. B., THE GREAT AMERICAN REVIVAL, Cincinnati, 1934.
Sweet, William Warren, REVIVALISM IN AMERICA: ITS RISE, PROGRESS, AND DECLINE, New York, 1945.
Thacher, Peter, A BRIEF ACCOUNT OF THE SOCIETY FOR PROPAGATING THE GOSPEL AMONG INDIANS AND OTHERS IN NORTH AMERICA, Boston, 1790.
Thomssen, G. M., SAMUEL HEBICH OF INDIA, Mangalore, 1915.
Tippet, Alan R., PEOPLE MOVEMENTS IN SOUTHERN POLYNESIA, Chicago, 1971.
Tracy, J., HISTORY OF THE AMERICAN BOARD OF COMMISSIONERS FOR FOREIGN MISSIONS, New York, 1842.
Trevelyan, George M., ENGLISH SOCIAL HISTORY, London, 1944.
Vedder, Henry C., A SHORT HISTORY OF THE BAPTISTS, Philadelphia, 1907.
Watt, Hugh, THOMAS CHALMERS AND THE DISRUPTION, Edinburgh, 1943.
Wanless, William, AN AMERICAN DOCTOR AT WORK IN INDIA, New York, 1932.
Wayland, Francis, MEMOIR OF THE LIFE OF ADONIRAM JUDSON, Boston, 1853.
Webb, Sidney & Beatrice, A HISTORY OF TRADE UNIONISM, London, 1894.
Webster, James, THE REVIVAL IN MANCHURIA, London, 1910.
Weigle, Luther A., AMERICAN IDEALISM, New Haven, 1928.
Wesley, Charles H., RICHARD ALLEN: APOSTLE OF FREEDOM, Washington, 1935.
Westin, Gunnar, GEORGE SCOTT OCH HANS VERKSAMHET I SVERIGE, Stockholm, 2 Volumes, 1928-1929.
Whitney, Janet, ELIZABETH FRY, QUAKER HEROINE, Boston, 1936.
Woodson, Carter G., THE HISTORY OF THE NEGRO CHURCH, Washington, 2nd edition, 1921.
Young and Ashton, BRITISH SOCIAL WORK IN THE NINETEENTH CENTURY, London, 1936.

INDEX OF PERSONS

Abraham, Bundara	123	Campbell, Mary	148
Abraham, K. E.	165, 166	Candler, Warren A.	73
Abraham Mar Thoma	160, 161	Carey, William	6, 10, 11, 12, 16, 19
Abraham, Vongole	67		21, 44, 45, 46, 48, 49, 96, 171, 173
Aitken, Hay	54	Carmichael, Amy	131, 132, 133
Alexander, F. W. N.	67	Carpenter, Mary	91
Ambedkar, B. R.	163, 175	Cassels, W. W.	86
Anderson, John	28, 46, 47, 192	Cattell, Everett	180
Anderson, W. B.	148	Chalmers, Thomas	2, 28
Andrews, C. F.	171	Chapman, J. Wilbur	82, 84, 99
Appasamy, A. J.	179, 183-185	Charles, Thomas	8
Archibald, R. T.	139, 183	Cherian, K. V.	182
Arulappan, J. C.	59, 61, 66, 169	Church, Joe	184
Asbury, Francis	22	Clark, Francis	54, 88
Augustus, John	91	Clough, J. E.	67, 68, 120, 122
Azariah, V. S.	127, 133, 159, 164	Coan, Titus	24
Backus, Isaac	4	Cochrane, Robert	96
Baker, Daniel	22	Coke, Thomas	10, 21
Baker, Henry	62	Collins, D. P.	184
Baker, James A.	120-123	Cook, Robert	158, 166
Bandela, Yesupadam	185	Cook, Thomas	110, 133
Barber, W. T. A.	110	Copleston, R. G.	71
Barnardo, Thomas	90, 91, 94	Craig, J. A.	119
Barratt, T. B.	158	Daniel, Nagabathula	165, 183
Battersby, Harford	83	Darby, J. N.	23
Beauchamp, Sir Montagu	86	Darling, C. M.	66, 67, 162
Beaver, R. Pierce	10	Darwin, Charles	53
Benjamin, Jacob	158	David, Tamil	133, 135-137, 161
Berg, George	158	Dickens, Charles	93
Berggrav, Eivind	102	Dixon, A. C.	82
Bentinck, Lord William	44, 46	Dolbeer, M. L.	126
Bird, Handley	129	Dorairaj, R. P.	178
Bliss, Philip P.	82	Downie, David	119, 120
Boardman, W. E.	83	Drummond, Henry	82, 85, 87, 88
Bœrresen, H. P.	69	Duff, Alexander	28, 46, 47, 58, 95
Booth, Bramwell	92		119, 171, 173, 192, 200
Booth, William	75, 76, 109	Dunant, Henri	93, 94
Bowden, E. S.	119	Dunlap, W. A.	181
Bowden, William	67	Dwight, Timothy	5
Bowen, George	58, 71	Eddy, G. Sherwood	75, 133, 159
Brand, Paul	96	Edwards, Jonathan	10
Brown, David	45	Engels, Friedrich	81
Brown, Edith	96	Fawcett, Millicent	92
Buchanan, Claudius	44, 45	Fenn, David	60, 61, 62
Buchman, Frank	157	Finney, Charles G.	22, 25, 78, 105
Burder, George	6	Fliedner, Theodor	3, 27, 36, 37
Burger, A. P.	111	Forman, John	87
Burns, Norman	179	Francke, August	36
Burns, W. C.	23, 64	Fraser, Donald	88
Butler, E. T.	153	Fry, Elizabeth	36, 37, 93
Butler, Josephine	55, 92	Gandhi, M. K.	173
Butler, William	29	Garden, J. H.	143
Buxton, Sir William Fowell	35, 44	Gee, Donald	158
Byu, Ko Tha	24	Goldsmith, H. D.	128

Gordon, A. J.	84
Graham, Billy	177, 186, 189
Grant, Charles	44
Grenfell, Wilfred	85
Groves, Anthony Norris	29, 59
Grubb, George	54, 71, 133, 135
Grundtvig, N. F. S.	23
Gupta, Paul	187
Hager, H. J.	180
Haldane, James & Robert	2, 3
Hammond, E. P.	76, 77
Hanna, Hugh	92
Hardie, Keir	55
Harris, E. C.	127
Hartog, Sir Philip	46, 47
Haslam, William	84
Haqq, Akbar A.	186
Hauge, Hans Nielsen	3
Haweis, Thomas	11, 14
Hebich, Samuel	24, 30-31, 140
Heinrichs, Jacob	120
Higginbotham, Sam	96
Hine, S. K.	180
Hislop, Stephen	28, 46, 192, 200
Hollenweger, W. J.	159
Hopkins, Ellice	92
Hopkins, Evan	84
Hoste, D. E.	86
Howard, John	36
Humphrey, Heman	13
Hyde, J. N.	108-109, 148-150, 168
Ingham, Kenneth	41, 48
Inwood, Charles	84
Jacobi, David	30
Jacob, C. K.	181
Jacobs, B. F.	77
Jenanian, Haratune	72
Johnson, Gisle	3
Jones, D. E.	116
Jones, E. Stanley	156, 161, 171, 181
Jones, John P.	130, 154
Jones, J. Pengwern	149
Joseph, Justus	60, 61, 62, 63
Joshua, P. J.	136
Judson, Adoniram	15, 16
Kadambavanam, P. T.	184
Katju, K. N.	174
Keller, Samuel	53
Kline, Frank	187
Kochukunju, Moothampackal	160
Krishnaswami, Dr. A.	175
Lancaster, Joseph	9
Lander, Gerald	85
Lang, G. H.	146
Latourette, K. S.	39, 40, 88
Lee, D. H.	153
Lindsay, A. D.	172
Lunde, Albert	102
Macauley, Zachary	46, 47
McConaughy, David	75
MacDonald, John	2
McGavran, D. A.	64
McNeill, John	54, 82
MacNicol, Nicol	145
Mammen, Oommen	135
Mammen, Punchamannil	137, 138
Manikam, R. B.	174
Manogarom, Victor	187
Mar Athanasius, Mathews	161, 181
Mar Athanasius, Thomas	181
Mar Chrysostrom, Philipos	181
Mar Theophilus, Alexander	181
Martin, Sarah	91
Martyn, Henry	18, 199
Marx, Karl	7, 98
Mason, J. M.	14
Mateer, Robert	53, 86
Mazamdar, P. C.	171
Mead, Charles	20
Mendus, E. L.	190
Meyer, F. B.	82, 84
Miller, William	27
Mills, Samuel J.	15
Moffat, Robert	24
Monahan, C. H.	130
Monod, Theodore	82, 84
Moody, D. L.	52, 78-87, 105, 107
Moorhouse, Harry	79
More, Hannah	9
Morgan, G. Campbell	82
Morgan, G. E.	73
Morgan, R. C.	79
Mott, John R.	54, 87
Moule, Handley	84
Muller, George	23, 79
Murray, Andrew	54, 84
Nagenda, William	184
Nee, Watchman	178
Nehru, Jawaharlal	97, 173, 174
Neill, S. C.	30, 32
Nettleton, Asahel	22
Newton, E. P.	150
Nightingale, Florence	37, 38, 93
Noel, Baptist	75, 92
North, Ian	189
Nyogi, M. E.	175
Oastler, Richard	39
Oommen, Aleyamma	164
Orr, J. Edwin	180, 181, 184, 185
Pamla, Charles	54
Pariat, U Paila	188
Parker, George	130

Paterson, R. McC.	149, 168	Smith, T. L.	94
Paul, Rama	166	Spurgeon, C. H.	51, 77, 79, 82
Payne, Ernest A.	10	Speechly, J. M.	62
Pennefather, William	79, 80	Speer, R. E.	58
Periah, Yerraguntla	67, 68, 199	Stanton, W. A.	164, 194
Philipos, C. P.	136	Stead, W. T.	92
Picket, J. W.	65, 162	Stebbins, G. C.	82
Pilkington, G. L.	135	Stock, Eugene	10
Plutschau, Heinrich	17	Studd, C. T.	85, 86
Polhill-Turner, Arthur & Cecil	86	Studd, J. E. K.	85, 87
Popley, H. A.	160	Sudhakar, Paul	187
Prasad, Rajendra	173	Sutcliffe, John	10
Prokhanov, I. S.	53	Swain, Clara D.	76
Radcliffe, Reginald	84	Sweet, W. W.	82
Radhakrishnan, Sarvapalli	171, 187	Taylor, J. Hudson	52, 193
Raikes, Robert	9	Taylor, Wm.	69-71, 80, 153, 193
Rajagopalachari, Chakravarti	173	Thoburn, J. M.	69, 107, 199
Rajamani, R. R.	178	Thommen, Kudarapallil	63
Rajaratnam, Bandela	165, 185	Thompson, Cyril R.	184
Ramabai, Pandita	110, 142-146	Thomson, James	24
Rees, Paul S.	179	Tilak, N. V.	144, 160
Revell, Emma	79	Timothy, Eleazar S.	163
Reynolds, J. B.	88	Torrey, R. A.	82, 84, 101
Rhenius, C. T. E.	19, 59, 200	Toynbee, Arnold	98, 99
Rice, Luther	16	Trevelyan, G. M.	46, 89
Ringeltaube, W. T.	19, 20	Trevelyan, Sir Charles	60
Roberts, Evan	82	Trumbull, H. C.	77
Roberts, John	112	Tucker, Frederic Booth	76
Romaine, William	8	Turner, George	149
Rosenius, Carl Olof	3, 23	Ullah, Ihsan	109
Roy, Ram Mohan	44, 46, 48, 171	Van Lier, H. R.	5
Ruotsalainen, Paavo	3	Varley, Henry	79, 82, 83
Russell, Bertrand	83	Vedamannikam of Mayiladi	19
Sahu, Subodh	187	Venkayya, Pagolu	66, 67, 162, 199
Salins, Augustine	186	Viljoen, D. J.	111
Samuel, P. M.	166	Walker, Thomas	136-139, 152-153
Sanyasini, Pennamma	164	Wanless, Sir William	96
Seamands, J. T.	182, 186	Walton, Spencer	54
Schrenk, Elijah	53	Ward, R. J.	108
Schwartz, C. F.	17, 19	Ward, William	19
Scott, George	3, 23	Wardsworth, L. M.	135, 137
Scudder, Ida S.	95	Wati, Imchaba Bendang	186
Scudder, John	29, 32, 95	Wesley, John	34, 36, 39, 69, 89, 105
Shaftesbury, Earl of	27, 38, 54, 79, 89, 90	Wherry, E. M.	150
Shea, G. Beverly	180	Whitefield, George	8, 34, 40
Sherring, M. A.	47	Whittle, D. W.	82
Simpson, A. B.	54, 84	Wilberforce, W.	2, 18, 21, 27, 44, 47
Singh, Bakht (Chabre)	167-169, 178	Wilder, Robert P.	53, 75, 87
Singh, Sadhu Sundar	157, 160	Williams, George	25, 79
Sitaramayya, Dr. P.	174	Wilson, Daniel	30, 43
Skefsrud, L. O.	69	Wilson, John	28, 46, 47, 192
Smith, Gipsy Rodney	54, 101	Wilson, T. Woodrow	53, 86
Smith, J. Blair	14	Wishard, Luther T.	53, 86, 88
Smith, R. Pearsall	83	Wood, John	39
Smith, Stanley	86	Yohannan, Poikayil	109
		Ziegenbalg, Bartholomæus	17

The author will be glad to correspond with any reader, foreign missionary or national Christian, on the subject of Evangelical Awakening in any country: address Professor J. Edwin Orr, 11451 Berwick Street, Los Angeles 90049.

BV
3777
.I4
O77
1975